CLASSIC REPRINTS

*Language and Logic
in Ancient China*

Chad Hansen

an exact reproduction of the text
originally published in 1983

Advanced Reasoning Forum

copyright © 2020 by Chad Hansen

reprinted with permission of the author

Advanced Reasoning Forum
P. O. Box 635
Socorro, NM 87801 USA
www.AdvancedReasoningForum.org

ISBN 978-1-938421-54-9 print

ISBN 978-1-938421-55-6 e-book

Preface

For the past half century, Anglo-American "philosophy" has carried the pejorative/honorific "linguistic analysis." Chinese philosophy, christened "nonlinear" and championed by a romantic counterculture, has played the part of the antithesis. This book, in presenting Chinese philosophies of language, challenges that distinction as a way of understanding Chinese thought. Its hypothesis is that Chinese thought is like modern Western thought in that both philosophical traditions focus on language and its role in culture; Chinese thought differs radically from traditional Western thought (as Chinese language differs from Western language) in what it *says about* language and culture.

The stereotypical contrast of Chinese thought and "analytic" Western thought has blinded Sinophiles to the ways in which attention to philosophy of language can aid in understanding Chinese philosophy as a whole. Virtually all students of Chinese thought have fondly contemplated the ways in which Chinese language might explain the differences in Chinese thought, but few convincing stories bridging language and thought have emerged. The chapters which follow set out to tell a plausible story in a focused example (the thought of Kung-sun Lung) by a less ambitious, more indirect strategy. The narrative focuses on philosophy of language as an explanatory link between language and other philosophical theories. The strategy is suggested by insights into language and thought derived from contemporary Western philosophy of language.

The "linguistic turn" in Western philosophy has raised the suspicion that the traditional perennial problems of philosophy are, in some sense, based on assumptions about language. Plato's views about definitions, meanings, and truth are held to explain both his formulation of the one-many problem and his theory-solution based on abstract forms (universals and instantiations). The Cartesian and Empiricist views of the mind-body problem, philosophy of mind, and theory of knowledge are undergirded by a peculiar view of language—including the identification of meanings with mental representations (ideas) akin to sensations. Neo-Kantians are seen as substituting the effects of language for the structuring activities of the mind in presenting phenomenal experience.

This view of the nature of philosophical problems is controversial, and I do not intend directly to argue for it in these pages. However, the very possibility of such an explanation of traditional Western philosophy should warn against any assumption that absence of these traditional philosophical concerns is evidence of nonrational thought. (And, of course, absence of such philosophical preoccupations by Chinese philosophers does not prove that the traditional problems are nonrational either.) The "philosophical problems are problems of language" view shows us that there could be a coherent theory of language which (1) could plausibly have been held by Chinese philosophers given their language and (2) would be less likely to motivate the traditional theories of abstract reality, mental representation, private meaning, propositional knowledge, and cognitive minds.

We understand the relation of thought and language in ancient China when we can present an account of the theories of language as influenced by the actual language and then an account of other philosophical issues as influenced by actual and implicit theory of language. The picture of ancient Chinese thought which emerges is significantly different from the accepted view. Radical reinterpretation is not the goal, however. This study revises the standard interpretation of Chinese thought only when that interpretation seems to have imputed an interest in issues which (1) are likely to have been generated by linguistic forms or theories about language which are absent in classical Chinese, and (2) are incompatible with other well-confirmed interests and approaches (on the standard interpretation).

The case for this strategy is buttressed by the fact that ancient Chinese thinkers shared modern Western philosophy's intense interest in language. Chinese theories of language have been largely ignored in traditional interpretations both because of their difficulty and because of the obscurity of some central texts (the Neo-Mohist Canon) which contain most of the technical detail of Chinese theories of language. The failure to understand the Neo-Mohist Canon, in turn, hindered understanding of Chuang-tzu and Hsün-tzu, who have the obvious focus on problems of language but presupposed (and drew heavily from) the Neo-Mohist treatment of linguistic issues.

This study touches on many contrasts in philosophical interests. However, it concentrates on one classical issue—the one-many problem.

Sinologists basically agree that Chinese philosophy has no obsession with abstraction, universals, or forms characteristic of the Western Platonic Realist view of the one-many problem. Kung-sun Lung is typically interpreted as the exception. His "white-horse paradox" ("white-horse not horse") is supposed to represent a classical Chinese counterpart to Platonism. The *locus classicus* of the standard interpretation of Kung-sun Lung is in the work of the best-known contemporary historian of Chinese philosophy, Fung Yu-lan. The Fung Yu-lan interpretation is consciously Platonistic. Fung suggests that the Chinese terms *ma* 'horse' and *pai* 'white' are being used to designate abstract objects—horseness and whiteness. Hence the paradoxical statement should be read as "whitehorseness is not horseness." Many were skeptical of Fung's Platonizing interpretation, but few more plausible theories have been offered. Thus the abstract view of Kung-sun Lung's enterprise has come to be widely accepted—if without much enthusiasm.

I will argue that there is indeed no Platonic Realism in ancient China (also no theory of abstract sets or classes), that Kung-sun Lung does not constitute an exception, and further, that the nonabstract orientation of philosophy can be (partially) explained using the strategy outlined above. The grammatical features of Indo-European languages which explain the impetus of Platonism in philosophy of language are not found in Chinese. Absent those motivations, there would be, I suggest, less reason to suppose Chinese thinkers have postulated such metaphysical curiosities as abstract or mental objects.

Essentially, I contend that a one-many paradigm for stating philosophical questions goes along with a count noun (nouns to which the many-few dichotomy applies) syntax. Chinese language, during this classical period, tends toward a mass noun syntax (based on nouns to which the much-little dichotomy applies). Mass nouns suggest a stuff ontology and what I call a division or discrimination view of the semantic function of words (terms and predicates).

The grammatical explanans tends to illuminate an extensive difference in "metaphysical" orientation; rather than one-many, the Chinese language motivates a part-whole dichotomy. And I argue that it helps explain not only the absence of Platonism, but, in turn, of mentalism and conceptualist philosophies of mind. These philosophical developments are based on the abstract scheme for dealing with meaning (e.g., conceptualism) and are even less to be expected in Chinese thought.

This study also draws from modern philosophy for its hermeneutic method. Chapter 1 presents an argument for justifying interpretations as we justify scientific theories, that is, as inference to the best explanation. Informally, the point is that the best way to justify an interpretation (or a philosophical view) is just to lay it out as completely and carefully as possible, then to highlight the advantages of the view one supports over the known rivals.

It will be treated as a drawback that an interpretation attributes a discredited Western traditional theory to a thinker in the absence of any adequate explanation of what could have motivated the doctrine. The tendency of interpreters to "discover" such views in Chinese thinkers seems to be connected with their own acceptance of a culture-invariant interest in the perennial Western philosophical issues. Believing that the problems are the genuine problems of philosophy and that they just "make sense," one charitably attributes the same insight to the Chinese thinker at the barest textual hint, thinking, "What else could this mean?" The insights of modern philosophy, in questioning these traditional issues, tend, therefore, to expand rather than restrict the coherent ways of assigning meanings to philosophical texts.

I accordingly regard the introduction of the discipline of philosophy into the study of Chinese thought as a liberating move. It gives the best hope of making headway on a project that all seem to accept—explaining how Chinese language influences Chinese philosophy. It is rather more than less likely to generate fresh, non-Western interpretations and demonstrate their relation to the unique features of Chinese language.

A defensive reaction, claiming for Chinese philosophy "everything found in Western philosophy," tends, I believe, to be counterproductive. The contexts into which these parallels are introduced fit the classical problems so poorly that any philosophically trained reader will find the Chinese thinkers confusing. The theoretical doctrines are attributed to Chinese philosophers who give no coherent arguments for the theories and demonstrate no insights into the classical positions they are supposed to be discussing. The defense typically asserts that they held the positions but did not believe in argument. Thus the view of Chinese thought as "irrational," "nonanalytic," or "inscrutable," is forced by the very attempt to glorify it.

There are issues of philosophy which Chinese philosophers do not see. The issues they do see are discussed competently. There are issues in traditional Western philosophy which no longer hold the interest of Western philosophers. That classical Chinese philosophers never worried such issues hardly undermines positive evaluation of their philosophical acumen.

Acknowledgments

I began work on these ideas eight years ago and I have received help from individuals too numerous to list completely here. I must, however, thank my teacher, friend, and colleague Professor Donald Munro for introducing me to Chinese philosophy and for his splendid ability to encourage my work while giving criticism and suggestions. Professor Munro first aroused in me the suspicion that concentrated study of Chinese philosophy (unlike the study of Western ethics) makes one a better person. One of his many contributions to the understanding of Chinese philosophy is his recognition of the importance of model emulation. His contribution to his students is himself as a model.

My heavy debt to Professor A. C. Graham is apparent from the notes to this volume. In the early stages of my work, Professor Graham gave me some vitally important advice ("Ignore Kao Heng's commentary on the Mohist Dialectic"). Throughout my development of these ideas I relied heavily on the textual studies and translations of Professor Graham that covered the philosophers I was analyzing. His own superb and massive analysis and translation of the Mohist dialectical chapters was being written at the same time I was working on this book. I had a chance to see the manuscript and profited from it. In places, I have continued to rely on his earlier published analyses. Professor Graham read my manuscript and criticized the translations. He advised revision of many key translations, especially those from the Mohist dialectical chapters. I am responsible for any errors which remain. I started from modern philosophical worries about the nature of 'meaning', but my interpretation of texts depends heavily on the prior work of textual scholars. Since I have selected from among textual emendations and textual theories, I must also take responsibility for any sinological errors in the analysis.

Professor Liu Yü-yün was the only person I could find in Taipei who would consent to guiding my reading of the Mohist dialectical chapters. Professor Liu taught my teacher and my teacher's teacher. So my debt to him goes far beyond the direct influence he exerted on this work.

Professor Chung-ying Ch'eng has also been working on issues which overlapped a great deal with my own work. I benefited from his published bibliographies on Chinese logic and from several lengthy discussions of various chapters of this manuscript. His comments and criticisms have always been appreciated, and his dedication to the growth of the philosophical approach to the study of Chinese thought have contributed enormously to encouraging me in this and related projects.

My colleagues at the Stanford Center in Taipei and the Universities' Service Center in Hong Kong listened patiently as I struggled to develop coherent, intelligible ways of presenting and developing the key ideas in this analysis of what they must have regarded as a historically obscure set of problems. My thanks to them and to those invaluable research institutions for the training and facilities they have provided to students of China.

In addition to Professor Munro, three scholars at the University of Michigan all made careful and helpful comments on the manuscript's early draft. Professor James Dew drew my attention to many problems in notation and linguistic issues related to my central claims. Professor Larry Sklar forced me to understand just what I could and could not claim to have proven and what kind of proof I should have to settle for for certain key claims. Professor Steve Stitch insisted that I should employ formal semantics consistently.

My colleagues and students at the University of Pittsburgh have read or listened to various portions of this work and made helpful comments concerning content, expression, and organization. Professor Henry Rosemont read the entire manuscript and was most encouraging. He gave me detailed criticisms and recommended some important and basic changes in organization which have been incorporated into the present text. Dr. Sally Gressens commented extensively and helped enormously with the final working of the arguments in the manuscript. My colleagues at the University of Vermont, Professors Philip Kitcher and George Sher, made many helpful suggestions, and Leslie Weiger patiently typed and retyped the successive approximations I generated. My thanks to all.

Finally I must thank Judy, my companion during all the time I was working on this project. I thank her not only for her support and patience but for all she taught me about writing.

Contents

Chapter 1.	Methodological Reflections	1
Chapter 2.	The Mass Noun Hypothesis and Abstraction in Chinese Language and Thought	30
Chapter 3.	Background Theories of Language in Ancient China	55
Chapter 4.	Neo-Mohist Philosophy of Language	100
Chapter 5.	Kung-sun Lung and the White-Horse Paradox	140
	Notes	173
	Selected Bibliography	195
	Index	199

Chapter 1

Methodological Reflections

Imagine a scene: A half darkened room is filled with incense and anticipation. A small huddle of humanity concentrates under the direction of a medium who is chanting. They are contacting a dead person to talk with him. A voice or voices are heard (perhaps that of the medium). The other participants ask questions to which the voice responds. If successful, the conversation should be the same as it would have been with the dead person. It should answer questions about the attitude of the dead person to issues which concern the participants.

The theory of the seance is that when people die their conscious life continues. The conscious life is embodied in an entity called a spirit. The rituals practiced by the medium or the mystic "contact" that spirit (a process analogous to finding the telephone number). The spirit's "speech" typically goes through the medium since the spirit lacks vocal cords, tongue, or lips with which to articulate its answers to the questions. The answers and responses are present in the spirit, as in our living mind, as curious things called "thoughts" or "ideas." The theory usually ignores the question of how the spirit hears, without eardrums. Presumably a parallel story could be told in which the spirit's thoughts are somehow conditioned by the thoughts in the minds of the participants. The conversation is just a convenient "linearization" of these spiritual interactions.

Now consider a second scene: The room is well lighted and dominated by a blackboard. The only smoke is from scholarly pipes. The people participating come from a quite different stratum of society. Papers, pens, books, and glasses are the main paraphernalia at this gathering. One participant reads from a paper. The topic of the paper is also what a dead person thought. But this is not a seance. No one here ever knew the deceased. It is a meeting of academic interpreters—intellectual historians, philosophers, anthropologists. They are concerned with a famous philosopher—specifically a Chinese philosopher, perhaps Confucius.

There are no subterfuges; the speaker uses his own voice and most typically uses *he* in discussing the views of the dead philosopher. He speaks in English in expressing his view, though we all know that Confucius spoke a precursor of modern Chinese dialects which no one now could understand. There are questions and answers. "If Confucius really meant that, why did he say . . . ?" "What would he say about a case where . . . ?" But these do not resemble a conversation with Confucius as much as a challenge to the speaker to defend his claim to be speaking for Confucius—a challenge from rival interpreters.

I describe these two activities to dramatize the differences between a theory of interpretation and a theory of spiritualism. An interpretation deals directly with a text, not a mind. Its first task is an account of the logical structure of that text and not directly of the psychological state of the author. It is first a theory about how best to understand that text; second, via some additional hypotheses, it can provide evidence for claims about the beliefs and attitudes of the author. The first aspect of an interpretive theory—how best to understand a text—may apply even to texts for which we think there was no single author. We can reasonably dispute about what is the best interpretation of a text whose compilation we agree was accidental. The interpretation would attribute presuppositions and generate implications of a text which no single author might have believed, formulated, or thought about.

One helpful metaphor used in illuminating the interpretation of texts is that of a conversation. Interpreters are not engaged in ordinary conversation but in radical translation which requires theory construction. Theorizing, even in the natural sciences, can be viewed as conversation with nature. But the conversational metaphor and the seance image together lead to the confusions involved in what I call the Chinese mind approach to methodology.

To see how the seance differs from the seminar, consider two different senses of meaning: the meaning (significance) of an expression in a language, and the meaning (intention) of a person in using that expression. In an ordinary conversation, we can use clues from our knowledge of our friends, the environment at the time of speech, or habits of expression to help tell when someone has intended an expression to have other than its normal meaning. In studying ancient Chinese philosophy we are under different constraints. We know almost nothing about the psychology of the authors of texts except what is revealed in the texts themselves. So interpretation cannot be based on any independent knowledge of a writer's psychology. Thus an interpretation must be concerned with the objective meaning first. Faced with apparent contradictions or conflicting approaches in a text, an interpretive theory attempts to reconcile the contradictions or select one of the approaches as more important, more central than the other. We are tempted to say, "This is what the author really believed," but the author might have had contradictory beliefs. That this does not invalidate this interpretive procedure shows we are concerned with objective meaning. We need not suppose that interpretation is a process of contact with the brain states, the thoughts, or the feelings of any supposed writer of the sentence. An interpretation is not a claim to have done what the medium does. It initially has nothing to do with psychological facts about some author. Talk of, for example, what Confucius really thought about X is just a metaphor misplaced from the seance room.

The object of interpretation is not a mind but a text. We intend to understand the text. An interpretation is a proposal about how best to understand it in our language. When we admit the obvious fact that there can be many ways to understand a text, the metaphor of the seance seems to provide us with a standard of objectivity. The "correct" interpretation, we suppose, is the one which harmonizes in some way with the subjectivity of the supposed author of the text. However, this characterization of the goal of interpretation is quite useless in deciding between competing interpretive theories. We have no access to the author's mental states except through the writings via a theory of translation and interpretation. So to justify an interpretive theory we must appeal to other standards of adequacy. This chapter spells out how we might construct arguments for interpretations of Chinese philosophical texts once we have realized that the mental metaphor is a useless runaround. I shall present an account of how to justify an interpretive theory and consider the most typical objections to the application of a coherence methodology of interpretation in dealing with Chinese philosophy.

The Coherent Theory Methodology of Interpretation

The method advanced is based on an analogy between understanding in the sciences and in interpretation of different cultures. Consider the initial state of a student of Chinese thought. She finds a book on some library shelf that is filled with inscriptions which she takes to be tokens of a written language. The book she holds was most likely printed twenty or thirty years before. It was set in type by reference to some other extant version of the text that was, in its turn, supposedly copied from a still earlier authoritative reconstruction of what is held to have been the original. The reconstructed version, however, was not produced by any direct contact with this original, but by comparing, consulting, reconciling, and theorizing about a number of earlier versions. The principles used in this reconstruction are sometimes conscious and deliberate and sometimes implicit and unformulated. The earlier versions were similarly compiled from still earlier ones (though, no doubt, the principles have changed) and so on to hand-copied or memorized versions reaching back beyond the horizons of textual history.

The text on the shelf was produced by someone who held an implicit textual theory. A textual theory explains the existence of the differing versions at present and through history. It may further postulate the existence of a single "original" which is represented by the reconstructed version. This textual theory is an empirical theory that seeks to explain the existence of versions of the text given an original version. Its aim is the "discovery" of a particular set of historical facts; for example, this graph was originally in this position on this line, or this sentence was added by a commentator not the author.

In the present study the concern is not as much with textual theory as with interpretive theory. I rely for empirical textual theories either on well-established tradition or on the textual research of clever textual detectives and theorists. Choices among the different textual theories is sometimes dictated by the ways they enhance the interpretation, and in some cases (though rarely) I have departed from both tradition and the authorities on textual matters on such interpretive grounds.

Interpretive theory is typically directed at the text selected by a textual theory as the most plausible candidate for the original. We can, in principle, interpret *any* of the versions of the text, and interpreting some version does not presuppose that it is the original version. It makes sense to say that two interpretations of competing versions of a text are both correct *for those different versions*. For example, disputes about the correct interpretation of the Wang Pi texts of the *Tao Te Ching* and the correct interpretation of the recently discovered Ma Wang Tui "legalist" version of that same work need not be rivals except via the rivalry of the respective textual theories—which version is closer to the "original."

There are good reasons for the usual assumption that we are interpreting the original. An interpretive theory, like a textual theory, can function in an attempt to explain the production of the text. An interpretation postulates a meaning for the sentences, terms, and expressions in the text in a way which is designed to explain how the author could have come to hold the theories hypostatized in the text. The interpretation of the original seems important because it is the main evidence for a historical psychological claim about the beliefs, desires, or assumptions of the author or authors of the text. The interpretation gives the grounds for further theorizing by fixing the referents of expressions in the text in the language of interpretation—say modern English. Thus an interpretation of the *Analects* furnishes evidence that Confucius believed that humans are good if, according to that interpretation, the doctrine in the *Analects* entails or presupposes that humans are good.

While the "best" interpretation of the "original" is the only access we have to historical claims about the beliefs of ancient Chinese philosophers, the correctness of the interpretation does not *entail* that the author had those beliefs. We all have the experience of saying or writing something we "don't mean." Still, the sentences we utter or write do mean something—albeit not what we actually believe. Also, an interpretation yields the set of sentences implied by the doctrine of the text, and no one believes all the logical consequences (most of which have never occurred to him) of his sincerely expressed views. Besides, quite simply, an author may lie, mislead, or deliberately confuse us. An interpretation is a theory of the meaning of expressions which may be used in a further explanation of beliefs but does not entail that all the ramifications of the theory given by the interpretation are "beliefs" of the author.

If we assume a common psychology, the interpretive theory can be part of an explanation of the "original" text. It will explain the expressions as arising from other expressions which are the presuppositions or reasons for the expressions or inscriptions in our library version. It functions as an explanatory theory via a principle of interpretation which Richard Grandy has tagged the "principle of humanity."[1] The explanation is relative to some audience, and we regard an explanation or interpretation as adequate when it reveals a "pattern of relations among beliefs, desires, and the world as similar to ours as possible." When we can "see" why, for instance, Mencius would have held some doctrine, then we have the grounds for the explanation of the utterance of sentences of Chinese which are consequences of his theory.

An interpretation, then, is a theory. Like other scientific theories, we judge the interpretation by how well it "fits" the facts to be explained. There is no exhaustive and definitive criteria of the "best fit" of a theory to a body of data. Philosophers of science have typically used such expressions as "elegance," "simplicity," or "neatness" in explaining the standards of theory choice. These standards, vague as they are, seem necessary because there can be a number of possible interpretations which fit the facts.

So the test of an interpretive theory, like that of a textual theory, is not a matter of comparing that theory with either the "original" or the psychological facts (what Confucius actually believed). We have no access to either fact *except* via the theories. What we must do is compare rival interpretive theories as we compare rival versions of the text. Anyone who rebuts an interpretive theory with the claim that the philosopher did not believe what the interpretation gives as the theory of the text has begged the question. We can only find out what some ancient Chinese philosopher believed by comparing and finding the best interpretation of what he allegedly wrote or uttered.

In the case of scientific theories, we can sometimes choose from among rival theories by testing their predictions. For most practical purposes we do not have this technique of theory choice available to us. In this respect, textual and interpretive theories are more like scientific theories that explain the origin of Earth or the evolution of certain species. These events happen only once, but the theories try to explain them on principles which have universal application. Usually the test of theories accounting for unique events involves the comprehensiveness of the theoretical account. Analogously, one of the criteria of a good interpretive theory is its coherence with more comprehensive theories about the corpus of texts of Chinese thought.

So an interpretation of a passage in a classical Chinese philosophical text should be coherent with an interpretation of the chapter, and that with one of the book. Our interpretive theory for a book, in turn, should be a coherent part of a theory of the author's philosophy, and that with a theory of the school of which he is a part, which should be a coherent part of the philosophical milieu of the time, which should be a coherent part of the theory of that tradition of philosophy, which should form a coherent part of one's theory of the nature of philosophy itself. The coherence test of an interpretation is not just relative to the doctrines, of course. We prefer an interpretive theory which is more coherent with our theories of political activity, social life, religious perceptions, and so forth wherever these overlap.

An interpretation, as opposed to other kinds of explanation for the production of a text, is an account of the background assumptions, theoretical motivations and considerations, and grammatical pictures involved in the production of the text. These explain in the sense of giving the rationales for the philosophical claims in the book. What counts as a reason or a rationale for some theory, as noted before, depends on our imputing to the Chinese thinkers roughly the same kinds of relations among beliefs we have. This is not a prejudice that ours is the only way to reason, but a formal requirement of any theoretical approach to interpretation. If we did not make such an assumption we should never know when one interpretation is a better explanation of the text than another. Judging among interpretations would be impossible without the principle of humanity or some similar principle.

The requirement that we compare interpretations with regard to how coherently, consistently, neatly, and elegantly they explain the statements in the corpus we call Chinese philosophy does not presuppose that the corpus can have no contradictions in it. It does not require that all Chinese philosophers must be consistent. But the principle of humanity does favor an interpretation which either renders the theory coherent *or* gives a coherent, elegant, persuasive account of why the inconsistency occurred, that is, what beliefs, presuppositions, or overgeneralizations might have led *us* to a similar error.

The concept of the best interpretive explanation is thus relative to an intended audience. It may be, for example, that a theoretically clear, elegant explanation of a text can be expressed in the language of fifteenth-century Urdu pirates. Even if that were true (and discoverable), it would be of minimal interest to us since we still have to produce an interpretation of the pirates' version of Chinese philosophy in English—our own conceptual apparatus. We might as well do it directly (though we can glean whatever hints are available from the Urdu account). Logically, of course, the same applies to modern Chinese and Japanese interpretations of ancient Chinese thought.

For the present purposes, the audience is the philosophically interested English-speaking student. The explanatory background is that of the philosophically informed native speaker of this particular modern language. The comparative features of the study of Chinese thought are not part of some special "comparative" methodology, but the inherent requirements of a theory-based understanding or interpretation in one language of philosophical texts in another language. The interpretation must be in the language and invoke the concepts and distinctions which are available in our own philosophical tradition. The comparisons and contrasts drawn with Western philosophy contribute to the informal task of explaining in our terms the production of philosophical writings which differ remarkably, as Chinese writings do, from our own background tradition.

Finally, an interpretive theory never starts from scratch. It inevitably inherits and builds on a tradition of interpretation of Chinese. In the first place, we get off the ground in interpreting by learning Chinese with the aid of dictionaries. Dictionaries are partial interpretive theories for the writings of a period in general. A dictionary purports to give us, for certain terms of Chinese, the term or terms of English which play the same roles in making English sentences true. Translation is not prior to interpretation in any other sense than this—that we construct interpretations against a background of interpretive theory in the form of translation conventions which we take for granted until problems, contradictions, incoherencies, or anomalies arise. *Then* we are likely to question a dictionary definition and to say that in the *Analects* the character *tao* 'way' has some special or more detailed interpretation than that captured in a dictionary entry. We also build on a tradition of interpretation of the philosophical works themselves and again usually depart only to avoid some problem in the explanation. Innovations in an interpretive theory are motivated only by conflicts and inconsistencies in traditional interpretations.

The "ideal" goal of an interpretive theory can be represented as a formalized semantic theory for the entire corpus found in the texts. It would translate each expression of the corpus into a formula in a calculus from which one could "calculate" the logical consequences and presuppositions. The calculus used for this purpose would have to be particularly precise and clear. It would have to be a language that could pair reference-fixing formulae to Chinese expressions with more elegance than ordinary English. Modern philosophy, in particular modern formal semantics, is concerned with the construction of languages which have that kind of precision and generality. Supplementing English with selected conceptual and logical tools from philosophical analysis should help render the precise logical and semantic structure of Chinese. The goal of such an interpretation is not a "literate" translation but a logically perspicuous one that brings to the surface the logical structure of the text. For purposes of philosophical analysis and exposition an accurate translation is not necessarily a word-for-word translation but a translation which reflects how the structure of Chinese sentences influences or explains the presuppositions and conclusions of the text. Most frequently, in fact, a literal translation hides this structure, with the result that we go from not understanding the Chinese original to not understanding the English translation.

Constructing an adequate interpretive theory is, accordingly, enormously aided by use of language which places a premium on conceptual clarity and clear distinctions. Philosophical language drawn from modern work on logic and semantics offers a wide range of tools of analysis which increases the means of accurate representation of the semantic structure of the Chinese philosophical theories studied here. Our taking precision and accuracy as desiderata in interpretive theory, again, does not assume that Chinese writers themselves were precise or were not precise. The point is that we have a clear account that aids our understanding only if the account itself is relatively transparent and precise. Assuming some Chinese term is vague, we need clear language tools to represent the broad reference potential of that term accurately. It is no help in understanding to be as elusive and imprecise as the original text, however much that might be a goal of beautiful or impressionistic translation.

The interpretation which follows will not be a formal theory in the above sense. I will appeal to tools and distinctions from modern philosophical analysis in giving a general account of how the structure of language affects the assumptions and outlooks of Chinese philosophy. Otherwise, this work will take the traditional form of a narrative, running commentary accompanied by translations. Still, the commentary will be theoretical. It is an informal theory of the assumptions and implications, the logical relations, and the model of reality which lie behind the philosophical doctrines from the classical Chinese period. It will draw on technical vocabulary when doing so can highlight the logical form of the text. Despite the common interpretive injunction "Think like a Chinese," thinking like a modern Western philosopher is the most reliable method of stating and defending a theory of what the injunction calls for. We must, that is, use our own language, and preferably precise and clear language, in giving interpretive theories. An interpretive theory of Chinese thought in classical Chinese is quite irrelevant.

Sociological, psychological, political, and other factors do enter into the comparison of interpretations. The approach of this study itself starts with hypotheses about some "psychological" motivations of philosophy—for instance, that philosophical issues are partly shaped and generated by reflection on puzzles which arise when thinkers try to describe the structure of their language. This is especially true of philosophies discussed in these pages that concentrate on philosophy of language, logic, and mind. We accordingly assume (1) that these texts are dealing with philosophical problems concerning language, problems set either by language or the implicit theories of the language in which they carried on their disputes; and (2) that the texts are partly to be explained as contributions to a philosophical dialectic—with some texts responding to, deepening the insights of, challenging, or presenting alternatives to others. That is a sociological assumption which justifies taking the texts also as falling into schools of thought sharing certain approaches and assumptions. The theory would, quite naturally, place texts at times that reflected their position in this dialectic—depending on what other texts they seem to be responding to or refuting.

Let us now consider a common objection to the method outlined here. In sinology the most common objection to an appeal to coherence, consistency, or rational standards in interpretations takes the form of what I shall call the Chinese mind approach developed through the special logic retort.

Objection: The Chinese Mind and the Special Logic Retort

Theories of method often face paradoxes. If they are plausible it must be because they accurately represent the logic of the practice they are trying to make explicit. But then they begin to appear useless. Consider the above view that an interpretation is a theory and that a theory would be deemed the "correct" theory if it is the best of the competing theories (interpretations) of the text, and that we show which is a better theory by showing which is more plausible, more coherent, more clear and precise an account of how those who fashioned the texts would have come to hold the views attributed to them by the interpretive theory. "Surely," a colleague has argued to me, "that is the way we in fact come to adopt interpretations. So is there anyone who ought to revise her method in the light of your reflections? Aren't you without significant opponents?" "Don't we inevitably think like Western philosophers in giving interpretations?"

Indeed, judgments about interpretations of Chinese philosophy *are* more or less in accord with the theory. The Fung Yu-lan interpretation of Chinese thought is influential *because* it is a comprehensive and uniform explanation of Chinese thought which *we* understand—since it is drawn from Plato and the Western tradition of abstract philosophy. The Needham interpretation, similarly, is a comprehensive vision of Chinese thought linked by its acceptance of a post-Einsteinian and anti-Newtonian scientific world view. In both cases the objections and reservations expressed to these theories is that while they do offer structures which could explain many of the philosophical theories in the tradition, they do not sufficiently explain why those philosophers would have come to hold such outlooks which in our own tradition are supported by elaborate theorizing and argument. In both cases the appeal, as this methodology urges, is that it is implausible to attribute the underlying theory without showing a rationale for the theory from the presuppositions of *these* ancient Chinese philosophers.

Still, there are opponents to this methodology even though normal interpretive practice may quite closely (and inevitably) reflect its basic outlines. There is widespread appeal to slogans and principles in criticizing and evaluating interpretations which are diametrically opposed to the coherent theory approach outlined here. The obstacle in the coherent theory approach is the principle of humanity which requires that in the judgment of the plausibility of the account we must take ourselves as a model or as a guide to what is a sufficient explanation of a belief from presuppositions, what considerations would incline us to a certain view or outlook. The opposed slogan is that we must "think like a Chinese" rather than like modern philosophers. The implied conclusion is that Chinese philosophers have a "special logic" which blocks rational understanding by "Western minds." Let us consider the two slogans and their validity as alternative methodological principles.

The slogan "Think like a Chinese" is quite an imposing one in the community of comparative philosophers. One hardly dares contradict it when talking about Chinese philosophy. But I want to argue that as a methodological suggestion it is either misleading or impossible to follow. As a purported aid in understanding ancient Chinese thought, it is a case of "going to Yüeh today and arriving yesterday." If we knew how to apply the slogan we should hardly need professional interpreters. We can establish how the Chinese philosophers in question thought only by determining the correct interpretation of their writings. Fully to think (ancient) Chinese would be to think in that same language, and not to interpret at all. In interpreting one must use some "home" language (metalanguage) or other. Earlier I argued that the home language should include many of the tools of modern philosophy. Thus one approach suggests that using the resources of our own language supplemented by the careful analytical tools of philosophy will help us in constructing clear, coherent, illuminating interpretive theories for Chinese philosophical writings. The other approach seems simultaneously to abandon the normal purpose of interpretation, that is, rendering understanding to an audience, and at the same time to presuppose that the audience one is addressing already knows the interpretation—without which they could not understand or apply the slogan.

The "Think Chinese" slogan could, of course, be interpreted in a way that is consistent with the interpretive approach suggested here. It could merely enjoin us to be consistent with our theories of the social, political, linguistic, and religious world of ancient China and to bear in mind the assumptions, attitudes, and presuppositions generated by the best interpretive theory that fits that cultural background to the philosophical texts that were produced. But if it is (as its use in criticism indicates) an objection to the coherent theory approach and especially to taking ourselves as models in judging what are explanations and motivations for holding certain theories and views, then it seems to be a theoretical sister to the claim that the dispositions of Chinese philosophers to accept theories are not reasonable or logical, in the ordinary (Western) sense of those terms—the special logic retort.

The special logic retort is an informal move in arguments about the correctness of interpretations of Chinese thought. It is used to attack interpretations and to defend them. As an attack, it suggests that an interpretation has relied on Western logic in reconstructing the philosophical views and hence has distorted the original intent of the Chinese philosopher in question. As a defense of an interpretation, it provides a catchall rebuttal to all objections that one's interpretation is inconsistent, incoherent, unclear, or imprecise.

Talk about "Chinese logic" emerged in a much earlier generation of sinologists. It is charitable to assume that it was initially motivated by a sincere effort to understand in a sense analogous to the one I developed earlier, namely, giving rationales for Chinese philosophical doctrines. But the doctrines themselves often appeared so bizarre (especially to the missionary generation of interpreters) that they could be characterized as reasonable only if logic were suspended or altered beyond our normal recognition. The talk was a manifestation, I believe, of tolerance and open-mindedness.

So "special logic" was originally thought of as a descriptive claim with a frankly racist content: people who are racially Chinese have different (and incommensurable) dispositions to draw conclusions from premises. The special logic claim was used to demand tolerance from Westerners who found Chinese philosophical theories—in a word which has become almost a specialized vocabulary item for things Chinese—inscrutable. Saying Chinese were illogical had a dual effect. It allowed us both to acknowledge our inability to understand the ideas and yet to regard those ideas as a "profound" alternative to our own world view. We could argue for the value of what we could not understand without threatening our own self-image as knowers: "After all, we can't be expected to understand this."

Later generations of sinologists, sensitive to the intolerant uses to which the special logic hypothesis might be put, have celebrated the evidence that Chinese thinkers are in fact logical. These scholars continue to assume that the special logic theory is a descriptive psychological claim and that the denial of the claim is likewise a descriptive psychological one—impugning the earlier one as being based on inadequate research or theory.

On examination, it will become clear that the special logic claim is not a straightforward empirical claim about Chinese thought. It is rather more like a methodological proposal—a hypothesis about which interpretative strategy will be more fruitful in generating illuminating interpretations: (1) one which holds basic logical structure constant and attributes a different set of background beliefs and assumptions, or (2) one which makes the background beliefs rather more like our own and varies or denies "logic."

There are, of course, certain straightforward empirical questions about Chinese logic, that is, about the existence and the content of texts and sections of texts which on certain interpretations discuss logical theories. But the special logic theory is hardly concerned with these. It is instead an account of the dispositional or underlying semantic structure of Chinese language. Of course no one would want to rule out that some aspects of the "logic" of classical Chinese will be different from the "logic" which forms the "base" of a semantic syntax for English. Logic is a very broad subject. It includes the study of inferences embodied in the structure of nouns, adjectives, adverbs, and tenses, as well as the study of traditional syllogisms and standard propositional calculus. But the dispute about logic in Chinese philosophy does not appear to be about such details nor even about the multitude of alternative logics of propositional connectives, mereologies, or the like. We can, in principle, discover such differences in detail—the mass noun semantics of Chinese nouns (chap. 3) would be an example. We use these detailed observations about Chinese logic to render the philosophical theories more consistent and coherent. A methodology based on the principle of humanity which commits us to consistency and coherence is, however, a presupposition of any argument for describing Chinese language in terms of an alternative logic. But the special logic theory makes no such appeal. Rather, it says that Chinese reasoning countenances contradiction and incoherence. In contrast with my generation of sinologists, then, I reject "no logic" or "special logic" theories of this sort not because I have discovered that they are empirically false, but because such approaches make it impossible to do interpretation. If Western minds are incommensurably different from Chinese minds then we could not discover anything at all about Chinese thought—including the actual details of the "logic" of Chinese.

The attempts to support or disprove the special logic thesis as an empirical claim have not, therefore, been particularly successful. This is in part due to the confusion between talk of (1) Chinese logic in the sense of philosophical texts whose subject matter is logical inference and structure, and (2) Chinese logic in the sense of the intellectual dispositions of people who are racially Chinese (speakers of Chinese) to relate their beliefs to each other and to draw inferences from evidence. There is no logical connection between the two notions at all. A philosopher can make sound, interesting, and coherent arguments without knowing any logical theory, and someone with a clear command of logical theory might, nonetheless, be a poor craftsman of philosophical arguments. So just showing that there were very few explicit texts dealing with logic does not show that Chinese inferential practices are radically different from our own.

The most common attempt to support the special Chinese logic thesis as an empirical claim supporting a "think like a Chinese" methodology is to note that one seldom finds deductive or "logical" arguments in the Chinese texts and that a great many of the "arguments" in the philosophical texts seem unconvincing to us. Derk Bodde gave such an argument (based on the Platonic distinction of philosophy and poetry, thought and feeling).

> Chinese philosophy, because of this special emphasis upon analogy, is rarely written in the form of logically developed essays, but usually consists of a series of picturesque metaphors, parables, and anecdotes

strung together to illustrate certain main ideas. Once more the result is to make Chinese philosophy poetic rather than logical. It tries to bring emotional rather than intellectual conviction and its main appeal is to the heart rather than to the mind.[2]

The characterization is not entirely accurate (witness the philosophers discussed in these pages), but even if it were it could not justify the special logic retort. If the use of analogy, metaphor, or parables to illustrate ideas makes searching for consistent, coherent interpretations a mistake, then very few of the luminaries of the Western tradition could be interpreted rationally. Plato's allegory of the cave[3] and Descartes's metaphor of the evil demon[4] are in fact powerful images motivating their creators' philosophical systems. Skillful use of analogy is crucial to philosophical exposition, and there are no obvious reasons why sound arguments cannot be expressed poetically. In fact, so few Western philosophical classics are written in strict logical form that the exceptions (e.g., Spinoza's *Ethics*) stand out like "cranes among chickens." So unless one regards Spinoza as the paradigm Western philosopher, we have no reason to suppose the interpretation standards for Chinese philosophy should differ radically from those for Western philosophy.

Another way that various scholars have tried to make sense of the special logic hypothesis is by detailing the differences between ancient Chinese and English grammar. Hajime Nakamura provides one of the best examples of this ploy.

> The non-logical character of the verbal expression of Chinese thought is, of course, intimately connected with the characteristics of the Chinese language. Words corresponding to the prepositions, conjunctions, and relative pronouns of Western languages are very rare. There is no distinction between singular and plural. A single character can denote "un homme, quelques hommes, or humanite." There are no fixed and definite forms for the expression of tense and mood of verbs. There are no cases. One word can be noun, adjective or verb.[5]

The observations Nakamura makes about classical Chinese grammar are commonplace. But there is no reason to suppose that any of those facts render verbal expression illogical. It is true that logics have been developed which include tenses,[6] but the absence of tense can hardly render the standard propositional calculus illogical. I know of no role for cases in logic, and the distinction between singular and plural is surely not logically basic (although mereology, a logic for substances, is different from a logic for physical objects). So there is no support for the special logic retort here.

That does not mean that these observations about Chinese philosophical style and grammar are not important in understanding Chinese thought. It is certain that stylistic and grammatical differences, because they affect the way philosophical questions are posed, can contribute to our understanding of Chinese thought. In chapter 3, I argue that the grammar of nouns to which Nakamura refers helps explain why systems of philosophy like Plato's are unlikely to develop in China. Language does influence philosophy. But differences in syntax do not justify the special logic retort. They do not, that is, give us any reason to consider Chinese thinkers congenitally inconsistent or to think that no coherent interpretation of their theories is possible.

Truth and logical consequence are relative to a language. And there are numerous inferences in a language like modern English for which no simple and direct corresponding inference can be found in classical Chinese (and vice versa, of course). Uncritically assuming corresponding inferences is a common source of distortion of Chinese thought. There are, for example, the inferences built into the meanings of individual words. *Ought* and *right* have the property in modern English that "education morally ought to be available to everyone" entails "everyone has a right to an education." "This object is round" entails "this object has the quality of roundness." Such inferences are analytic (i.e., follow by meaning alone) in English.

Now if we were to translate some sentences of a Chinese text as, say, "Everyone ought to have education" and "this is round," we may not use these sentences as proof that the thinkers in question advocated equal human rights or theories of abstraction. Such inferences cannot be attributed to Chinese thinkers on that kind of evidence. The failure of these inferences, while important to understanding the differences in Chinese thought, does not justify the special logic retort since it does not betoken any inconsistency in the thought at all.[7]

So far, then, we have found no factual justification for the special logic retort. Chang T'ung-sun has argued at great length for the different logic view. He says:

> The differences between Latin, French, English and German grammatical forms do not result in any difference between Aristotelian logic and their respective rules of reasoning, because they belong to the same

language family. Should this logic be applied to Chinese thought, it will prove inappropriate. This fact shows that Aristotelian logic is based on the structure of Western systems of language.[8]

Chang's observations do little to justify or clarify the special logic retort. It is not clear why the application of Aristotelian logic to Chinese thought is inappropriate. All the propositional forms (A, E, I, O) are expressible in classical Chinese.[9] Some inferences licensed in Chinese cannot be put in the form of an Aristotelian syllogism, but that does not provide any contrast with Western languages. In fact, some of the most important of Aristotle's own reasoning cannot be cast in syllogistic form.[10]

To support the special logic retort descriptively, Chang's claim would have to be that Chinese regularly and legitimately token and accept arguments which "Aristotelian" or Western logic would call invalid. But that hypothesis gives far too much potential for strange beliefs to Chinese people. Suppose, contrary to fact, that Chinese reasoning regularly and legitimately tokened arguments of the form found in Kung-sun Lung's dialogue:

> All yellow horses are horses.
> No yellow horse is a white horse.
> Therefore, a white horse is not a horse.

With a minimum of imagination, one could convince any Chinese thinker of a plethora of weird beliefs: Confucius was not Chinese since Mencius is Chinese and Mencius is not Confucius; chickens are not alive since snakes are alive and snakes are not chickens. No culture that routinely accepted such inferences could have had sagacity enough to rule that empire for two thousand years!

Logic and Languages

The panoply of systems known as Western logic are not the logics of any specific Western language, but are themselves "artificial" languages. The valid inferences of such a language are not linked to any specific natural language. When we learn to test "ordinary" reasoning in English by some system of logic, we learn to translate the English sentence into the syntax of the formal language of logic. Now it is well known to all logic students that the classical symbolic logic of even the simple predicate calculus does not translate exactly into English. Some examples: English *and* is not always commutative, while the formal *&* is; "I took off my clothes and went to bed" is not equivalent to "I went to bed and took off my clothes." English *if* . . . *then* . . . requires the antecedent to be relevant to the consequent; "if the moon is made of cheese then I am Rudolph Nureyev" would not normally be judged a true conditional in English, while the classical logical form would.[11] English *or* is usually exclusive disjunction, while logical *v* is not; we would regard it as misleading for someone to say, "Either Harrisburg is the capital of Pennsylvania or Albany is the capital of New York." Natural languages like English may indeed have a logical structure, but logicians do not claim to have captured more than a fragment of the logic of English.

So the logic of which we normally speak is not the logic of any specific natural language. It can be used, via translation, to test inferences in any language. Once we do accept a translation of a sentence of English into the logical symbolism then we can test its validity. But exactly the same is true of German, Swahili, Farsi, *and* Chinese (ancient and modern).

Remembering that logical systems are themselves languages can help us see why the special logic retort raises methodological issues—in fact creates methodological paradoxes. Suppose an interpreter asserted that some sentence *(A)* of Chinese were to be translated in formal logic as "P & Q" and yet he claimed that it was both appropriate and common to deny one of the two sentences he had translated as "P" or as "Q" while asserting *A*. Has he proved that his Chinese speakers are illogical? Or is that the kind of result that should be taken to show that he had mistranslated the Chinese connectives?[12] Ultimately, any assertion of illogicality is going to assume some translation-interpretation. And as long as an interpretation is available which is not incoherent, the incoherent one is suspect.

So the special logic retort just cannot rest on any "bare facts" about Chinese. Its implications are methodological.

There is, as noted earlier, a factual issue about the existence of logic in Chinese philosophy. That is the question of whether or not Chinese philosophers ever engaged in the study of logic or in erecting theories of logic. That query is settled by empirical research and evidence. Of course, Chinese philosophers might have failed to do this or might have done it in ways that are fundamentally different from the way logic was or is done in the West. But the existence of such theories of logic is a totally different issue from the special logic retort and bears on interpretation in exactly the same way any other background theory or doctrine does. It becomes part of the sets of beliefs with which any proposed interpretation must be coherent. It thus influences our interpretation *qua* being a philosophical theory, not *qua* explaining how Chinese people think.

Whether or not Chinese philosophers expounded theories of the inference structure of, say, the sentential connectives (e.g., *if . . . then . . . , and . . .*) or the truth functional or modal operators of their language (*not . . . , necessarily . . . , all . . . , some . . .* , etc.) is an empirical question. If and to the degree they did so, they have theories of logic. The empirical question can be settled by inventorying the corpus of classical philosophical works to see if there are doctrines which, on a reasonable interpretation, are about logic in anything like the Western sense. On the other hand, that Chinese philosophy is logical in something like a dispositional sense is not a discovery but a decision. It is a decision to propose, criticize, and defend interpretations in a particular way, using consistency and coherence as critical standards.

The dispositional logic claim could be viewed as empirical, as a kind of second-level discovery. We may find that interpretations following the rule of coherence and consistency are possible, enlightening, more informative about the culture, or suggest many new hypotheses and provoke deeper insights. Or we may continually fail to find valuable interpretations which are coherent. Then we should think that the special logic retort may indeed have some merit. But then we should see that the retort can never be a valid *objection* to any coherent interpretation. The only evidence for it is the lack of coherent interpretations. If a given interpretation is rational and coherent, then any claim of the innate illogicality of Chinese thought would be undercut by the very possibility of that interpretation.

The Empirical Study of Chinese Implicit Logic

Another way to show that the special logic question is essentially methodological is to consider attempts to *disprove* it as an empirical claim. We will find that if we were to attempt any such proof we would *necessarily* end up doing what the coherent theory methodology outlines—taking our own patterns of drawing inferences for granted in giving our account of Chinese thought.

There are two scholars who have been engaged prominently in

proving that Chinese thought is *not* illogical or fundamentally different from our own logic: Janusz Chmielewski and Chung-ying Cheng. Both treat the hypothesis and its denial as empirical claims to be settled by a survey of the body of texts that make up the extant evidence of the philosophical thought of the period. Chmielewski, first, describes his investigative procedure as follows:

> The task I have set myself may be briefly stated in the following terms: without losing sight of the philosophical and historical background (which I believe is always the necessary prerequisite in sinological research) I propose to single out some more or less typical forms of reasoning (whether already interpreted by others or not) occurring in early Chinese philosophers; to define them from the standpoint and in terms of elementary symbolic logic; to find out general logical laws and notions underlying them; and, as far as possible, to compare them with the ancient logical theory of the West.[13]

Chmielewski goes on to suggest that the *only* problem with claims like those of Chang Tung-sun is that the investigators were familiar with only traditional logic and could not "see" that there were logically defensible arguments in the corpus.

> . . . in the sense that practically all scholars, both Chinese and Western, so far working in the field never used modern symbolic logic (mathematical logic, logistics) as a tool for their research; instead, they have all adhered to the traditional conception of logic, hardly going beyond syllogistics (in its traditional, not truly Aristotelian form), or some kind of "philosophical logic."[14]

The error, according to Chmielewski, is essentially hasty generalization—helped along by inadequate understanding of logic techniques which would have aided them in noticing counterexamples to their claim.

But as we have seen, the special logic retort is not an empirical generalization at all. It is a cry of despair. Unable to make sense of Chinese philosophical doctrines to critical Western audiences, the sinologists, in effect, give up. The vague form of the special logic retort then goes, "What makes sense to Chinese does not make sense to Westerners." What is needed to alleviate the despair is not a compendium of dialogue sequences that can be translated into valid arguments in some logical system or other, but coherent, rational philosophical interpretations of Chinese thought.

Chmielewski's approach offers scant comfort here. He manages interpretations in which the arguments are formally valid, but grotesquely unsound. He removes the nonsense from the structure of the argument to its content.

> In particular, I have demonstrated positively that the early Chinese thinkers correctly used some simple but important laws of the propositional calculus—even if at the subconscious level and even if to the purpose of epistemologically indefensible speculation.[15]

Chmielewski thus perpetuates the confusion not only by treating the question as an empirical one but by suggesting that the dispositional sense of Chinese logic (which he calls "implicit logic") and the writings about the subject matter of logic are equally logical *theories*. Hence, after collecting his samples of reasoning in Chinese texts, he proposes to "find out the general logical laws . . . underlying them." In doing so he suggests that we will find something comparable to logical *theory* in the West. But treating the dispositional sense of logic as a form of logical theory tempts one to the confusion that there is really, underlying the explicit-implicit distinction, a single logic of China—a little of which was brought to consciousness and the rest of which remained hidden awaiting Chmielewski's reconstruction efforts.

The direct consequence of blurring the distinction between the two kinds of issues is Chmielewski's sliding from a description of a purported structure of one of Kung-sun Lung's arguments to attributing the theory used in the description to Kung-sun Lung.[16] A. C. Graham has already called attention to this lapse.

> He also complicates the issue by slipping from the tenable claim that the argument may be tested by applying the algebra of classes into the highly questionable assumption that Kung-sun Lung was actually studying logical classes.[17]

Professor Chung-ying Cheng follows Chmielewski in distinguishing between "implicit" and "explicit" logic. But also, like Chmielewski, he covertly collapses them. He too refers to the dispositions to reason in certain ways as being "theories" to be reconstructed from the empirical evidence.

> For the purpose of elucidating the nature of Chinese logic, we may suggest that the goal of study and research in classical Chinese logic

should be envisaged as a critical analysis of the explicit logico-methodological issues in Chinese classical discourses on the one hand, and a synthetic reconstruction of the implicit logico-scientific theories, on the other.[18]

Cheng implies, in effect, that studying implicit and studying explicit logic are merely different approaches to the same subject matter. He says:

Chinese writings in the classical period can be studied with regard to their explicit formulation of problems in logical theories of inference and argument and in scientific methodology of explanation and confirmation. Second, they can be studied with regard to their implicit patterns of logical semantic and synthetic connections and categorizations. Finally they can be studied with regard to their philosophical concerns with problems of truth, necessity, reality, experience, and related subjects.[19]

In a later article, he characterizes the above as a "three level study in Chinese logic."[20]

Both of these proposals to refute the claim of a distinctly Chinese logic can be used to show that the special logic retort *and* its denial have methodological rather than empirical significance. Consider Cheng's procedure outlined above. In an interpretation we do frequently attribute implicit or presumed premises to an argument, but we understand the implicit premise to be that premise required to make the argument formally valid. We can speak of premises being presupposed in this way and even of whole theories being presupposed. We prove that premises or theories are presupposed by showing that they are logically necessary for the supposed argumentative purpose—the conclusion.

Thus any claim to have found a presupposition must take logic as given. We could never hope to find the entire system of underlying logical rules in this way because we invoke them in the process. Unless we have some conception of the logic to use in interpretation, the statement that some doctrine presupposes another doctrine becomes meaningless. The end result of the procedure outlined by Cheng—that Chinese thought is logical—is not difficult to predict.

Chmielewski's method, too, can illustrate the same point. His "discovery" is also presupposed in his method. Suppose we have isolated and formalized some argument in some classical text. Formally complete deductive arguments are rare in any philosophical work, so let us suppose that what we have isolated is one of the incomplete arguments. We have two choices. We may pronounce it a non sequitur (invalid argument) or an enthymeme (incomplete argument). If we regard it as a non sequitur we either include it in the corpus to be formalized or we do not. If we include it and write rules which will validate such arguments, then (as with the white horse example earlier) it will only take a little imagination to prove innumerable absurdities in this "Chinese logic." If we leave the non sequitur out of the corpus, we do so because it is *not logically valid*—a judgment which presupposes some account of logical validity. The result, that Chinese logic is like ours, is dictated by our use of "Western logic" in doing the study.

Suppose instead that we treat the argument as an enthymeme and supply the missing premise. Then the situation is again that we can know which premise is missing only by having some antecedent conception of logical validity. Supplying the missing premise automatically makes the argument valid (perhaps unsound, but valid). Again the formalized result is not going to differ from the logic used either in supplying the missing premise or in rejecting the argument as a non sequitur and therefore not part of the corpus which will be used to define "Chinese logic." There appears to be no interesting sense in which we could be said to be discovering some culture's implicit "logic" by such a procedure. We are simply employing our own logic as a methodological device in developing interpretations.

The Dilemma of the Chinese Mind

As we saw, then, either the slogan "Think like a Chinese" is just a misleading proposal that corresponds to the procedure of theoretical interpretation or it supposes some kind of incommensurable and contradictory or incoherent special Chinese logic. But it offers us, given this second interpretation, no escape from an impossible methodological box. We have no way to prove there is a different Chinese logic except by deciding what is the correct interpretation of the extant texts. As an objection to the coherent theory approach to interpretation it counsels nothing except paralysis. (One may, uncharitably, suspect that the real moral behind the ploy, when used in disputes, is, "Trust me, your intuitively in-tune master of the mysteries—and don't you dare contradict or question my interpretations.") The only evidence against the coherent theory approach would be its failure to produce any intelligible explanations of Chinese philosophy. But we can never be sure that some other proposal will not succeed. So the special logic version of the Chinese mind methodology can *never* count as a valid objection to an interpretive theory.

The methodological import of the special logic retort and the Chinese mind approach to interpretation is basically defeatist. There is no guidance to be gained from the injunction to be *in*coherent—there are simply too many ways to be incoherent. Could we seriously apply the suggestion that the less consistent of two given interpretations is the more plausible one? In principle the retort totally disparages any attempt to understand Chinese philosophy through its rationales.

In its more respectable use in sinology, the retort is linked to some other restriction on methodological practice. Some positive, though nonrational, characterization of Chinese thought is offered, for example, that Chinese thought is poetic. This is simply a factual-sounding methodological proposal that in textual reconstruction, punctuation, and assignment of meaning we should choose that alternative which renders the outcome more poetic, evocative, stylized, or otherwise aesthetically pleasing no matter what nonsense it makes of the philosophical doctrine of the text.

The "poetic" methodological bias described above is, in fact, tacitly assumed by a great many sinologists because of the research and breakthroughs in reconstructing the phonemic system of ancient Chinese. Any such characterization becomes, as it has in sinology, a self-fulfilling prophecy because it shapes the methodology. If we regard as illegitimate any construal of a text which makes coherent sense whenever the choice is between rational coherence and preserving the rhyme structure, the sentence length patterns, or parallel couplets, then it should come as no surprise that the interpretations that emerge will not be philosophically as good as they are poetic and graceful.[21] A poetic characterization which dictates accepting textual variations, punctuations, or emendations which preserve rhythm over those which preserve sense is not *always* a bad idea.[22] When we have other reasons to suspect that the works being studied are poetry, then we ought to adopt such a method. But when we think the works are philosophy, we ought to adopt interpretive standards appropriate to philosophy.

The methodological bind emerging from the "think Chinese" slogan can have other, even less attractive methodological implications. Consider the following pair of observations by H. G. Creel:

> In approaching things Chinese we might attempt, first of all, to appropriate to ourselves the Chinese point of view, so that we regard any particular thing not as a Westerner would, nor even as a Hindu, but as a Chinese.[23]

> The crux of the matter is that the ancient Chinese were on the whole neither systematic nor orderly thinkers. . . . They were indefatigable cataloguers; they were not systematizers.[24]

The implication for our methodology should give anyone pause. In general, the exhortation to approach Chinese thought from the Chinese point of view is paradoxical. We do not know what the point of view is until we have approached it. In the "first of all" we do not know if some Chinese thinker is systematic or not. The failure to find a system by a particular interpretation, say of the *Chuang-tzu*, does not establish that incoherence is a characteristic of the thought since a subsequent interpretation may render the structure in a thoroughly coherent and systematic way. We should then want to withdraw the characterization of Chuang-tzu as a cataloguer.

Notice that it is not a case of *assuming* that Chuang-tzu's thought is coherent. We are only arguing that there can be no good reason to put an upper bound on the degree of rational coherence we may regard as plausible in Chinese thinkers. Any time the injunction "Think like a Chinese" carries such an implication, it is a mistake. When the injunction is given content by characterizations such as "poetic," "intuitive," "mystical," or "unsystematic," these characterizations become a priori methodological predispositions which are self-fulfilling.

In any case, I have never seen, on *any* interpretation, an account of some sentence or doctrine of, say, Chuang-tzu, saying, "I am really trying very hard to be unsystematic and just to catalogue as many disparate items of information as possible," or Lao-tzu implying, "It is more important that your phrases be balanced than that your principles be correct." I am naturally suspicious of anyone who implies that this is the way ancient Chinese thinkers viewed themselves. In fact, for the most part, on most plausible interpretations, all these thinkers had just the opposite view.

So critical, analytic, logical, and coherent standards should be used in interpreting Chinese thought. That methodological conclusion does not arise from any hypothesis about the nature of Chinese thought but from the nature of the interpretive enterprise. Since an interpretation is a theory and is designed to advance understanding it should be guided by the same rigorous principles which produce understanding in other theory-guided activities.

The rest of the methodology follows from the presupposition that we are interpreting philosophical texts. This part of the method is defeasible. It could in principle turn out to be the case that there is only poetry in China. But, as with the coherence standard, we will not know philosophically interesting doctrines are absent unless we fail to find them. And even then our proof is never complete.

I do not mean to deny that the style of Chinese philosophical writing does differ from that of the West in important ways—it is relatively more poetic and balanced, and the arguments are not typically as careful nor as complete. But the explanation of these differences in style does not require any assumption about fundamentally different thought processes. Chinese thinkers, from Mo-tzu to Mao Tse-tung, were social-political activists. Their concern in writing was to inspire and move the readers to action in accordance with certain ethical-political doctrines. They saw the function of language and theorizing as its impact on behavior. Hence they did stress forceful, attractive, moving, gripping, even poetic slogans and expressive style over convincing argument. But the latter was neither absent nor ignored. Even if adumbrated in style, the rationales were there and gave the content for the style to operate on. Nothing in the style entails that coherent, interesting, and understandable interpretations of their ideas is impossible.

Methodology Summarized

The methodology outlined here starts from the premise that interpretation (which includes translation) is a theory. It is an attempt to explain a text—to render it understandable. As such it is (1) inescapably relative to the intended audience (English-speaking philosophy students), and (2) appropriately wedded to the critical, rational, logical evaluation procedures appropriate to other theories. The main evaluative feature on which we have concentrated is the coherence of the theory. Can it explain and be explained by other, more inclusive theories, and is it the most elegant theory which accounts for the data—the texts?

The methodology by itself does not commit us to the view that the Chinese thinkers themselves are logical or not logical. Our assumption that we are interpreting philosophical texts commits us to constructing theories about the rationales for the sentences we find in the texts. The availability of a coherent, rational system for a fragment of Chinese thought *is* to be taken as confirmation of the claim that it is philosophy and that the philosopher in question was a coherent thinker.

The special logic retort and the "Think like a Chinese" slogan are neither intelligible objections to such a methodology nor explicable by any other defensible methodology. The upshot of both, taken seriously, is that we cannot understand Chinese thought at all. Thus, the only appropriate conclusion to be drawn from them is "Give up" or "Trust me, your master and guide" (spoken by the scholar who claims to have penetrated the mystery).

There is no factual basis for any associated "Chinese logic" hypothesis. The features of Chinese thought usually associated with the antirational slogans just cannot prove that a radically different (inconsistency-justifying) implicit logic is at work. And for similar reasons, the attempts by modern formally sophisticated philosophers to prove the opposite also fail. The issue is a methodological one and not an empirical one. The only factual question is whether or not the theoretical methodology can work, and this translates into the question of whether or not these writers are philosophers or not.

The intermediate positions, formed by joining the special logic retort or the "Chinese mind" slogans to some characterization of Chinese thought as "poetic" or "cataloguing," are similarly not straightforward descriptive claims but methodologies. These methodologies are widely respected and followed in theorizing about Chinese philosophy despite the fact that in practice they mitigate against philosophical interpretations. The special logic retort is just the limiting case of methodologies which treat coherence of reasons for views as unimportant relative to some other constraint on emendation, textual reconstruction, punctuation, and translation and interpretation. Since our interests are philosophical and the texts we study are uniformly regarded as philosophical, there is no a priori reason why we should adopt restrictions on interpretation appropriate to poetry or religious incantations.

There is more involved in the methodology than just a kind of charting of frequent tendencies of Chinese thought. The ideal should be to explain *why* these characterizations should hold. A theory, say of the tides, does not just chart the highs and lows. That kind of a chart is not an explanation. So the mere litany of recurring patterns of thought is not an adequate interpretive theory until the patterns have been explained as based on beliefs or attitudes which we can regard as reasonable for a Chinese philosopher to hold.

The above explanation of the apparently poetic, metaphorical character of many Chinese philosophical writings is an example. The explanation attributed an activist motivation to the philosophers in question. While, in principle, we could insist on a further rationale for the motivation, it is not necessary for our understanding, for, even though many professional philosophers disagree with others who "popularize" their philosophy, we do understand the rationale for doing so. The understanding could be regarded as complete as soon as we can free it from any appeal to grasp intuitively "the Chinese mind."

In what follows I apply the theoretical interpretation methodology to one of the most recalcitrant puzzles of classical Chinese thought—the white-horse paradox of Kung-sun Lung (see chap. 5). Chapter 2 argues for a very general interpretive hypothesis about the way Chinese language might have influenced the conceptual scheme of the classical philosophers in ways which illuminate the thought in contrast to our own philosophical tradition. I argue that the mass-noun-like syntax of Chinese nouns motivates an implicit "substance ontology" as opposed to our "physical object ontology," and that it renders less appealing a whole host of philosophical views which have characterized Western thought from its outset. These conceptual differences include a different concept of mind, of language, and of thought. The argument rests on the claim that the Chinese assumptions are more coherent with (explained by) their language than our own assumptions are. In chapter 3, I develop and argue for compatible interpretations of the philosophies of the period prior to and surrounding the thought of Kung-sun Lung. There I discuss four presuppositions about language which are reasonable for Chinese philosophers to have held, which explain many of their views about language and thought, and which explain many of the fundamental differences between Chinese and Western thought. Chapter 4 deals with a particular school which focused on questions of language, logic, and semantics. I argue that their views develop out of the presuppositions outlined in chapters 2 and 3 and, in turn, explain the motivation and justification of the white-horse dialogue in chapter 5.

So, consistent with the methodological view, there is a kind of inverted pyramid of explanations focused on that one paradox: broad theory about all of Chinese thought, an embedded theory about Chinese thought in general prior to Kung-sun Lung, an embedded theory about the development of semantic thought from that broad tradition, and finally the interpretive theory explaining the white-horse paradox. The broadest theory is confirmed by the insights it yields and the explanatory power it has at all the other levels. The interpretation of Kung-sun Lung is confirmed (relative to other available interpretations) by its coherence with the text and with the entire historical period. The other two levels of interpretive theory are confirmed both by their coherence with the more inclusive level and their explanatory power in illuminating the lower-level texts.

Chapter 2

The Mass Noun Hypothesis and Abstraction in Chinese Language and Thought

The basic interpretive hypothesis underlying the following study of classical Chinese thought is that Chinese philosophical theories all presuppose a common model or picture of the relations between language and the world and between language and the mind. This model or picture explains characteristic pre-Han Chinese philosophical presuppositions. The model and the presuppositions are plausible either on their face, or are plausible beliefs for thinkers using a language like ancient Chinese. In this chapter, I want to develop an account of the major differences between the pre-Han scheme and traditional Western views of semantics and philosophy of mind and to show how the differences are explained by features of Chinese language.

Briefly, we can characterize Chinese semantic theories as a view that the world is a collection of overlapping and interpenetrating stuffs or substances. A name (term or predicate—*ming* 名) denotes (refers to, picks out—*chü* 舉) some substance. The mind is not regarded as an internal picturing mechanism which represents the individual objects in the world, but as a faculty that discriminates the boundaries of the substances or stuffs referred to by names. This "cutting up things" view contrasts strongly with the traditional Platonic philosophical picture of objects which are understood as individuals or particulars which instantiate or "have" properties (universals). In a Platonic scheme the concrete instances of any abstract property stand in a one-many relation to words which stand for or "have as a meaning" the universal or repeatable abstract component (property, essence, or attribute). Similarly, the Platonic view of the mind is one in which the mind knows (has or contains) these "meanings" or intelligible abstract objects. Chinese philosophy has no theory either of abstract or of mental entities. The "individuals" in Chinese theories of language are "unit parts" of the "stuffs" picked out by names.

I stress the negative side of this hypothesis, the antiabstraction, antimentalism side, to cure the temptation to regard the traditional Western philosophy of mind and philosophy of language as obvious to everyone. We tend to regard that model as so inescapable that we can only make sense of Chinese thinkers by invoking metaphors from this tradition: ideas, concepts, objects in the mind, or the like. Stressing this negative theme is intended to sensitize readers and make them conscious enough of the metaphors and the picture they impose that, by careful attention, they can avoid it. That the abstraction model is not the Chinese picture is argued in detail in the following chapters by showing that more coherent interpretations emerge when we assume the background scheme to be that of mass substances rather than that of objects and properties. In this chapter I argue that the mass alternative is the more plausible model for humans doing philosophy in Chinese.

Behavioral Nominalism

Behavioral nominalism[1] captures both "negative" features of the philosophical perspective of Chinese thinkers. I use *behavioral* because, in the place of internal mental representations of particulars and properties, the Chinese view of mind (heart-mind) is dynamic; the mind is the ability to discriminate and distinguish "stuffs" and thereby to guide evaluation and action. I use *nominalism* because the Chinese philosopher is not committed to any entities other than names and objects. There is no role in Chinese philosophical theories like that played by terms such as *meaning, concept, notion,* or *idea* in Western philosophy.

Positively characterized, the Chinese picture went as follows. Language consists of *ming* 名 'names' which have a one-to-one relation to *shih* 實 'stuffs'. Chinese ontology, I suggest, is mereological. For every abstract *set* of objects one can construct a concrete mereological object by regarding all of the members of the set as one discontinuous stuff. Identifying different members of the set is the same as identifying spatiotemporally different parts of the same stuff. In learning names we learn to discriminate or divide reality into these mereological stuffs which names name. Naming is not grounded on the notion of an abstract concept, a property, an essence, or an ideal type, but rather on finding "boundaries" between things. Accordingly, Chinese philosophers view minds not as repositories of weird objects called ideas, but as the faculty encompassing the abilities and inclinations to discriminate stuffs from each other. This mass stuff view can be explained by special features of the logical structure of Chinese nouns. The explanation, again, is via our own perception of what would be a reasonable or plausible way to talk about words if our language had the grammatical features of Chinese.

The Logic of Mass Nouns

The syntax of Chinese nouns is strikingly similar to that of "mass nouns" in English.[2] English mass nouns include *water, rice, paper, furniture,* and *grass.* Mass nouns contrast with other common nouns like *cat, pebble, photograph, lamp, pea,* and *lake.* These rather more "common" common nouns are, by contrast, called count nouns, since one can "count" them: seven cats, twelve peas, one lake. Count nouns take pluralization. They can be directly preceded by the articles *a* or *an.* They stand alone as a noun phrase only when plural or preceded by articles, demonstratives, numbers, and so forth; "horse is brown" is not grammatical in English though "furniture is brown" is.

Mass nouns, by contrast, do not take pluralization and cannot be directly preceded by numbers or indefinite articles; *seven grass and *a furniture are improperly formed. Instead, mass nouns are associated with certain other expressions (let us call them measures or sortals) which allow one to divide up the substances into countable units: a *cup* of water, a *blade* of grass, three *pieces* of furniture. Characteristically, we can "count" mass nouns in a number of ways. We might have had, for example, a *drop* of water, a *lid* of grass, and a *roomful* of furniture. Mass nouns can stand alone as noun phrases in sentences.

In most modern Chinese dialects the syntactical parallel with English mass nouns is almost exact for all nouns. Chinese nouns have no ordinary plural. They cannot be directly preceded by numbers or indefinite articles or demonstratives.[3] Each noun is associated with appropriate sortals (called classifiers or measures in most language texts). Thus in (Mandarin)

Chinese, one says ⌜one *pen* book⌝, ⌜three *ko* persons⌝, and ⌜this *chih* pencil⌝. The nouns by themselves are complete term expressions.

Another characteristic distinction between the two groups of nouns in English is their association with either *much* or *many* (or the opposites, *little* versus *few*). Mass nouns go with *much* (e.g., much wood, much money); count nouns go with *many* (e.g., many trees, many dimes). Chinese *to* 多 'many-much' and *shao* 少 'few-little' go with all nouns (and adjectives).

Classical Chinese is slightly different from modern Chinese in a few of these respects. The concrete nouns in the language of the pre-Han philosophers seemed like hybrids. They had no plural; they were associated with sortals or measures, and there was no *many-much* distinction. They functioned as basic term expressions. But sortals did not become grammatically necessary until sometime in the Han Dynasty. So nouns might be preceded directly by numbers, and this produced puzzles for pre-Han semanticists, the Neo-Mohists.[4] But the nouns otherwise had all the grammatical trappings of mass nouns.[5] These masslike nouns of classical Chinese are what shape the intuitive picture of the language-world relation in Chinese philosophy.

A Comparison of Noun Interpretations

Given this unique grammar of classical Chinese nouns, the question is, how shall we characterize these nouns—as count nouns with some peculiar properties or as a transitional stage leading to mass nouns? I contend that the count noun alternative is much less natural and elegant an account than the mass noun one. Consider the usual translation conventions for Chinese nouns. One translates concrete nouns as count nouns whenever the nearest equivalent is a count noun in English (and picks according to context when equally common mass and count equivalents are available, e.g., *mu* 'tree', 'wood'). Choose the plural or the singular depending on the context and render *to* 多 and *shao* 少 as "many" and "few" when the English noun is grammatically count, otherwise "much" and "little." This commonsense approach involves an embarrassing wrinkle, however. Since these nouns frequently refer to the species as a whole, translators are tempted to talk as if there were a twofold ambiguity in all nouns, that is, as if these were count nouns which were not only ambiguous between singular and plural, but also between concrete and abstract.

Consider, for example, the complexity of this description of Chinese nouns by Dobson:

> An important observation must be made here about nominal usage in LAC [Late Archaic Chinese]. A word used nominally denominates indifferently both species and specimen or specimens of the species. Thus, *jen* 人 in a nominal usage is indifferently "homo sapiens," "man" as a species, or "a man, the man, men" as a specimen or specimens of the species. It is not merely that number (the difference between one, two, or more than two instances of) is not differentiated, but that both class and member are comprised in one term. Certain of these distinctions are imposed in determination, and the noun is then said to be "committed"; otherwise, it remains neutral in its indications as to these distinctions. A noun determined by, for example, a numeral or a unit of measure becomes immediately "an enumerated instance of" or "a quantified unit of" the thing it signifies.[6]

Despite his assimilation of Chinese "nominals" to count nouns, Dobson uses the language of mass and stuffs, for example, "a quantified unit of *the thing* it signifies," "class and member are comprised in a single term." But his choice of language forces him to postulate that nouns have some abstract reference too—to classes, to species, to that of which things are instances, namely, universals (though he avoids that term). However, this tortured analysis can be avoided if we give up the class-member picture for a more masslike part-whole picture. Then we never need to import any Platonism into Chinese graphs. Their reference is always concrete, always to stuff or bits of stuff in space-time. We are not forced to say a graph refers to a mathematical entity (a class), an abstract one (a universal), a mental one (an idea), or a semantic one (a meaning). So the masslike characterization is the simpler, the more elegant theoretical model on which to talk about Chinese nouns.

There is an ambiguity remaining in even the masslike description. Classical Chinese nouns, as noted above, do have some countlike features. That turns out to be a virtue of the theory, for that ambiguity helps explain a number of semantic puzzles considered by the Neo-Mohists (see p. 124) and it is an ambiguity that is removed by the subsequent development of the language—the strict use of sortals after the Han Dynasty. Now if the ambiguity in nouns were the fourfold one of singular-plural/concrete-abstract, then that development of the language did nothing to remove it and just added a tedious and unnecessary grammatical complication. Modern Chinese nouns are still ambiguous in all four ways if they ever were. It is significant, then, that when the choice came between resolving the ambiguity in favor of mass or count nouns it was resolved in favor of mass nouns.

The Stuff-Kinds Picture of Reality

The grammatical parallels between English mass nouns and Chinese nouns give initial plausibility to the hypothesis that the Chinese assumptions about language would be something like the assumptions we might be tempted to use in explaining the semantics of mass nouns. The picture outlined above of interpenetrating stuffs or substantives organized basically under the part-whole relation is only one of the ways of modeling a semantic universe for mass nouns, but it is an intuitively natural one and, as the study of the Neo-Mohists shows, there is strong evidence that this rudimentary mereology was indeed the model that informed their semantic theories.

To see how masslike nouns contribute to mereology, consider how they function as terms or individual constants. Mass nouns, unlike count nouns, play the same role in sentences that proper nouns do. This makes it natural to regard the mass nouns as logically singular terms—as names. Thus, in Chinese semantic theory, *ming* 名 'name' is rather like English "word." It encompasses not only proper names but all nouns and adjectives.[7] Then the question, "Of what is *ma* 'horse' the name?" has a natural answer: the mereological set of horses. "Horse-stuff" is thus an object (substance[8] or thing-kind) scattered in space-time.

Notice that there are differences between these mass nouns and proper nouns, despite their surface similarity. Mass nouns can be modified (e.g., red ink), while proper names cannot (*Green George). Similarly, mass nouns are grammatically distinct from adjectives. Again, however, mass nouns are more like adjectives than are count nouns, and the similarities are even more striking in Chinese. As a result, Chinese theories of language tend to treat adjectives as terms denoting mass substantives; for example, red is the stuff that covers apples and the sky at sunset.[9]

This way of picturing the language-world relation is reinforced by a tendency common in both China and the West. Both traditions treated all words as names and regarded naming as the main semantic relation. We name children, pets, favorite places, or toys. Naming is a one-to-one relation. However, this common form of oversimplification motivates traditional Platonic problems when we ask about count nouns, "What does *X* name *really*?" We look for the "one" that the many "instances" or "members" have in common. With mass nouns, the one is simply the whole substance. A naming paradigm in conjunction with count nouns, but not mass nouns, generates the traditional one-many problem of philosophy and explains the appeal of Platonism.

The line of reasoning is familiar: what does *horse* name? Not Dobbin in particular, nor Secretariat. It applies to *each horse separately,* so it must name something in each individual horse which is the same in all its instances. This thing-in-common surfaces in metaphysical, semantic, and epistemological guise as the essence, idea, or property. That line of reasoning would not emerge from similar reflections on masslike nouns. Instead, the puzzle would seem to be how the extent of reference of the term could be specified. *Ma* 'horse' in term position might refer to the entire mereological object—the concrete species, or to some part, specific herd, team, or an individual horse, depending on the context. The central problems in Chinese semantics revolve around the ambiguity of part-versus-whole reference. Taoist skepticism grows mainly out of reflection on the relativity of the scope of ordinary nouns to context. There is no philosophical concern formally corresponding to the classical Western grammatical problem of the one and the many. The name denotes a stuff which functions as a rather amorphous "one"—a one which is scattered in different places. But like water, gold, rice, and wood, it is regarded as a stuff. When speaking of localizable bits of the stuff, it is natural to think of them as parts of the single whole stuff picked out by the name, not as a "particular" with some common or universal property.

This difference in semantic perspective is fundamentally central to the explanation of other differences between the two philosophical traditions. The argument for a something-in-common which functions as the meaning of count nouns has had an enormous impact on the Western tradition and, if absent from the Chinese tradition, would account for much of the disparity between them. Great chunks of the history of Western philosophy are involved in elaborating the line of reasoning leading to the postulation of abstract objects like horsehood. The examples range from Plato's forms or *Ideos* to the Realists' universals, to Locke's abstract mental images, to the logicians' classes, and to metalanguage functions to possible worlds. The absence of such concerns in Chinese thought should not make us suspect they lack a gift for philosophical thought. There is a far simpler answer close at hand: the differences in the grammar of nouns contributed to the survival of an intuitively natural nominalism in which each graph is taken to name scattered aggregate stuffs or masses.

It is hard to characterize the effect of having a different conceptual scheme in a nonmisleading way. Of course, we must suppose that someone with whatever language still has the same visual presentations when looking at horse-stuff. But all the ways of talking about it would be correspondingly altered. We would know that such stuffs come in regular shapes. The shape can even be regarded as one of the key ways we use to distinguish that stuff from ox-stuff. But we could do this without suggesting that the shape was a property which the individual horses shared or had in common. It is just a fact about this kind of stuff that it comes in regular shapes. Learning to recognize the shape is a key in distinguishing the stuff—and in knowing, therefore, how to use the word.

Abstractions in Chinese Language and Thought

In chapter 1, I use the vehicle of hermeneutic method to tackle one of the standard issues in interpreting Chinese philosophy—the question of Chinese logic. Here I want to use these observations about grammar and this hypothesis about the intuitive picture of language and the world appropriate to Chinese grammar to analyze another old question—does Chinese have abstractions?

Again, the tides of academic favor seem to have a generational history. The generation which first encountered Chinese thought was struck by the absence of abstract metaphysics and suggested that Chinese language could not form abstractions. The later generation, sensitive to what seemed to them the implicit intolerance of this view, has mostly rejected it. My view is that the question has been misconstrued by both sides. The question is not what language *can* do, but what theories *do* do. Classical Chinese philosophical theories had no roles for abstractions.

The Functions of Abstract Theorizing in Philosophy

I am inclined, in a qualified way, to side with the earlier generation on the question of abstraction (as in a qualified way I supported the later generation on the question of Chinese logic). I would like to argue for the claim that no Chinese philosophical system of the classical period in China was committed to the existence of or had roles for abstract (universal) entities in any of the traditionally important ways that Western semantics, epistemology, ontology, or philosophy of mind had roles for abstractions. Plato's *Ideos*, or forms, for example, served all of these branches of philosophy. In semantics, forms stood as the embodiments of meaning, corresponding to definitions; in epistemology they represented the objects of knowledge; in ontology they constituted a realm of unchanging objects outside the space-time realm; and in philosophy of mind they came to represent the content of the mind, the thoughts or ideas. I shall briefly expand on the function of abstractions in these kinds of theories to underline how traditional Western philosophy differs from Chinese.

Semantics is the study of meaning, and for Plato the main focus of philosophical activity was a search for the meaning of a word conceived of as finding the correct definition. His theory of forms or *Ideos* was intended as an account of the nature of ideal meanings and was motivated in part by the line of argument about the meaning of count nouns discussed above. Abstract entities in semantics act as the single object "meant" by general terms and adjectives. The words denote objects in the world only indirectly—via the abstract forms. The objects "resemble" the form and via the form we are able to connect them with their name.

Epistemology is the account of knowledge and ontology is the account of reality. Plato shared the Ionian (and Indian) view that what could be known must be "truly" real and thus could not change. Familiar physical objects exist in time and undergo change. Thus our ordinary awareness of them cannot be knowledge since knowledge concerns what is necessarily or always true.[10] The abstract forms, by contrast, exist in a timeless realm. They are thus appropriate objects of knowledge and candidates for the "really" real.

The philosophy of mind application of abstract entities was not one of Plato's purposes. Still, our modern term *idea* stems from his *Ideos*. This variation on the abstract theme was a product of the Cartesian mentalism behind modern Western thought. Post-Enlightenment Nominalists, while rejecting abstract universals, clung to the philosophy of language underpinnings of Platonism. There were no ontologically fundamental nonphysical entities like manhood, horseness, or virtue. The semantic and epistemological functions of abstractions were attributed to the mind. Thus there were the ideas of manhood, horseness, and virtue. Meanings of the words *man, horse,* and *virtuous* are entities present in the minds of those who know those words.

Now my denial of abstraction in China amounts to a denial that there is any similar interlocking set of philosophical theories. In the absence of an explicit theory, I argue that we can satisfactorily interpret Chinese philosophical writings without attributing a philosophical commitment to abstract or mental entities. To know a word is simply to be able to discriminate. That such a nominalist interpretation is possible is an empirical historical issue, and I shall argue for it by exhibiting nonabstract interpretations of the general direction of philosophy in the classical period (chap. 3), the highly developed epistemological and semantic theories of the Neo-Mohists (chap. 4), and the most commonly cited counterexample to this claim, Kung-sun Lung's white-horse dialogue (chap. 5). The first step in this argument is that the primary grammatical motivations for such abstract theorizing were absent in China. The features of Western languages which explain the traditional fascination with such issues are not features of Chinese. This argument from the logic of Chinese nouns establishes the initial plausibility of such a nominalist interpretation of Chinese philosophical theories. If mereological interpretation of the philosophical writings of the period is possible, then given the explanatory significance of the grammar of Chinese nouns we should prefer nominalist interpretations to traditional, Western-style, abstract interpretations.

Confusions about Abstraction in Chinese

This way of framing the abstraction issue is rather more involved and delimited than is usual. One may likely object, as a result, that I am not addressing the actual abstraction controversy. The typical statement of the issue focused on whether or not there were (or are) abstract *terms* in Chinese or whether Chinese language could express abstract concepts.[11] The issue I am addressing is whether or not there were *theories* dealing with abstract entities in anything resembling the way Western theories of abstract entities did. I shall show that there were only nonabstract theories. The explanation for this fact about Chinese thought stems partially from the grammar of Chinese. I do not mean to suggest that, had they been motivated to formulate them, Chinese philosophers *could not possibly* have expressed such abstract theories. The question is not what philosophical theories *could* they have invented, but what *did* they invent and why? In the absence of any theory of abstractions or mental entities or substances, or some structurally similar theory, there is no point in saying that some Chinese character means the same thing in Chinese philosophy as an abstractly inflected noun does in Western philosophy. To mean the same thing, it must function in the same way. With no such theory for it to function in, no term has the same function.

There are ordinary grammatical functions of abstract terms which *are* regularly filled by Chinese graphs.[12] Let us look at the grammatical parallels and see how they could be interpreted.

Consider first a kind of parallel grammatical function which most typically results in translation using inflected abstract terms of English (horseness, triangularity, childhood, etc.). For virtually all Chinese graphs, there is some grammatically possible context in which they function as terms. For example, the predicate *ta* 'large' in "*x ta*" can replace *x* in "*x fei y yeh* (particle)," that is, *ta* 'large' is a term in "*ta fei hsiao yeh*." It is common to translate such tokens into English abstract terms: "greatness is not pettiness." The Chinese, however, has no distinguishing inflectional shape such as *-hood*, *-ness*, *-ity*, or *-tion* to support this reading against, say, "that which is great is not that which is small," or "its being great is not its being small," or "the great is not the small," or "big-stuff is not small-stuff," or even " 'big' is not 'small'." So the mere grammatical fact that these graphs sometimes have the grammar of a singular term is not enough to show that they are abstract terms. Considering these grammatical structures along with the masslike grammar of nouns, it would be more plausible to read these tokens either as singular mass nouns, propositional contexts, or mentions.[13] In the absence of any characteristic inflection, there is no special reason for identifying term use of adjectives or verbs with English abstract terms.

Hermeneutically, the question becomes, "Is an interpretation which identifies the term uses of nouns and adjectives with abstract terms the most coherent theory for understanding the texts?" The answer is that there is no special reason to translate these terms as abstract terms other than the easy familiarity of the English translation which results. Any adequate account of Chinese semantics must already allow the embedding of sentences as terms in certain predicates, and treat a lone adjective or one-place verb (intransitive verb) as a sentence. So a problem sentence like "*ta* 'great' *fei* 'is-not' *hsiao* 'small' *yeh* (particle)" can have the several plausible nonabstract interpretations discussed above: the mass substantive interpretation ("big-stuff is not small-stuff"), the mention interpretation (" 'big' is not 'small' "), and an embedded sentence interpretation ("the '. . . is big' is not the '. . . is small' "). Which translation to use depends on the context, of course. But there are almost no contexts, given these alternatives, in which we would be forced to use a translation committing us to abstract objects. In many contexts, in fact, such a translation is palpably incoherent; for example, "*pai* 'white' *pu* (negative) *tai* 'depend' *yu* 'in' *wu* 'thing' *erh* 'and': yet *pai* 'white' *tzu* 'self' *pai* 'white'."[14] Now an interpretation of this sentence as entailing the claim that "whiteness is white" produces a category mistake. White *things* are white; white stuff is white; whatever satisfies ". . . is white" is white; and so on. But only extended things are colored, abstract objects are not extended, hence no abstract thing is colored. Whiteness (the abstract object) is *not* white.[15] The upshot of these grammatical structures and the semantic strategies available is that in the absence of an explicit philosophical theory of abstract objects, we would never be required to render such terms of Chinese as abstract terms.[16]

The crucial issue becomes, then, whether or not the term use of adjectives and nouns functions implicitly or explicitly in *philosophical theories* as abstract terms do in the West. The presence or absence of a particular inflectional shape is quite irrelevant to that debate. Plato did not have *–ness*, or *–hood,* or *–ity* forms either. He used classical Greek in novel ways to generate a novel philosophical theory. Someone generating a similar theory for Chinese would have used Chinese in novel ways in the context of presenting his theory. The absence of a *–ness*like suffix does not prove that there was no theory, nor could its presence prove that there was such a theory. In a sense, the absence of *any* novel conceptual apparatus at all *is* evidence that there was no such philosophical theory since usually in the spelling out of such a theory one creates linguistic forms. In the absence of either theory or conceptual apparatus there is no reason to attribute subconscious reference to the nonexistent abstract objects. Borrowing a metaphor from the *Tao Te Ching,* the language and the theory "give birth to each other."

Now the proof that there was no such theory requires analysis of the purported example of abstract theorizing—Kung-sun Lung. Unless the white-horse dialogue is more coherently interpreted as a theory about abstract objects than about mereological objects or mentions, there is no reason to hold that this particular Chinese philosopher is committed to abstract entities. What has been shown in this chapter is that the grammar of Chinese would not have motivated the postulation of such philosophical theories—not that it makes them impossible or inexpressible in Chinese. The grammatical point does have some evidential impact on the interpretation of Kung-sun Lung, however. If the abstract and nominalist interpretations turn out to be *equally plausible,* other things considered, then these considerations argue for opting for the nonabstract interpretation as more consistent with the nature of the language. It tends to confirm the hypothesis that there were no such theories by offering a partial explanation for the adoption of a nonabstract explanatory theory and by showing how the key motivations for abstract theorizing which are present in, say, English, are lacking in classical Chinese. The alternative mass noun ontology and semantics is a more appropriate ontology for the language with the grammatical features of Chinese.[17]

The Argument against Chinese Mentalism

The argument against mentalistic interpretation of Chinese philosophical theories in general and of Kung-sun Lung in particular is parallel to that given against abstract interpretation. We often use terms with abstract inflection as the names of mental entities—ideas, concepts, or the like; for example, we use "whiteness" as interchangeable with "the idea (or concept) of white." And like the abstract object, whiteness, the concept of white is not white—or any other color, nor is the concept of nothing (nothingness) nothing. So for the same reasons, unless there are explicit theories of mentalism, it will never be necessary to translate term use of common nouns or predicates *(x)* as "the idea of *x*." Thus, neither in semantic theory nor in epistemology should we saddle Chinese philosophers with the confusing notion of a Lockean "idea" unless there is independent evidence of similar theories.[18]

The explanation for this difference in epistemology and philosophy of mind lies in the same considerations which motivated a different ontology. The Western theory of mind as a mental substance, with idea as "modes" of that substance, mirrors the structure of the Greek ontology. In Aristotle's influential metaphysics, for example, reality consists of a substratum (substance, matter) which instantiates the universal forms common to many objects (properties, attributes, etc.). For the British Empiricists, the same forms, realized in mental substance, are the ideas which correspond to the individual physical objects. Knowledge, meaning, thought, and truth were traditionally explained via this substance-quality or individual-property picture. In China there is no account of *parallel* realms of substrata for properties in part because there is no account of qualities, attributes, or properties in substrata in the first place.

This explanation of the absence of abstract or mentalistic philosophizing in Chinese thought has the logical features of all negative explanations.

We can explain why something is lacking only by showing that the plausible explanations of its existing do not hold. No such argument could be complete unless we could eliminate all possible motivations for such theorizing. I do not claim to have eliminated all possible or actual rationales for these theories. But I can show that several obvious and historically important lines of thought which might motivate talk of mental concepts would lose their force given a language like classical Chinese. The various arguments follow.

The Argument from Names

The argument from names starts from a common (and questionable) assumption of both traditions, namely, that all words are names. Talk about meaning rests on the model of the proper name that has a one-to-one relation with some entity—its referent. If we ask what is the "one" of which count nouns like *horse*, *man*, and *chariot* are names we generate the Platonic puzzle. It begins to seem that there must be a something-in-common to all horses or men which the noun "names." That something-in-common can then count as the "real" referent of the general noun. So we postulate that there are, for example, properties, essences, concepts, and ideas (like horseness and manhood).[19]

The assumption of a naming model in theory of language does not motivate the same puzzle in Chinese. As we saw earlier on pages 34–37 an alternative and much simpler scheme is immediately available to answer the question, "What is *ma* 'horse' the name of?" It is the name of a mereological object, a stuff, of which individual horses are parts rather than copies. The semantic model of naming does not lead one to look for "the one" outside of the concrete realm as long as all nouns are sufficiently masslike in syntax. The mental version of the argument purports to explain what it is to understand a word or expression. In the Chinese scheme, as I noted earlier, knowing a word is having the ability to discriminate or divide according to the conventional practices associated with that word and to evaluate the division in guiding action. Lacking the Platonic "knowledge as representation" model, Chinese philosophers had no motivation to explain the ability to discriminate as the mind's comparing objects to ideas.

Mystique of Semantic Ascent

One feature of classical Chinese is that like spoken English it lacks a clear quote convention to distinguish the mention of an expression from the use of an expression. In written English, italicizing or quoting expressions (names, clauses, sentences, etc.) converts them into terms denoting themselves—names of the linguistic roles they play in a language or theory. Contrast, for example, "fighting is dangerous" and "*fighting* is a gerund" (we don't conclude that some gerunds are dangerous). This distinction between use (unquoted) and mention (quoted) is prominent in contemporary philosophy. Linguistic analysis is characterized by the view that philosophical issues can be more clearly understood as pragmatic questions about how best to use language or what language to use. In particular, traditional talk of abstractions can be viewed as veiled talk about the use of some term or expression; for instance, "being is prior to nonbeing" unpacks as "the phrase *there exists* plays a more basic role than the phrase *there does not exist*." Since Quine, the move from talking about abstract things to talking about language has been tagged *semantic ascent*. The typical function of abstract theorizing in Western philosophical discourse is held to be semantic ascent.

In Chinese philosophy, without inflections or punctuation, there is no clear distinction between abstraction and semantic ascent. But semantic ascent treatment of candidate structures provides a more uniform treatment and reflects Chinese grammatical structures more closely. The syntactic mobility of graphs can be largely explained by use-mention distinctions. Nouns, for example, occur frequently as two-place predicates (transitive verbs). The translation convention is to render those uses as "treat as *N*" where literally Chinese has "*N* it." Grammarians have called these *putative* or *mental action verbs*. But they could with equal justification (actually greater, given the absence of the philosophical doctrine of a mental life and mental contents) call them language-action verbs. Literally, we should read them as "*N* it" in the sense of "include it among the stuff picked out by the term *N*." Conversely, operators and verbs frequently occur as nouns such as *yu* 有 'has', 'there is . . .' and *wu* 無 'lacks', 'there is no . . .'. The translation convention, again, is to convert the verb into an abstract term (in the above example, *being* and *nonbeing*, respectively). But these are sometimes unmistakable mentions—as "*wu* 'lacks' *ming* 'names' *wan* '10,000' *wu* 'things' *chih* (possessive) *mu* 'mother'" ("*Wu* names the mother of all things."). (Note: nonbeing is not a name of anything and *nonbeing* is the name of nonbeing.) So we should understand "*yu* 'have' *wu* 'lack' *hsiang* 'mutually' *sheng* 'born'" as "(the expressions) *yu* and *wu* arise together" rather than as "being and nonbeing arise together."[20]

The Argument from Adjectival Nominalization

In English sentences, subject and predicate usage routinely requires inflectionally distinct forms of most adjectives. We say, "Bobby is wise" and "Sally is wise." If we want to shift *wise* to subject position we must convert it into a grammatical noun: "Wisdom is a virtue." The grammar suggests that *wisdom* is a singular term intuitively assimilable to *Bobby*. What does it name? At this point the argument borrows from the argument from names. There is something which both Bobby and Sally are—something they have in common that justifies saying of each that he or she is wise. That thing which they have in common is wisdom. We employ the apparatus of Platonism to explain what it is to be wise via having some metaphysical relation to an abstract entity, wisdom. The theory may call the entity a property, characteristic, attribute, or something like that.

In Chinese the distinctions between what we would describe as nouns and adjectives are rather subtle. There are no inflectional markings. Most graphs can occur either as terms or predicate expressions. A celebrated example is Confucius's sentence, "*fu* 'father' *fu* 'father'." There is no *is*, no predicate expression denoting identity or inclusion, in Chinese. The juxtaposition of two terms (usually followed by the particle *yeh*) is a relational sentence which is roughly equivalent to sentences asserting identity or inclusion. These expressions could be analyzed as one-place predicate expressions in which the second term is a predicate (is a horse). The focus of chapter 5, *pai ma ma yeh* 白馬馬也 'white-horse horse' is an example of this sentence structure.[21] Thus the distinction between nouns and adjectives hardly stands out. It was natural for Chinese thinkers to miss the structural differences between terms (nouns) and predicates (adjectives and verbs). So the nominal use of an adjective was not seen to raise any special kind of problem for semantics. Like any noun, it is the name of all the stuff that satisfies the predicate . . . *is F*. The masslike nouns are relatively more adjectivelike and the adjectives relatively more nounlike, and Chinese semantic theories quite naturally assimilated them in the mereological model. There was no inclination to postulate special abstract objects to account for adjectives.

Furthermore, since the subject term of Chinese sentences is frequently not expressed in literary Chinese, subject-predicate sentences like *ma pai (yeh)* 馬白也 '(it is the case that) the horse-stuff is white' and open sentences *pai ma yeh* 白馬也 '*x* is white-horse' seem to differ only in the order of the graphs. Thus, as we shall see in discussing the Neo-Mohist semantics, Chinese semanticists had no clear concept of a sentence as a grammatical structure. They defined *ts'u* 辭 merely as a string of names. That the order of graphs made a difference was clear, but their semantics included no theory of what functional elements were involved in sentences nor any use of the notion of semantic truth—the semantic correlate of sentences. Chinese semanticists simply lumped adjectives and nouns together as expressions denoting a segment of reality. Thus, they regarded all graphs, the simple expressions, equally as *ming* 名 (names) and they regarded *ts'u* (complex expressions—phrases or sentences) as no more than combinations of names used to express or convey speakers' *i* (intentions).[22] Some *ming* 名 (names) referred to corporeal stuffs like water, wood, man, grain, while others referred to stuffs which could "interpenetrate," like white, hard, wisdom, and benevolence (see p. 148). So adjectives, even in term position, did not prompt any revision of the basic stuff ontology (though it does prompt us to note that stuffs need not be physical masses. In general, the conception of a mass term is not limited to terms which denote corporeal substances; *information* is a mass term. Even *white*, though normally an adjective in English, functions sometimes as a mass term: "There was too much white on your paper for you to get a passing grade.")

Adjectives were usually indistinguishable from nouns in noun modification as well as in predicate use. Noun modification could result from either an adjective or a noun preceding another noun. All basic expressions (*ming* 名 [names], nouns and adjectives) were taken to pick out *shih* 實 (stuff, reality).[23] The main focus of semantic study in classical times was on the theory of modification. The Chinese semanticists, the Neo-Mohists, treated all modification as compounding of names and understood that modification yeilded a *ming* 名 (name) with an altered range or scope.[24] So modifiers generated no need to distinguish nouns and adjectives. Where any two *ming* were juxtaposed to form a new *ming*, the result was viewed as a compound term denoting the intersection of the stuffs; for instance, *white-horse* denoted that stuff which was both white and horse (or their sum [see p. 148]).

So when adjectives are used as terms, rather than thinking of their referent as an abstract or mental property or characteristic, the natural tendency in Chinese semantics was to regard adjectives as stuff-names—just like ordinary nouns. Adjectives like *pai* 白 'white' and *chien* 堅 'hard' were stock examples of "names" in the studies of modification (compounding names). We can understand this way of viewing adjectives most easily for these examples of adjectives because related adjectives occur as nouns in English without inflection: "There was a lot of white in paintings from his blue period." The grammar of adjectives, then, and the ways Chinese philosophers were inclined to talk about adjectives, does not motivate postulation of abstract repeatable entities characteristic of realist metaphysics and philosophy of mind in Western thought.

The Semantic Mediation Argument

There are some lines of thought about mental entities which seem to be generated by reflections on our ability to master an inflected phonemic language which would lack appeal if one's model of language were nonphonemic, that is, "pictographic" or "ideographic."[25] An ideographic or pictographic "character" is taken to represent conventionally not the word's sound but its meaning—some kind of presentation or representation of the class of things denoted by the character.

Written Chinese has no alphabet. Each character has a one-syllable pronunciation.[26] The character was viewed as the basic unit of language and was the natural focus of interest for anyone who was literate in ancient China. The characters provided a shared mode of communication among the different Chinese languages since it did not represent any particular pronunciation. Thus, as in China today, people speak different languages but write and read "the same."[27]

Consider now how a typical argument for the existence of mental ideas as the meaning correlates of words would look from a Chinese perspective. We are inclined to say that a written and spoken pattern are both "the same word." When one writes phonetically, one naturally tends to think of a word as what is represented in both forms—the sound. When we reflect on the meaning of words, we are immediately confronted by the arbitrariness of the association of words (sounds) and the things they denote. It seems necessary to invent a mechanism to bridge the gap between words and objects; by what mechanism does the word (sound) *cow* manage to get us to pick out and notice cows? The mechanism characteristic of British and American Empiricism (the abiding "commonsense" view) is a mental representation—the image or general idea *cow-ness*. We have learned to associate the sound with the mental image. It would not work to associate the word with any particular cow (see p. 43), so it must be some kind of generalized image of a cow. That image is not part of the natural world or it could not do its job: explaining how we discriminate cows from horses. It must therefore be in the mind—an idea. We associate the sound with its written phonemic representation, and the mental image with the sound, and the object with the mental image which it resembles. Thus we are able to make the connection between language and the world.

The philosophical tradition of explaining our understanding of a word as mediated by some inner mental presentation associated with words is really much older than early modern Empiricism. The Aristotelian semantics is close to such a view. Aristotle says:

> Now spoken sounds are symbols of affections of the soul, and written marks symbols of spoken sounds. And just as written marks are not the same for all men, neither are spoken sounds. But what these are in the first place signs of—affections of the soul—are the same for all; and what these affections are likenesses of—actual things—are also the same.[28]

This traditional conception of a mental mediator to explain the connection of names and things is developed into the classical Empiricist account of abstract ideas by combining the semantic mediation argument with the argument from names. Locke's description is the paradigmatic one which still counts as the "commonsense" view of Anglo-American popular authors.

> It is not enough for the perfection of language, that sounds can be made signs of ideas, unless those signs can be made use of as to comprehend several particular things; for the multiplication of words would have perplexed their use, had every particular thing's need of a distinct name to be signified by. To remedy this inconvenience, language had yet a further improvement in the use of general terms, whereby one word was made to mark a multitude of particular existences: which advantageous use of words was obtained only by the difference of the ideas they were made signs of; those names becoming general, which are made to stand for general ideas, and those remaining particular where the ideas they are used for are particular.[29]

Thus, starting from the assumption that words must be associated with mental representations, Locke moves on to assert that some representations must be general or abstract, separated from "any other ideas that may determine them to this or that particular existence." These "abstract ideas" are "vague" images mediating between count nouns (general terms) and the multitude of objects they denote. Neither the semantic mediation argument nor the argument from names portion of this proof would be likely to appeal to a Chinese philosopher given the language with which he is familiar.

The core of this line of thought is that mental picturing must lie at the base of language's relation to the world. But the Chinese can rely on picturing or representing as the method of tying language to things without having to invent a detour through the mind and mental images. The picture is itself the linguistic entity, the character. The written form is not a representation of the sound but of the thing. Hence the mediation between sounds and objects in the world is not provided by the inner, private subjectivity (an idea or other "affection of the soul") but by shared social convention—by the character. Accordingly, there is no positing of private mental states to explain or describe thinking or meaning.[30] The medium of thought, in the ancient Chinese view, is language, not ideas. In this respect, classical Chinese philosophy is rather more akin to very recent Western thought than to that of the Enlightenment. Of course, Chinese thinkers never put the view as an explicit denial of mental ideas because there was no development of the "idea" theory around to be denied. The behavioral nominalist view was their commonsense view just as the Lockean one is ours. They never were motivated to postulate a mental image or concept to mediate between sounds and objects; their characters performed that function and made it clear that language and its semantics are shared social phenomena—not individual, solipsistic ones.

The Argument from Translation

One of the natural roles for terms like *concept, idea,* and *universal* is to explain translation. Words like *knife* and *tao* 刀 are related. We say they "mean the same thing." What is the "thing" they mean? Again, the mechanism of the idea comes into play. The meaning of a word must be the concept, the idea—the abstract or mental entity that mediates between language and the world. The possibility of translation between two different languages seems to depend on the existence of such ideal or mental or metaphysical meaning-entities. Otherwise there is no objective reality on which to base the claim that words in those languages have "the same meaning."

This line of thought helps to soften the shock of the awareness that language is conventional.[31] We can limit the conventionalism of language to the words (sounds) while keeping objective (constant across different cultures) the ideas or concepts which are the important components of thinking and on which language is parasitic.

In Plato's *Cratylus*, Socrates defends against conventionalist skepticism of language by just such an argument. Following Plato's practice of assimilating his subject matter to skills, Socrates argues that a name is like a shuttle:

> And suppose the shuttle to be broken in making, will he make another, looking to the broken one? or will he look for the form according to which he made the other? . . .
>
> Then, as to names: ought not our legislator also to know how to put the true natural name of each thing into sounds and syllables, and to make and give all names with a view to the ideal name, if he is to be namer in any true sense? And we must remember that different legislators will not use the same syllables. For neither does every smith, although he may be making the same instrument for the same purpose, make them all of the same iron. The form must be the same, but the material may vary, and still the instrument may be equally good of whatever iron made, whether in Hellas or in a foreign country;—that makes no difference.
>
> Very true.
>
> And the legislator, whether he be Hellene or barbarian, is not therefore to be deemed by you a worse legislator, provided he gives the true and proper form of the name in whatever syllables; this or that country makes no matter.[32]

The Chinese equivalent of Plato's "ideal name" which is constant among different linguistic groups would not be an ideal or mental entity, but the Chinese character. It could be expressed in different syllables in the different languages in the Chinese cultural area. The characters provide a single nonphonemic written form common to all languages—which are simply different ways of pronouncing each character. The natural way of describing translation in a Chinese cultural milieu is to say that it consists in giving the pronunciation or reading of the characters in the different languages, rather than considering languages to have different words. The words are common to all (represented by the characters) and allow one to understand something like translation without any refuge to ideas or concepts. This view of translation persists even when non-Chinese languages like Japanese are encountered. Rather than saying the Japanese word *iku* means the same thing as the Chinese word *sheng*, one says *iku* is the Japanese *yomi* (pronunciation, reading) for 生 . If our culture had been dominated (rather than merely fascinated) by Chinese culture, we might now regard *life* as the English reading for 生 rather than saying they mean the same thing.

The Argument from Communication

There is a line of thought leading to talk of mental or ideal abstract entities that proceeds from worries about how communication takes place. This story is common in psychological, linguistic, and commonsense accounts of oral communication even with modern scientific embellishments. The speaker passes air through a vibrating and articulating medium; the air transmits the sound waves; the ear receives the impulses and translates them into nerve stimulations going to the brain, which somehow decodes them into phoneme sequences. But this story of communication leaves questions at both ends. Something lies behind the speaker's forming the words. The hearer, furthermore, may hear the string of words without communication in the full sense. The presence of homophones, ambiguous words, equivocation, or the like prompts us to say that successful communication requires some deeper correspondence than that between the sounds intended and received. The hearer must form "the same idea" on hearing the sounds that the speaker had when he spoke. The bare sequence of sounds seems as inadequate to our notion of communication as it does to our notion of meaning.

Again, Locke gives us the classical statement of this picture of communication.

> Concerning words also it is farther to be considered. *First*, that they being immediately the Signs of Men's *Ideas;* and, by that means, the Instruments whereby Men communicate their conceptions, and express to one another those Thoughts and Imaginations, they have within their own Breasts, there comes by constant use, to be such a Connexion between certain Sounds, and the Ideas they stand for, that the Names heard, almost as readily excite certain Ideas, as if the Objects themselves, which are apt to produce them, did actually affect the senses.[33]

The alternative account of communication available to a Chinese speaker, also in the face of homophones and ambiguity, is fascinating and instructive. There are a high number of homophonous characters, so the character provides much more specificity than the sound. A person's understanding oral communication is characteristically seen as his knowing which word (character) the speaker intended. When breakdowns in communication occur, Chinese write the character on their hands, in the air, or describe it in conventional ways.[34] The elements in the implicit theory of communication are all public, social, and linguistic. The way of describing and facilitating communication does not turn on achieving coincidence of private mental ideas, but on knowing which "name" was used.

The Argument from General Learning

Baby Susie learns to utter "doggie" in the presence of Fido (the family dog—a collie) and the neighbor's German shepherd and a few other occasional mongrels as examples. However, the first time she sees Uncle Harry's Afghan hound, she promptly chirps, "Doggie!" How did she know? We tend to say she has learned to abstract from particular examples —learned abstract thinking. She has abstracted from all the particular dogs she had encountered the features common to all dogs. Seeing that the Afghan hound had these features, even though quite different in other respects, she correctly classifies it as a dog. This classification depends on her having learned an abstract idea.

Baby Mei-ling, on the other hand, has learned to use the word *kou* 'dog' for that stuff which she encounters again at Uncle Jang's. But the story told does not involve any abstracting. Rather one says that she has acquired the ability to distinguish dog-stuff from non-dog-stuff. She is, in effect, not seeing a different object, but a different part of the same stuff.[35] The problem of learning for Mei-ling is how she is able to reidentify the same stuff. But expressing the problem in that way makes us less likely to talk of abstracting properties from different objects. As we shall see (see pp. 124–37), the philosophical problem corresponding to the possibility of abstract knowledge generated by the Chinese picture is rather how we can possibly know or love some mereological whole rather than just knowing or loving those parts we encounter in our vicinity.

On Arguments from Chinese Language to Chinese Thought

Western sinologists have long been fascinated with the possible effects that Chinese characters might have had on Chinese thought. The suggestions have at times discredited the very attempt to theorize about any possible relations between written style and philosophical content. But despair is not justified. The arguments cannot be as strong as many have hoped; they cannot support conclusions of the form, "Chinese cannot say or think. . . ." Nor can the argument from characters to lack of abstract theorizing be as simple and direct as, for instance, Nakamura's assertion that because characters are pictures they cannot express abstract ideas.[36]

Still, the assumption that modes of expression influence the content expressed is too plausible to abandon. The above arguments attempt to give the kind of explanation of the relation of language to thought that *is* defensible. One cannot argue that a nonphonemic writing system is a necessary and sufficient condition for philosophical nominalism. One *can* plausibly argue that characters (which are viewed as representing semantic content directly) can serve theoretical or explanatory functions which those without such a writing system are inclined to assign to abstract or mental entities. The characters thus render such theorizing less attractive to philosophers. By eliminating or filling some of the explanatory functions of concepts or ideas, the pictographs or ideographs reduce the motivation for abstract or mentalistic theorizing.

Our conclusion is simply that it should not be taken as unreasonable or lacking in philosophical depth that Chinese thinkers never developed theories of abstract entities like ideas, concepts, or universals. These kinds of theories, either in ontology, semantics, philosophy of mind, or theory of knowledge (epistemology), are motivated and stimulated by features of language which divide the Chinese family of languages from the Indo-European family.[37] Since philosophical questions are generated out of our ordinary ways of speaking and writing, we can expect that the different forms in which philosophical questions are posed will push theorization in different directions. It is not that abstract theories are impossible for Chinese; it is only that they are not necessary.

Chinese Grammar and Ontology in Review

A pair of hypotheses about Chinese thought in general in the classical period make up this chapter. One is positive. It is the hypothesis that a stufflike ontology and semantics were implicitly operating as a background assumption behind pre-Han philosophy. The other is a negative corollary. It is the hypothesis that an abstract or mentalistic ontology and semantics of the type common to Western thinkers were not implicit assumptions behind pre-Han philosophy.

The positive hypothesis is generated by noticing the mass-noun-like features of Chinese nouns (especially as a historical development). The way in which such nouns can be assimilated to proper names suggests an elegant and simple picture. All terms pick out a segment of reality. The segment is not necessarily physically contiguous but is roughly a stuff-kind. This picture rests on an assumption common in the beginnings of semantic theory, the assumption that all words are names. We have seen how the syntactic mobility of graphs in Chinese grammar allowed this assumption to survive considerable analysis.

The issue linking Chinese semantics and theory of knowledge, given this picture, was the cognitive ability of speakers to distinguish the stuff-kinds from each other. For a great many stuff-kinds, like the stock example *ma* 'horse', the distinguishing characteristic could be the shape of the bits. So *horse* can be held to be the name of a mereological object—a thing-kind, and we can explain our ability to distinguish horse-stuff from ox-stuff as our ability to distinguish characteristic shapes.

That the grammar provides an explanation for an alternative mass-stuff picture of reality is, at the same time, evidence that the grammar would not explain, as our grammar would for Indo-European languages, an abstract or mentalistic theory of reality. The question about abstraction in Chinese philosophy should be a question about theory, not about the presence or absence of inflection nor about the possibility of referring to abstract objects if there are abstract objects. I have, however, produced several arguments from language to the implausibility of such abstract theorizing (and thus against abstract interpretations of philosophical theories when concrete interpretations are equally coherent). Chinese language, I assume, could perfectly well have expressed abstractions if a Chinese philosopher had been motivated to construct theories about semantic abstraction and abstract objects, but the common motivations from language (grammatical structure and writing system) for such abstract or mental speculation are absent in the case of Chinese. There is no reason for Chinese philosophers to have invented such objects.

This ends the initial phase of the argument that a mereological or mass ontology and a nominalist philosophy of mind are the foundation assumptions of classical Chinese thought. The next step is to see how these assumptions structure and illuminate the philosophical texts of the period. In the subsequent chapters, I argue that nominalistic interpretations of the traditional schools of classical thought are more philosophically interesting and coherent than those based on the traditional assumptions of Western philosophy. The thought of the Neo-Mohists and Kung-sun Lung in particular are made much more intelligible by the present strategy than when viewed as pale, inaccurate reflections of Western traditional philosophical theories.

Chapter 3

Background Theories of Language in Ancient China

A long time ago in a far-off place (though still on Earth and in history) a philosophical tradition arose. The tradition developed issues, theories, criticisms, and controversies. Our evidence for what these were is found in texts preserved by a tradition. In explaining those texts we propose accounts of what the controversies were.

The philosophical controversies in China differed in some well-known ways from those of ancient Greek and European philosophy. Interest in metaphysics, epistemology, and logic, topics which have virtually defined "philosophy," do not dominate Chinese thought. It had social-political theory, ethics, philosophical psychology, and philosophy of language. The latter is of special interest because the language itself is fascinating.

In the preceding chapter, I began an explanation of some of the differences. Against a background belief that we think alike, I showed that having a different language would make us less likely to postulate certain philosophical objects—mental concepts, meanings, ideas, abstract objects or forms. Other differences have to be accepted as starting contingencies. Our accounts must simply accept that philosophy starts with certain interests dominant. Thales is interested in explanation; Confucius is interested in social activism.

Plausible stories can be told that explain certain broad orientations of thought from various "material" conditions. Explanations of this sort may be based on geography, sociology, political history, growth of technology, or something similar. Language is thus just one of the factors influencing the development of a philosophical tradition.

There is no need to speculate about which factors are most important in explaining a whole tradition. Different factors explain different aspects of philosophical theories. Language as an explanatory factor has two advantages relevant for the present study. It explains better the kinds of issues under discussion here—abstraction, mental theorizing, and (obviously) the theories of language.

In this chapter, I look at the direct and indirect assumptions and claims made about language, knowledge, and mind in the writings of the major figures of Chinese thought who provided the philosophical milieu out of which the School of Names arose. I discuss the Neo-Mohists and Kung-sun Lung in separate chapters. My purpose here is to defend the attribution of four assumptions about language to the tradition as a whole. These four claims about the view of language help both to explain many traditionally Chinese philosophical issues such as the rectification of names, and to anchor the argument for a nominalist treatment of the Neo-Mohists and Kung-sun Lung.

In the place of an intuitive grasp of the "Chinese mind," I have outlined an argument for an interpretive theory that takes behavioral nominalism as a plausible perspective through which to understand both the background tradition of philosophy and the semantic theories which later emerged from that tradition. That perspective methodologically embodies a preference for coherent, philosophically defensible interpretations which need not presuppose any theories of abstract or mental entities. The preference, of course, could be overridden by texts which can only be interpreted as expressing lines of thought which motivate abstraction.

The assumption that we are dealing with philosophy also has a metaphilosophical perspective. We identify philosophical theories as those which can be informatively cast in the rubric of questions about language. Broadly stated, philosophy is regarded as an attempt to clarify and perfect the use of language as an information processing and socializing tool. This is done by analysis of meanings, uses, assumptions, or theories found in both ordinary and specialized language. The formulation of philosophical questions and philosophical theories in, for instance, ontology, logic, epistemology, or ethics can be expected to reflect the structure, idioms, social uses, and history of a particular language.

The language-focus perspective turns out to be a particularly appropriate one for interpreting Chinese philosophical theories. It is notoriously difficult to find clear counterparts of metaphysics and epistemology in Chinese thought. But the entire classical period reveals a fascination with problems of language, its semantics, and especially pragmatics (the relation of language and users of language). Trying to force metaphysics, ethics, or epistemology on unwilling texts has resulted in simultaneously distorting and debasing the philosophical theories of classical China. The infatuation of Chinese thinkers with language is widely recognized and accepted by even the most traditional scholars, but it is pushed aside in interpretation because these scholars themselves do not fully appreciate the ways in which language is central to philosophical thought. (I do not mean to single out Western interpreters by this remark—the same comments apply to Buddhist-infected traditional Chinese scholars in union with the philosophical heirs of the anti-language innatism of Mencius, that is, Neo-Confucianism in general.)

Early in chapter 2, I explain the features of Chinese which would motivate nominalist presuppositions about language—presuppositions which, though close to some modern nominalism, contrast strikingly with the dominant traditional assumptions of Western thought. In this chapter, the nominalist hypothesis is broadened into an account of four assumptions about language which lie behind the key doctrines from traditional thought which led up to Kung-sun Lung.

The philosophical doctrines of the major pre-Han traditions I examine are primarily those which plausibly involve implicit or explicit theories about language. I contrast the assumptions about language in those doctrines with Western "conventional wisdom" about language. The nominalist assumptions, I argue, explain the texts more coherently than the abstract or mental-conceptual assumptions. Given these nominalist presuppositions and their other explicit philosophical attitudes, the differences between Chinese and Western philosophical views can be understood as reasonable developments and inferences from these different assumptions. The underlying hypothesis, then, is that Chinese views on language are interestingly different from our own and that the difference explains (gives the rationale for) their differing philosophical views.

The Four Assumptions

The assumptions that are implicit in classical thought about language fall into four categories: (1) assumptions about the function of language, that is, what is language for?; (2) assumptions about the way in which language relates to the world, that is, what model of reality informs the account of the function of language?; (3) assumptions about the origin and status of language, that is, how do languages come to be and what kind of knowledge do we have when we know how to use them?; and (4) miscellaneous contrasts in assumptions about the relation between language and mental or abstract objects—thoughts, meanings, universals, classes, and the like.

Ancient Chinese philosophy contrasts with ancient Greek philosophy in lacking a preoccupation with meanings as expressed in definitions. Socrates and Plato regarded their attempts at definition as the crucial method of gaining real knowledge. Neither Confucius, Lao-tzu, nor Mencius ever viewed the philosophical task in that way or used definition as a discovery of a deeper truth. It would be contrary to the tenor of the Chinese approach to admonish an interlocutor as Socrates does, "Tell me what it means, don't give me examples." There is in Chinese thought no theory of semantic correlates of words, i.e., "meaning" in the sense of something conveyed in a definition. And meaning's theoretical and philosophical associates, such as universals, intensions, ideas, senses, concepts, or connotations, are similarly absent from pre-Han philosophical discourse.

Of course Chinese literature includes dictionaries—and these have definitions, that is, words or strings of words which can replace the word being defined. There seems to have been no attempt to capture the "real essence" by a definition. Synonym definition, definition by ostensive listing, and etymological explanation can be found alongside genus-species definitions[1] in dictionaries and in the Neo-Mohist Canon. Dictionaries, in other words, list words or expressions which have the same use as the term being defined and hence are interchangeable with it in sentences. There never appeared to be any assumption that fundamental knowledge about reality was being conveyed by definitions. This was merely knowledge about names—how to use them.

We might best understand the thrust of Chinese thought in this period by thinking of the philosophical schools as being interested in the use of language; they would be interested only in accounts of the way words functioned in, say, socialization, problem solving, or behavior modification.

Given the division of the study of language into syntax (the interrelations of linguistic entities), semantics (the relation of language and extralinguistic reality), and pragmatics (the relation of language to the purposes of language users), Chinese thought may be said to concentrate on pragmatics. Thus, Chinese thinkers, relatively speaking, are concerned less about semantic truth and more about pragmatic acceptability. That is not to claim that their language is in some fundamental way different, such that the criteria of truth cannot be applied—it can. But the broadly pragmatic test of appropriateness of utterance, or k'o 可 'acceptability', was more often appealed to in their own statement of philosophical issues and in dealing with disputes than any notions resembling a semantic truth concept. Hence, instead of asking if a philosophical claim was true, Chinese philosophers asked if it was assertable (k'o).

The Regulative Function of Language

The function of language that seemed to preoccupy Chinese thinkers was the regulative, as opposed to the descriptive, function. Words have an impact on people's attitudes and inclinations to act. Chinese philosophy tended for the most part to focus on ethical terms for which the Positivist metaethical philosophers used the term *emotive*. Confucianism (the Confucius-Hsün-tzu wing) and Taoism (especially the *Lao-tzu*) exhibit this assumption most plainly. Confucius and Hsün-tzu regard "rectification of names" as an important facet of the art of governing, and the *Lao-tzu* adduces a strong causal link among naming, desiring, and acting. Taoism discusses terms, desires, deliberate action, and similar matters as if they formed a system. Even where the focus is on seemingly nonevaluative distinctions like upper and lower, the Taoist assumes a (perhaps misguided) tendency in a linguistic community to prefer one of the contrary aspects.

This traditional Chinese attitude toward language's function is often characterized as a naively primitive belief in the "power" of words. Describing this assumption as a belief that words can magically exercise a psychological compulsion is merely presupposing our own view of a language-independent psyche and of a relatively inert language system. Thus Nivison may be taken to have noticed this same underlying feature of Chinese thought when he speaks of "a primitive and persisting belief in the magical properties of words: words properly used and combined had power to compel action."[2] But Chinese thinkers would have no reason to regard the rather mundane truth that language learning and acquisition of dispositions to behavior go hand in hand as "magical." That characterization is for our benefit. But it has drawbacks since it suggests that one cannot give a rationale for the Chinese assumption. It is implausible, given the absence of any direct textual assertion, to suggest that Chinese thinkers themselves regarded this feature of language as magical, beyond natural process.

Herbert Fingarette has recognized the significance of language perhaps more than any modern commentator on Confucianism, but he too persists in using the metaphor of magic in describing it (although for Fingarette *magic* is not supposed to have the pejorative, condescending tone we normally associate with it).[3]

The interest in the regulative function of language is also taken as primitive by some Chinese writers. Chang Tung-sun wrote:

> Primitive man, we are told, often takes language as a concrete entity. The lower the culture, the greater the power of words. In primitive society language has magical power, therefore there is a direct connection between language and thought. If a primitive man is accused of being a thief, he most certainly becomes angry. But in modern society a sophisticated person can turn aside this accusation by a smile, provided he is innocent. We may take the degree of the power of words as a gauge to measure the development of an ethnic intellectual development. This point has been sufficiently demonstrated by modern students of child psychology and "primitive mentality" so we do not need to dwell upon it any further.[4]

An analytic American philosopher like Fingarette, noticing essentially the same concern with "the force of speech acts," would characterize them as "distinctive insights . . . close in substance and spirit to some of the most characteristic of the very recent philosophical developments."[5] In itself, the awareness of the regulative function of language is neither sophisticated nor naive—but it does contrast with the dominant assumption of the Western philosophical tradition.

One of the most convincing characterizations of the way Chinese think can be seen as a consequence of this characteristically Chinese assumption about language. It has been noted by Munro:

> In China, truth and falsity in the Greek sense have rarely been important considerations in a philosopher's acceptance of a given belief or proposition; these are Western concerns. The consideration important to the Chinese is the behavioral implications of the belief or proposition in question. What effect does adherence to the belief have on people? What implications for social action can be drawn from the statement?[6]

The stress on behavioral implications of doctrines can be seen as a natural consequence of the underlying view that the function of words is to engender and express attitudes with implications for action rather than to express some "content" such as the speaker's thoughts which either reflect or fail to reflect reality.

The relative stress on the attitude-forming functions of language versus the content-expressing function is one of the crucial and most frequently ignored contrasts between the Western and Chinese traditions. It is ultimately central to the perspective of dominant schools of Confucianism and Taoism. Even for those schools for whom the assumption is less central (the Neo-Mohists, the Dialecticians, and Chuang-tzu's Taoism—for whom a representing function of language is relatively more prominent) the influence of the regulative view is clearly evident.

Division and Discrimination

The dominant traditional answer to the second question—how language relates to reality—employs the metaphor of cutting, dividing, or discriminating. Again the Taoist position is the strongest expression of this attitude (and again, especially in the *Lao-tzu*). Terms of language divide or cut the universe of discourse into portions or opposites. To have a language is to distinguish or discriminate stuffs in a given way.

The dividing metaphor gives a model of how language performs its functions both when the function is regulative and when it is descriptive. To use language in a certain way is to grade the world into portions evaluated positively and negatively, into that desired and that abhorred, that allowed and that forbidden. The link between the regulative function and the dividing technique can be illuminated by considering different interpretations of a line from chapter 32 of the *Tao Te Ching*. This line is developing the metaphor of the "uncarved block." D. C. Lau renders the line, "As soon as it is cut, there are names,"[7] and W. T. Chan gives, "As soon as there were regulations and institutions there were names."[8] The intuitions of these two translators could easily be harmonized if we attribute to Chinese a background understanding of language—a system of names—as a conventional institution or social practice of dividing and discriminating. When there are institutional practices of dividing or discriminating there are names. (I am using *institution* in the sense in which morality is an institution—not in the sense in which Chase Manhattan Bank is an institution.)

Even where the descriptive function of language is relatively more important in Chinese thought, the division- or distinction-making model of the language-world relation still applies. One can find it expressed in the Neo-Mohists and in Hsün-tzu. When we regard language as an institution for dividing reality[9] the story interlaces nicely with the claim, defended in chapter 2, that terms of Chinese are taken as singular names of mass objects. The institutions of language divide the world into, say, horse and nonhorse, hard and soft, white and dark. So a "one-name-one-thing" formula for rationalizing a language is based on taking mass kinds as *things* divided off from one another by the linguistic practices of the community.

Naturally, working with this rudimentary intuitive semantic picture is going to lead to quite different ways of talking about modification and to some special problems: is white-horse two things or one? If two, is one of them "the white"? In fact, the problems which emerge in the Neo-Mohists' and Dialecticians' arguments about names and things are just those which we could predict would arise for a mass stuff ontology. And they are quite unlike the kinds of problems which would be generated in a Platonic scheme. Ultimately, as we shall see, the difficulty in dealing with the problems as cast in their mereology and the failure of any schools to produce an alternative semantic theory confirms for Chinese philosophy, over time, the skeptical view of the Taoist with regard to language, namely, that consistent semantics is impossible for languages.

Conventionalism

The third presupposition, conventionalism, has two versions. The weaker version of conventionalism treats the sounds or symbols we use as social conventions, properly used as long as they are mutually recognized by a language community. Simply put, what we call *horse*, we could as well have called *ox*. The stronger version holds that not only the sounds and symbols are conventional, but so is the associated practice of division. The way of dividing reality into objects to be named (totally apart from what symbols or sounds the community uses) is also a function of common acceptance of a shared and conventional practice of classification or division.

The conventionalism in China tends toward the stronger version. Naming is just making the distinctions, and the distinctions themselves are merely conventional—socially agreed-on ways of dividing up the world. This does not necessarily land one in Taoist relativism, for one may allow that there are in some sense "correct" distinctions which should be reflected in socially accepted language, that is, the theory of rectification of names. Alternatively, one could become a Taoist skeptic and say that there are no "real" distinctions and that any way of dividing the world is social convention. There is no basis for evaluation of distinctions except some shared practice. This seems to be the central philosophical claim underlying Taoist skepticism and mysticism.

The recognition that language is conventional is, of course, also a feature of Western philosophy. But the Western version tended more to weak conventionalism. So conventionalism's implications emerge as more skeptical and nihilistic in China. This is in part due to the absence of theorizing about real meanings, forms, ideas, or universals. The skepticism-conventionalism link would have seemed less compelling if one believed either (1) that there are stable ideal entities which stand as the meanings of words, or (2) that we have language-independent access to the real things or real distinctions against which to check the conventions in our use of names. In general, only the latter approach was employed by Chinese realists.

Nominalism

Chapter 2 includes a partial explanation for nominalism in Chinese thought. The claim from that point on is just that there is no reason in the texts to reject that explanation. No concept of "real" meaning nor of any abstract entity such as universal, idea, concept, or sense is employed or hinted at by early Confucians, Taoists, or Mohists. Further, none of these notions are presupposed or are explanatorily helpful in understanding their other doctrines. The presupposition is not that the philosophers of the period denied that there were universals but that there was never a theory of universals, implicit or explicit, around to deny.

Nominalism, as a distinguishing assumption of Chinese thought, is the absence not only of a specific form of metaphysical theory (universals) but also of characteristic Western theories of language, philosophy of mind, and theory of knowledge. In general, early Chinese philosophical texts do not show any tendency to assume or postulate subjective mental ideas either to explain the meaning of words, to attribute beliefs, or to be evaluated as knowledge. The words *idea* and *thought* play all these roles in the Western tradition, and there are no equivalent theories in classical Chinese philosophical discourse.

Nominalism in the Philosophy of Mind

Nominalism in the areas of epistemology and philosophy of mind in China is reflected in pre-Han Chinese grammar of propositional attitudes: *believes that, thinks that, knows that,* and so on. Traditional empiricist Western epistemology rested on a widely articulated theory of mind. The mind was viewed as a container of items called *thoughts* or *ideas* which potentially correspond both to words and to objects or states of affairs in the world. That commonsense philosophy of mind is easily correlated with our own grammar of propositional attitudes—of *know* and *believe*. Both verbs take sentences or that-phrases as their "objects." Similarly, we take the sentence or proposition to be the "content" of the belief or knowledge state—the content of the mind. Hence a mind's believing is just its containing thoughts or ideas. The thoughts are things which, like sentences, may be true or false—depending on whether or not they correspond to the way the world actually is. This picture of inner, conscious, or mental states suggests that belief is a subjective representation and that knowledge is the representation's corresponding to the way things are. The belief-knowledge distinction is a prominent feature of English grammar.

Now ancient Chinese has two quite different and grammatically complex expressions which are routinely translated into the propositional attitudes—*chih* 知 'know' and *i wei* 以爲 'believe'. Because the two expressions are grammatically quite different, Chinese theories of knowledge virtually never used that contrast to formulate skepticism. Instead, knowing was presented as a kind of skill. Think of it as skill in applying names (discriminating according to community practices). Propositional knowledge was implicitly treated as knowing how (according to the accepted practice) to apply expressions (predicates) to things. Propositional belief, similarly, was a disposition of a speaker to apply such expressions to objects in a particular way and then to behave in the ways conventionally associated with that predicate; for example, to believe Nixon is evil is to "evil" (apply the term *evil* to) Nixon and to vote against him or to demonstrate in the streets.

The grammar of the belief context in Chinese is that of a three-place predicate: x *i* y *wei* F (where x is a person, y an object and F a property), for instance, "Nancy *i* John *wei* the most handsome man in Kansas." Translators are sometimes careful to replicate this structure yielding the translation, "x deems y to be F." The difference between *chih* and *i wei* can be represented as analogous to that between a disposition or habit and an acknowledged skill. A skill has a success component; it is done correctly. The disposition may or may not also be a skill. The success element in the meaning of *chih* is what makes the translation *knowledge* (versus *belief*) work. Knowledge, too, has a success or objective component which belief lacks. But the background philosophical account of what this component is in Chinese and Western systems is rather different. The simple word-by-word association hides that underlying structure which shapes the different formulations of skepticism in the two traditions. The Chinese case leads quite naturally to a skepticism based on conceptual relativism where the classical empiricist belief-knowledge distinction led to skepticism of the senses. The "correctness" or skill in the application of an expression to an object is much more obviously dependent on the conventions of a language than is the notion of a correspondence between ideas or thoughts and reality. So the Chinese concept of knowledge *(chih)* is of a skill that is relative to some practice or institution of distinguishing and naming—that is, to some language.

Chinese skepticism is thus quite different from classical empiricist skepticism in the West. The Taoist skeptic does not doubt that we have knowledge; rather, he treats it as obvious that we do but recommends that we jettison the "knowledge" that is the conventional discriminatory and manipulative skills which we learn in acquiring names. What this version of skepticism rejects, then, are not subjective ideas, beliefs, or views of a thinking individual, but the learned practices of dividing the world shared by a linguistic group.

The nominalist assumption thus explains a broad range of Chinese thought. What follows is a survey of the theories of language and related views in ontology, philosophy of mind, and epistemology of the pre-Han thinkers who formed the background philosophical milieu out of which the study of naming grew. The order of exposition is the *Tao Te Ching*, Confucianism, Mo-tzu, and Chuang-tzu.[10]

The *Tao Te Ching*

The *Tao Te Ching* is usually regarded as an edited collection of aphorisms, poems, and fragments of politics, metaphysics, ethics, and psychology. There is a central philosophical core linking these disparate elements (of course how they are linked and harmonized depends on one's selection and reconstruction of the parts). This core is a theory about names and language, knowledge, learning, desires, distinctions, and practical action. The theory is that knowledge, wisdom, and learning are matters of mastering a linguistic practice. These intellectual virtues are thus relative to language. Language is viewed as a collection of names which mark conventional distinctions and correspond to and cause conventional ways of responding to the world—attitudes and actions.

Conventional Knowledge

Knowledge is used in the *Tao Te Ching* in ways which are quite different from the ways it is used in the West. While the *Tao Te Ching* is a skeptical document, its skepticism is not a traditional, empiricist skepticism of the senses. This difference is signaled by a central slogan of Taoism: "Abandon knowledge." Rather than doubting that we have knowledge, the Taoist questions its worth. The slogan is paradoxical unless we assume the Taoist has something in mind quite different from warranted true belief when he uses the term *knowledge*.

Lao-tzu[11] recommends abandoning a whole complex: (1) names, (2) distinctions, (3) desires, (4) specific moral virtues of Confucius, (5) learning, cleverness, knowledge and wisdom, and sageliness, and (6) action caused by 1–5. The connection of these elements forms the core of the Taoist theories of language.

There is a useful philosophical distinction for understanding the Taoist theory, that between knowing that (propositional knowledge) and knowing how (skill). Knowing how need not involve conscious, propositional knowledge. I may know that gyroscopic forces act in a certain way, yet knowing that does not entail my knowing how to ride a bicycle, nor can I necessarily learn how to ride a bicycle quicker or more certainly than the person who has never heard of a gyroscope. There is yet a third type of knowledge—knowledge by acquaintance. The three different senses of knowledge may be illustrated by the different senses in which I can know the frost is on the pumpkin. I can know *that* it was below freezing last night; I can know *how* to recite the piece; and I can know *of* the poem—I have encountered it before; I know what you are talking about.

References to knowing *(chih)* in Chinese philosophical texts are most naturally treated as either knowing how or knowledge by acquaintance.[12] Knowing the virtues (e.g., knowledge of benevolence), can be read as either knowing (how) to be benevolent or knowing of (being acquainted with) benevolence.

Knowledge is a product of learning in the sense of training, not in the sense of the acquisition of data items called concepts and facts. The paradigm of what is learned is the traditional Confucian virtues (though the Taoists' argument is perfectly general, i.e., it applies against *any* acquired system of discrimination, naming, evaluation, and conventionally guided action).

What is it to know a virtue? It is at root a kind of knowing how. How to what? How to make certain distinctions and how to desire and act according to the virtue. That involves being able to make discriminations or distinctions (dividing the world) which have, via the attitudes that go along with the division, implications for action.

Our "knowledge," "wisdom," and "sageliness" (when condemned rather than praised) are best viewed as our mastery of a particular system of name use—knowing how, according to that system, to divide the world and how to "desire" in consequence of our division. "Knowledge" is akin to "culture." It is skill in evaluative distinction making of the type recommended by Confucius. Knowing how to use a name is knowing a culturally accepted way of distinguishing and discriminating for guiding our action.

If we think of *tao* as a "way" of acting, then a total system of names, distinctions, and evaluations corresponds to a *tao*. A *tao* is the concrete set of actions corresponding to a system of discourse—its embodiment in behavior (human social behavior for Confucians, natural "behavior" of all things for Taoists). The notion of *tao* is closely linked to theories of language in Taoism. The first chapter of the *Tao Te Ching* begins with two parallel assertions, the first about *tao*s and the second about names. The translation for the verbal use of *tao* is simply "to speak." Thus a *tao* reflects the features of discourse or language. It is essentially regulative, and it "creates" things.

Negative Knowledge

There seem to be three kinds or levels of learning, knowledge, or wisdom operating in early Taoism: conventional, negative, and mystical. There are the systems of naming, distinguishing, and desiring typical of Confucianism: the culturally dominant conventions of language and behavior. Any such system of distinguishing and desiring, including a prudential or "selfish" one, should be abandoned. One is urged not only to forget benevolence and righteousness but also "self."[13] There is a kind of negative knowing or learning which consists in the injunction to abandon conventions—knowing to refrain from the conventionally approved evaluative or discriminatory practices.

> He learns to be unlearned and returns to what the multitude has missed.[14]

> To know your not knowing is best.[15]

> A wise man has no extensive knowledge; he who has extensive knowledge is not a wise man.[16]

In the *Tao Te Ching* this negative knowledge consists primarily of exposure to a *tao* in which evaluations are reversed. Using negative knowledge helps us see that the conventional *tao* is not invariant. Our tendency is to desire or abhor certain things associated with certain conventional descriptions or names. The evaluations that typically go along with our names can be reversed; we could value a lower position, and disvalue wealth or beauty in certain circumstances or in the long run.

The submissive, the negative or lacking (*wu* 無) aspects of a system *can* be regarded as having value. This second, "negative" kind of wisdom—that valuations conventionally associated with distinctions in language are not invariant—is what is "taught" by the *Tao Te Ching*. Since the mystical "wisdom" cannot be spoken, the *Tao Te Ching* can only propose abandoning conventional knowledge; its stated doctrine can coherently be only negative knowledge. One does have a kind of knowledge[17] when one realizes that the emotive valuations typically associated with the distinctions of the naming system are "inconstant"—that in particular circumstances or in the long run one would value the opposite of the conventional values. However, taking this second level alternative valuation scheme as *the* Taoist philosophical alternative to Confucianism is to miss the deeper, mystical point. Such a misconception lies behind the practical "scheming" interpretations of the *Tao Te Ching* that have bothered interpreters and drawn two millenia of Confucian criticism. The *Lao-tzu* cannot consistently simply advocate another system of desiring which is the polar opposite of the conventional system. Its critical philosophical theories imply that we must eventually abandon all such systems, including the negative one.

Mystical Knowledge

Now, if we are to make sense of the tradition attributing a mystical reading to the text, then we must posit still another species of "knowledge." There must be a positive kind of "wisdom" which, descriptively, is the mystical identification with extralinguistic reality and which, regulatively, is a pattern of behavior guided by some immediate, natural responses. About this "knowing," if it is part of Taoism at all, the *Tao Te Ching* can only hint since it cannot be put into words. However, certain passages suggest that there are certain sagelike attitudes and behavioral characteristics. But it does not distinguish between characteristics arising from some sort of profound identification with a "constant but unspeakable *tao*" and the characteristics of someone who has abandoned all spoken *taos*. The descriptions could fit either picture. There can, by the very nature of the supposed mystical knowledge, be no evidence from a text like the *Tao Te Ching* that its theory included a commitment to a mystical realm of knowledge.

The psychological characteristics and "inner state" of the wise man in either the negative or the mystical state will be the same: he will not speak, desire, make distinctions, or have a purpose.

> He who knows does not speak.
> He who speaks does not know.
> Close the mouth.
> Shut the doors (of cunning and desires).
> Blunt the sharpness.
> Untie the tangles.
> Soften the light.
> Become one with the dusty world.
> This is called profound identification.[18]

> Mine is indeed the mind of an ignorant man.
> Indiscriminate and dull!
> Common folk are indeed brilliant!
> I alone seem to be in the dark.
> Common folks see differences and are clear-cut;
> I alone make no distinction.
> I seem drifting as the sea;
> Like the wind blowing about, seemingly without destination.
> The multitude all have a purpose;
> I alone seem to be stubborn and rustic.[19]

Language Dichotomies

In Lao-tzu's view, language not only makes distinctions and arouses desires, but does so largely through dichotomies. Every term in language has its opposite. Any time a name is used to mark a distinction there must be an opposite name to apply to the complement. Hence, strictly speaking, for any one distinction there are two names. They mark the same distinction, so in a sense they are the same. Taoist relativism seems to be the claim that we could draw the distinction almost anywhere. But since the main point of the distinction is its effect on our evaluation, it is enough to show that, given the distinction already conventionally marked, we can conceive of a system of evaluation that completely reverses the standard, conventional attitudes. Since the evaluations can be completely reversed, the distinction could, in principle, have been drawn anywhere. Hence the seemingly opposite names have no "real" evaluational significance. The differences are merely a product of conventional recognition.

> That the whole world knows the beautiful's being deemed "beautiful" is sufficient for "ugly." That the whole world knows the good's being deemed "good" is sufficient for "evil." Thus "having" and "lacking" produce each other. "Difficult" and "easy" complement each other. "Long" and "short" offset each other; "high" and "low" incline toward each other; "note" and "sound" harmonize each other; "before" and "after" follow each other.[20]

Each dichotomy could, in principle, be reversed, and then we would appreciate what we now call *ugly* and admire behavior that we now call *evil*. The conclusion has two forms that relate to the ontological and normative interpretations respectively of *tao*. The distinctions marked by language are not really in the world, and the recommendations for behavior embodied in the distinctions are not invariably sound recommendations. The distinctions are created by a conventional use of words. "Infinite and without boundaries, it cannot be given any name."[21] "Only when it is cut are there names."[22]

On this interpretation, Lao-tzu's opening chapter is a concise presummary of his underlying view. It also gives us strong reasons to prefer the reading which punctuates after *wu* and *yu* in lines 3–6. (These considerations apply only to the traditional Wang Pi version of the *Tao Te Ching*—this chapter is buried in the middle and the punctuation altered in the recently discovered Legalist text dating from the Han dynasty [see pp. 19–26.]) *Wu* 無 'there does not exist' and *yu* 有 'there exists' must surely be the most inclusive dichotomous distinction in the language. But they, too, just create a division. Each term carries with it a pattern of attitudes, interests, and behaviors. Here, as before, there is a hint that the attitudes generated by *wu* 'nonbeing', which are normally ignored, are as valuable as, if not more valuable than, the *yu* 'being' attitudes and purposes. Ultimately, again, the distinctions marked by *yu-wu*, like those marked by other language distinctions, are in reality one. Understanding that is the gateway to ten thousand mysteries.

> Speaking what can be spoken is not invariant speaking. Naming what can be named is not invariant naming. *Wu* 無 ['there lacks . . .'] names the beginning of the universe. *Yu* 有 ['there is . . .'] names the mother of all things. Invariantly *wu*–ing, one desires to use it to see the subtleties. Invariantly *yu*–ing one desires to use it to view manifestations. These two are the same, but in issuing forth are differently named. Their being one is mysterious—mystifying it deepens the mystery—the gateway of ten thousand subtleties.[23]

Conventional moral terms and distinctions are introduced, the argument continues, only because of breakdowns in the natural order of things. The Confucian distinctions do not really alleviate the breakdowns but in a perverse way perpetuate them. The preferred policy would be to abandon the distinctions and words entirely and eliminate all learning (which is mere skill in word manipulation) and return to "natural" behavior.

> When the great Tao declined,
> The doctrines of humanity and righteousness arose.
> When knowledge and wisdom appeared,
> There emerged great hypocrisy.
> When the six family relationships are not in harmony,
> There will be advocacy of filial piety and deep love for children.
> When a country is in disorder, there will be praise of loyal ministers.
> Abandon sageliness and discard wisdom;
> Then the people will benefit a hundredfold.
> Abandon humanity and discard righteousness;
> Then the people will return to filial piety and deep love.
> Abandon skill and discard profit;
> Then there will be no thieves or robbers.[24]

The *Lao-tzu*'s only discussion of the senses illuminates the differences between this linguistic skepticism and skepticism of the senses. The Taoist version is based on a distinction-making rather than an object-marking account of the way words relate to the world. The sense organs distinguish sensible qualities rather than mirror or represent objects in the world. The distinctions the senses make are distorted by the classifications in language.

> The five colors cause one's eyes to be blind.
> The five tones cause one's ears to be deaf.
> The five flavors cause one's palate to be spoiled.[25]

The suggestion in the passage is that the conventional language-based distinctions distort or limit the function of our organs. This Whorfian variation of the Taoist theme is the only hint in Taoism of skepticism of the senses. Still, the relevant distinction for skepticism is not an appearance-reality distinction, but a language-reality one.

In summary, there is a quite elaborate theory of language in the *Tao Te Ching*. It presupposes first, that language and names mark distinctions (usually dichotomous ones); second, that the distinctions involve attitudes, desires, choices, purposes, and ultimately action; and third, that names and valuations attached to them are conventional—as is all language and all learning. There is nothing constant, invariant, or ultimate in the conventional practices. Not only do names arbitrarily mark certain distinctions; the distinctions themselves are merely a result of the social practices fixing a name's use. Finally, nothing in the *Tao Te Ching* requires explanation by means of definitions, universals, concepts, ideas, or senses. There is no reason to suppose that Taoist philosophy is other than nominalistic. The Taoist view is adumbrated nicely in the *Lao-tzu*'s well-known image: "the nameless uncarved block which is just freedom from desire."[26]

Confucius and the Rectification of Names

The Confucian theory of language is embodied primarily in the doctrine of rectification of names (正名). Formally, the doctrine urges that *ming* 名 'names' and *shih* 實 'actuality' be *ho* 合 'united'. As a political doctrine, the rectification of names concerns names of government hierarchical positions. Still, the general formula of rectification is ambiguous. It might require that actual states of affairs be changed to coincide with naming conventions or that names be manipulated to apply only to actualities which deserve the names.[27]

The characterization "rectification of names" favors the sense in which names are manipulated to match reality—and this is theoretically the most interesting sense. Confucius's *Analects* contains some famous illustrations. This seems also to be Hsün-tzu's approach to the doctrine in his more detailed and elaborate account of the rectification of names. He deals at length with how names are to be assigned and controlled by political authority. The primary import of the theory of rectification of names, then, seems to lie in the manipulation of naming conventions rather than in manipulation of states of affairs (i.e., nonlinguistic states of affairs).

Despite the assertion that rectification of names is fundamentally important to Confucian thought, this passage is the only direct mention of the doctrine in the *Analects*.[28]

> Tzu-lu said, "The ruler of Wei is waiting for you to serve in his administration. What will be your first measure?" Confucius said, "It will certainly concern the rectification of names." Tzu-lu said, "Is that so? You are wide of the mark. Why should there be such a rectification?" Confucius said, "Yu! How uncultivated you are! With regard to what he does not know, the superior man should maintain an attitude of reserve. If names are not rectified then language will not be in accord, if language is not in accord then things cannot be accomplished. If things cannot be accomplished, then ceremonies and music will not flourish. If ceremonies and music do not flourish then punishment will not be just. If punishments are not just, then the people will not know how to move hand or foot. Therefore, the superior man will give only what can be carried out in practice. With regard to his speech the superior man does not take it lightly. That is all."[29]

In this passage, the rectification of names appears to consist in making names accord (with something). The converse notion of making things or people accord with names is tokened in other passages, but these are not explicitly identified as rectification of names—in fact do not deal directly with names at all. In the first such passage (which follows) the term *rectification* (*cheng* 正) but not *rectification of names* is used.

> Chi K'ang Tzu asked Confucius about government. Confucius replied, "To govern [*cheng* 政] is to rectify [*cheng* 正]. If you lead the people by being rectified yourself, who will not be rectified?"[30]

The other most frequently cited passage for discussing the rectification of names is also a notorious example of the use of nouns as verbs in pre-Han philosophical Chinese.

> Duke Ching of Ch'i asked Confucius about government. Confucius replied, "Let the ruler be a ruler, the minister be a minister, the father be a father, and the son be a son." The Duke said, "Excellent! Indeed, when the ruler is not a ruler, the minister not a minister, the father not a father, and the son not a son, although I may have all the grain, shall I ever get to eat it?"[31]

The other sources of the meaning of this Confucian theory are indirect. Confucius was traditionally credited with having written the

Spring and Autumn Annals as an example of the rectification of names.³² The traditional interpretation of this work should give us a good idea of what the tradition of rectification of names involves or was thought to involve.

Basically, the *Spring and Autumn Annals* is a historical document which records events in Confucius's native state of Lu. It is written in terse chronicle form. According to the commentaries, the laconic entries are not just recordings of the events, but are simultaneously evaluations of the moral significance of the events. Words with moral implications were carefully selected to make moral judgments self-evident. Hu Shih (1891–1962), for example, lists eight different examples of assassinations in the *Spring and Autumn Annals*.³³ However, not all of them use the word *assassinate* (弒). Some use the milder term *kill* (*sha* 殺) to imply that the person killed was not a just ruler. In some cases the killer is identified, thereby condemning him. In other cases, the killing is said to have been done by the people, which implies that the ruler was a tyrant.

In another more detailed and very illuminating example, the *Spring and Autumn Annals* records the following event: "The Earl of Cheng subdued Tuan at Yen."³⁴ The commentary points out that the Earl of Cheng and Tuan were brothers. This fact was deliberately ignored by the chronicler to chastise the brothers for failing to behave in a "brotherly" way. The younger brother, Tuan, had rebelled against his older brother, the Earl, so he is not called younger brother. The older brother is deliberately misranked—he was, in fact, a duke. By failing to record the escape of Tuan, the *Annals* accuses the older brother of having murderous intent. All these "Confucian slips" are designed to convey an evaluation of the events.

Tung Chung-shu (179–104 B.C.) summarizes the typical Confucian assessment of the *Spring and Autumn Annals:*

> The *Spring and Autumn Annals* examines the principles of things and rectifies their names. It applies names of things as they really are without making the slightest mistake.³⁵

Mencius, for his part, never directly discusses the doctrine of rectification of names, but the most famous example of rectification occurs in the *Mencius*. His goal is to rectify the name *king*. The term is to be applied only to a person with the proper Confucian ruling attitude. The relation of the rectification of names to the traditional code is made obvious. The code clearly condemns the assassination of the ruler. Yet Confucian scholars usually approve of dispatching the supposedly wicked last king in a declining dynasty. Mencius was asked about this apparent inconsistency:

> The King said, "Is it all right for a minister to murder his king?" Mencius said, "He who injures righteousness is a destructive person. Such a person is a mere fellow. I have heard of killing a mere fellow Chou [the supposedly wicked ruler], but I have not heard of murdering the ruler."[36]

Thus Mencius, too, rectifies names in order to escape problems arising from conflict of rules or else to make apparent exceptions consistent with the rules. This kind of problem was a common one for Confucians because of their stress on obedience to the traditional code. This body of rules, which had supposedly been handed down from ancient times, was called the *li* 礼 . Early Confucians neither investigated nor developed normative mechanisms like theories of moral responsibility or excuse conditions for resolving conflicts between specific rules or *li* or for specifying exceptions to the rules. Naturally, however, such problems were posed to both Confucius and Mencius at various times. Confucius was asked about the famous conflict of filial and state obligations—should one report his father for stealing sheep?[37] Mencius was faced with problems of extreme exceptions to the rules of *li*—should one rescue one's drowning sister-in-law with one's hand, given the traditional prohibition of touching between sexes?[38]

In place of a theory of subjective versus objective rightness (e.g., a theory of conditions of responsibility or of excuses), the technique of rectifying names was the Confucian way of dealing with conflicts and exceptions. How this doctrine functions can be understood by looking at the counterformulation of the problem by opponents of the doctrine—the Mohists. In the Mohists' attack on this Confucian doctrine, they used killing thieves as a paradigm example.[39] Obviously, the traditional rules condemn killing other men. These same rules will allow, perhaps even require, the killing of thieves. Both Confucians and Mohists can agree that these two rules are part of the code to be followed. How are they to be reconciled? The doctrine of rectification of names, as in the king-versus-merefellow example, entails that one has killed a thief and not a man and therefore the two rules do not conflict. A thief fails to have the pattern of action which would merit application of the term *man*. The Mohists, on the other hand, accept "a thief is a man," but deny the inference to "killing a thief is killing a man." This formalized paradigm shows rather clearly how philosophical speculation was focused on the problem of avoiding conflict among a fixed set of moral rules. The rectification of names achieved the goal by denying simultaneous applicability of names to a thing whenever the names were used in potentially conflicting rules. This amounts to giving all terms a grading use and building the code's moral judgments into its names.[40]

The theory of rectification of names is an expression of a basic underlying philosophical attitude toward theories that is still reflected in contemporary China's "sinification of Marxism." Mao's attitude toward theory reflects the same skeptical awareness of the gap between an instruction and its application—an awareness that something unstated, some intuition, is crucial to any "knowing how." It is the emphasis on this awareness that directs Confucianism away from rule-systems accounts of morality and toward intuitionism.

Generalizing from the man-thief example along with Mencius's rectification of "king" and the traditional view of the *Spring and Autumn Annals*, it appears that the process of rectification of names consists in manipulating the line of division, the linguistic distinction, between positively and negatively evaluated persons and events in such a way that the attitudes engendered by rectified use of the language will produce exactly correct conduct. Hu Shih has suggested that the doctrine of rectification of names is a kind of positivism and involves a commitment to an ideal language.[41] The parallel is illuminating even if not exact. Where positivism's commitment to scientific realism led it to envision a language in which the real structure of facts could be accurately mirrored, Confucianism's belief in a moral reality impelled it to advocate conceptual reorganization of language in its regulative function so it would accurately reflect (and imbue) moral distinctions. Since an ideal language would not allow for conflict and ambiguity in prescription, rectification of names had to eliminate rule conflict.

The doctrine of rectification of names characteristically deals with exclusive distinctions, as opposed to inclusive relationships among names. The word *man* is simply not appropriately applied to a thief or to a person who allows his sister-in-law to drown. If the word *thief* applies to a person, the word *man* or *king* or *gentleman* should not—since moral rules attach to one and not the other of these descriptions. Thus the moral version of rectification of names inclines toward a formula to be found in Kung-sun Lung—one-name-one-thing.

The doctrine of rectification of names presupposes the same set of attitudes about the nature and function of names and language outlined earlier.

The Regulative Function

The terms and names involved in the rectification of names are those that function in the traditional code: *man, king, brother, son*. The purpose of the rectification is to create an ideal language for moral discrimination, evaluation, and action. It is supposed to eliminate the problematic ethical questions.

> Confucius said, "In hearing litigations, I am as good as anyone. What is necessary is to enable people not to have litigations at all."[42]

Thus, while in early Western philosophy there is a kind of assumption that the primary role of language lies in describing the world and communicating ideas or beliefs about the world, Confucian *cheng-ming* 正名 'rectification of names' operates on the presupposition that the primary function of language is to instill attitudes guiding choice and action. Language use should be manipulated as a means of social control. The moral ruler can thereby control and influence action by inculcating skill in making moral discriminations. "If language is in accord then things will be accomplished," "*li* and music will flourish," and "the people will know how to act."[43]

Between the rectification of names and its supposed consequence of widespread moral conformity lies a psychological assumption. Once names are rectified, once we distinguish among things, events, and people in the ways the sage kings did, those learning the language will "emote" and therefore act in perfect accord with the conventional rules laid down by those same sage kings. The regulative function of language is paralleled by an assumption of the emotional malleability of people. For the Confucius–Hsün-tzu "realistic" wing it is this assumption which justifies the Confucian dictum that all can become sages with proper education.

The Mencian, "idealist" wing of Confucianism had a quite different basis for the dictum. People were indeed malleable, but only toward the good. Everyone can become a sage but not via an external *tao* or acquisition of discriminatory abilities from some conventional system. These Confucians believed that it was natural for someone to be moral. Moral behavior was not learned behavior but "human" behavior (of course, learning could help!). The point was not that people simply were virtuous, but they had an innate inclination to acquire the correct rather than incorrect discriminatory abilities. This is evidenced in the tendency to emulate virtuous rather than wicked models.

The idealist version of Confucianism does not deny the regulative function of language, but it does undercut the importance of language as a tool of social control. It is easy to read Mencius as saying that, in principle, people could be perfectly moral (i.e., be a sage) and never learn a single ethical formula. The natural growth and development of our inborn inclinations to act will eventuate in the same outcome (sagelike behavior) that rectification of names plus the sage's *li* 礼 (the traditional code) would produce. Mencius does not deny the regulative efficacy of language, but he objects to relying on it for moral development.

Distinction Marking as the Name-Reality Relation

The *Tao Te Ching* evinced an intense concern with complementary pairs of words. In Confucian rectification of names there are still complementary pairs—father-son, ruler-minister—but they express role relationships rather than evaluative divisions of the world. Thus the pairs of words which interest a Confucian and which dominate their interest include ruler-minister, father-son, older brother–younger brother, and great man–small man. All these dichotomies are practical and political; this branch of Confucianism lacked interest in pure ontology—the science of being. The distinction-marking function of language applies primarily to grading words. We apply a word to the thing if it "deserves" it. Conferring a name is declaring a value—assigning a grade.

Thus, this second assumption of Chinese theories of language is related to the first—the regulative function of language. In evaluation, the function of language is to identify those events, persons, or policies which are to be the objects of choices—to be accepted (emulated) or rejected (shunned). Choices are dictated by the divisions made in language. Persons or events are distinguished according to their "grades" or "merit" and names are assigned to the objects in the different grades. The names used—*gentleman, small man, king*—are terms which occur in conventional descriptions of role behavior. The combination of rectification of the line of division and sage-given rules provides the causally sufficient conditions of correct behavior. Preferences and choices will be stabilized in a kind of harmony with those of the sages.

> . . . when sage-kings instituted names, the names were fixed and actualities distinguished. The sage-kings' principles were carried out and their wills understood. Then the people were carefully led and unified. Therefore the practice of splitting terms and arbitrarily creating names to confuse rectified names, thereby causing much doubt in people's minds and bringing about much litigation, was called great wickedness. . . . Now the sage-kings are dead and the guarding of names has become lax, strange terms have arisen, and names and actualities have been confused. As the standard of right and wrong is not clear, even the guardians of law and the teachers of natural principle are in a state of confusion.[44]

All four of the presuppositions outlined for early Confucians underlie the theories of Hsün-tzu as well. He concurs in the assessment of the role of language as primarily a moral one, helping to regulate people and to provide order in the land. Hsün-tzu differs, however, in that he does acknowledge a descriptive function as well. This is probably due to the influence of his contemporaries—the Neo-Mohists and Dialecticians. Hsün-tzu says:

> Therefore men of wisdom sought to establish distinctions and instituted names to indicate actualities, on the one hand, clearly to distinguish the noble and the base and, on the other, to discriminate between similar and different.[45]

Distinguishing between noble and base refers to the grading or regulative function of words. Discriminating similar and different appears to be a descriptive function.

Conventionalism

The doctrine of rectification of names is conventionalist in the following senses:

1. The doctrine implies that actual name boundaries are determined by their actual use. The return-to-the-sage aspect of the doctrine entails that the names have been corrupted and changed by historical patterns of use and by gradual introductions of new distinctions. Furthermore, that political techniques on the part of the ruler can reestablish the boundaries set by the sages entails that the actual criteria of name use are changeable social practices.
2. The "realist" Confucian version of the rectification of names

theory is seldom cast in terms of absolute correctness of the sages' use of names. Rather the argument (both in *Analects* 13:3 and *Hsün-tzu*) is that the sage provides a single model which can coordinate and harmonize the way people make evaluative distinctions, cultivate attitudes, make choices, and act. The objection to nontraditional use of names is not simply that they are wrong, but that they confuse, complicate, and disorder the society. Implicitly, the argument seems to allow that *any* way of assigning names that was universally adopted (and met survival and effectiveness criteria[46]) would be acceptable.

Confucian and Burkian traditionalism have in common this appeal to an argument from anarchy. They do not claim that the traditional values are rationally justified, but that messing with it will create chaos. The penchant for order and the distrust of human reason are the common themes behind Confucian and Western conservatism. They seem to be saying, "These various changes might each separately seem wise, but the whole system of naming from the wise old kings has been tried and tested. The little changes upset the overall balance and create disorder and risk chaos and anarchy."[47]

3. For the "idealist" version of Confucianism, a different argument can show the conventionality of actual language use. The rules for the application of names fixed by the sage kings are important because of their necessity for the smooth functioning of the code of rules called *li* (rites). The degree of absolutism of language is paralleled by the degree of absolutism of *li*. But the *li* is not absolute for this wing of the school. For the idealist wing of Confucian moral philosophy, *li* (ritual:rites) is neither the totality of morality nor the final arbiter. The arbiter function belongs to the "moral mind" or *jen* or *liang-chih* (intuitive wisdom). The *li* are rules with a function: they help to cultivate the moral mind and bring it to active fulfillment. In the interim, they have the purely instrumental function of preserving order and peace, which are the prime conditions for individual cultivation of the innate patterns of behavior.

The Mencian theory does conflict more directly than the Hsün-tzu version with strong Taoist skeptical conventionalism. Names indeed *are* "disordered" by actual use, but there is a nonhistorical standard against which they could be rectified—the internal moral sense. By contrast, Hsün-tzu's embracing even *strong* conventionalism can be quite consistent with his Confucianism, if not logically required by it. Hsün-tzu is the only Confucian openly to acknowledge that names are just conventional—even those created by the sage-kings:

> In this way [rectifying names] the traces of their accomplishments spread. The spreading of traces and the achievement of results are the highest point of good government. This is the result of careful abiding by the conventionality of names.[48]

Hsün-tzu believed that a sage-king appearing now would not even necessarily retain all the old conventional names. "Should a true king appear, he would certainly retain some old names and create new ones." Hsün-tzu expounds both negative and positive aspects of conventionalism:

> Names have no correctness of their own. The correctness is given by convention. When the convention is established and the custom is formed, they are called correct names. If they are contrary to convention they are called incorrect names. Names have no corresponding actualities by themselves. The actualities ascribed to them are given by convention. When the convention is established and the custom is formed, they are called names of such and such actualities.[49]

Nominalism

The main reason for mentioning nominalism in connection with the rectification of names is to make clear that the most plausible and interesting account of that doctrine does not require any implicit abstract or mental constructs. Obviously none of the accounts explicitly appeals to mental, abstract, or ideal entities. But there are a number of accounts of rectification of names which interpret it as a Platonic theory. Hu Shih, for example, says of the rectification of names, "Words are to express the 'ideas' or 'ideals' (what things ought to be) from which real things and institutions have deplorably deviated and which they should always seek to approximate."[50] Fung Yu-lan says:

> Every name possesses its own definition which designates that which makes the thing to which the name is applied be that thing and no other. In other words, the name is that thing's essence or concept. What is pointed out by the definition of the name "ruler" for example, is that

essence which makes a ruler a ruler. In the phrase, "Let the ruler be a ruler," etc., the first word "ruler" refers to ruler as a material actuality while the second "ruler" is the name and concept of the ideal ruler.[51]

And Clarence Day says:

> As a first step, Confucius wished to make the actualities of life—things, people, events—correspond to the essence of each which is conveyed by its name.... He thought that if each person could get the "idea" or "ideal" clear in his mind, he would naturally try to measure up to this norm for his particular role in an orderly society. To the end that names be used judiciously, Confucius instituted the early study of semantics and insisted that his students make precise definitions of terms. He also regarded as essential clearer definitions of the personal virtues.[52]

But nowhere in any of the traditional accounts of the rectification of names was there any mention of definitions, ideals, ideas, ideal types, concepts, essences, or even of meanings.[53] The interpretations above import these notions wholesale in an attempt to buttress the Confucian position against charges of dogmatic traditionalism. Without including in the theory objective and absolute "ideals," "truths," or "universals" the basis of the rectification just is accord with the intent behind a traditional, culture-specific code.

Aside from the lack of textual basis, a coherence-based objection to these interpretations is that they make rectification of names just another adventitious view Confucius happened to hold. It has no important theoretical role to play in the ethical system. It does not illuminate or contribute to joining the major Confucian conceptions of evaluative decision making: the intuitive-instinctual or the conventional-formal. It adds another irrelevant conception of morals as intellectual-ideal. There appears to be no sound reason for adopting a Platonic interpretation of the theory of rectification of names.

Mo-tzu and Early Mohism

Confucius did not found Confucianism, a fact partially attested to by the well-known disclaimer by Confucius himself that he was only a "transmitter," not a "creator."[54] As the ground of his teaching and innovating, Confucius had a rich intellectual and literary tradition, including the *Book of Rites*, the *Book of Songs*, the *Book of History*, and, some believe, parts of the *I Ching* and the *Spring and Autumn Annals*—all important sources of the *tao* of Confucianism. Although Confucius was almost certainly being modest in saying he created nothing, he is theoretically committed to fidelity to his inheritance. He simply took over the elaborate religious and proprietary code of *li* (rites) with almost no attempt to synthesize the rules of *li* into a rationalized autonomous morality.

By contrast, Mohism seems to have almost no independent intellectual tradition. The ideological wellsprings of Mohism appear to be just peasant common sense sprinkled with some random (perhaps unconscious) borrowings from the "scholar" tradition. This fact, along with Mo-tzu's obvious intimacy with the details of Confucian social doctrines, suggests strongly that Mo-tzu was at one time a disciple of some Confucian (probably a second- or third-generation disciple of Confucius). His writings leave no doubt that he rebelled against this training; whatever unconscious encumbrances he retained, he opposed almost anything that he consciously considered Confucian. Mo-tzu's underlying theory of language, like much of the rest of his philosophy, is relatively more similar to the dominant Western tradition than are Confucianism or Taoism. But the presuppositions we have identified in Taoism and Confucianism still have a large role in Mo-tzu's thinking. For example, while he is more inclined to discuss examples which involve descriptive rather than evaluative terms, such as black and white, ox, or dog, he characteristically uses such examples to support evaluative conclusions. His point in these cases is, for example, the need to generalize in ethical reasoning, to be consistent, or to universalize. His underlying concern (and one which eventuates in the Neo-Mohist interest in logic) is with the bases for language-based evaluative judgments. The standards of reasoning he enunciates are almost all ethical standards.

The Standards of Language Use

Outside of the dialectical chapters (discussed in chap. 4), the *Mo-tzu* has about the same amount of explicit theorizing about names and language as the other two schools. Thus we will be looking at related discussions (especially about judgment and dispute) to reconstruct and illuminate the underlying theory of language. The dialectical chapters, with their definitions and rules, are a development and elaboration of Mo-tzu's concern in the ethical-political chapters with standardization and with the techniques for resolving differences in standards of linguistic and political performance.

The *Mo-tzu* constantly stresses the importance of standards, including the will of heaven, agreement with the superior, and ways of the sage-kings. The role of such standards lies in providing a technique for harmonizing linguistic practice—particularly evaluations expressed in language. Mo-tzu proposes a political doctrine of "agreeing with the superior," which has the structure of a Hobbesian justification of authoritarian rule. But the equivalent of a "state of nature" is not violence and war. It is inefficiency and disorder arising from disagreement about *i* 'morality'. The concern of the theory is on conflicting evaluations:

> Mo-tzu said: In ancient times, when mankind was first born and before there were any laws or government, it may be said that every man's view of things was different. One man had one view, two men had two views, ten men had ten views—the more men, the more views. Moreover, each man believed that his own views were correct and disapproved of those of the others, so that people spent their time condemning one another.[55]

The proposal was for a hierarchical society with evaluations or judgments at each level coinciding with judgments at the higher level. The goal was the social efficiency guaranteed by total agreement in evaluation.[56] By each level agreeing with the higher level, there was ultimately a single authority on evaluative distinctions for the society.[57]

The *Mo-tzu* contains other standardization techniques. In addition to the conforming to the judgmental practices of a human authority figure, Mo-tzu frequently utilizes the notion of impersonal, mechanical standards. In fact, the notion of Heaven, which Mo-tzu insists is personal, is as often explained by the analogy of a tool of measurement as it is by the analogy of anthropoid decision making:

> Therefore Mo-tzu said: The Will of Heaven is to me like a compass to a wheelwright or a square to a carpenter.[58]

The Three Standards

This concern for a mechanical standard is a step from the search for another authoritative opinion toward the logical concern with evidence relationships—standards of correct argument. Mo-tzu initiates interest in this question of standards of argument by proposing his famous "three standards of language."

> Now how are we to go about clearly discriminating these views? The Master Mo-tzu said: There must be a standard erected, using language

without a standard is like trying to establish the direction of sunrise and sunset with a revolving potter's wheel: right and wrong, the distinctions between benefit and harm, cannot be distinguished and understood clearly. Therefore there must be three standards for speech. What are the three? The Master Mo-tzu said: There must be that which is the basis, that which is the inquiry, and that which is the utility. In what way do we provide it with a basis? Looking up, we base it on the ways of the sage kings of antiquity. How do we inquire into it? Looking down, we study it in what the ordinary people have seen and heard. How do we utilize it? Propagate it as law and governmental policy, observe how it accords with the benefit of the people and the state. This is what is called "there are three standards for language."[59]

The "basis" standard is clearly related to the Confucian appeal to tradition. Mo-tzu takes this Confucian attitude to be a kind of argument from precedent and constantly tries to use even earlier historical precedents than those in the traditional literature (very probably drawn from his imagination or folk traditions). Mo-tzu appeals to no known body of ancient literature.

The later Mohists, because of their increased confidence and independence, rejected this standard, arguing that techniques which worked in ancient times just are not suited to the present time.[60]

The other two standards in this passage perhaps sound more familiar. But it is easy to exaggerate the similarities to Western theories of knowledge. The tendency in interpretation has definitely been to project this relative similarity into full-blown recapitulation of Western epistemological doctrines. The source of the error lies in attributing a concern with the semantic notions of truth and meaning to Mo-tzu and then regarding him as an ancient pragmatist or empiricist. But the three standards are not tests of the truth of sentences or judgments, but of *yen* 言 'language' use. The question is not what is true but what is an appropriate way of talking about, describing, distinguishing, and naming—in short, using language.

Because it uses the words *eyes and ears* the second statement has been the springboard for considerable "discovery" of empiricism in ancient China. In discussing the application of this criterion to the question of the existence of ghosts, Needham, Mei, and Hu all see visions of empiricism, foundationalism, and sense-data theory.[61] But the surface similarity is misleading. Mo-tzu is not concerned with "eyes and ears" as a phenomenal, inferential base for knowledge of the physical world.

Consider this standard against the kinds of judgments Mo-tzu wants to make—judgments about the appropriateness of language use. Then it becomes the perfectly sensible suggestion that language should be used in ways (should make discriminations) which coincide with people's sensory abilities and inclinations. He is not claiming that all sense data statements are true, but that we ought to accept language use which accords with the actual patterns of the people's sensory discrimination.

Taking this as phenomenalist empiricism has led to undue celebration of Mo-tzu's "modernity" and also undue criticism of him as a shallow empiricist. Hu Shih compares him to J. S. Mill in ignoring "the possibility of error and hallucination and other limitations of sense observation,"[62] while Needham puts in Wang Ch'ung's mouth a lecture to the Mohists that sounds like Kant warning a British empiricist: "What status have sense-impressions compared with the synthesizing mind?"[63] In fact, this tenet of Mohist methodology, both in statement and (despite the occurrence of *eye* and *ear*) application is less reminiscent of philosophical empiricism than of poll taking. Y. P. Mei calls it the Testimonial Argument.[64] That is more accurate.

An even more elaborate case of philosophical reincarnation is the third standard. Most interpreters have followed Hu Shih's lead and declared Mo-tzu a pragmatist. Hu Shih explains his interpretation:

> Dissatisfied with the method of Confucianism, Moh Tih sought a criterion by which to test the truth and falsehood, and the right and wrong, of beliefs, theories, institutions and polities. This criterion he found in the practical consequences which the beliefs, theories, etc., tend to produce.
> Briefly stated, Moh Tih's main position is this: that the meaning of every institution lies in what it is good for, and that the meaning of every conception or belief or policy lies in what kind of conduct or character it is fitted to produce.[65]

Similarly, Y. P. Mei argues, "Strange though it may seem, considering the time span and the cultural distance that separate the ancient Chinese and the modern American, perhaps the Western expression that comes nearest to this idea of Mo-tzu is to be found in William James."[66] It does seem strange, of course, and not just because of time and place separation. So far, as we have seen, Chinese philosophy has not confronted the problem of providing an account of "truth" or "meaning." And that, in turn, is related to a stress on the evaluative, prescriptive functions of language as opposed to the descriptive functions. Notice that Mo-tzu is interested in the acceptability of doctrines that can be promulgated as law—prescriptions. He clearly does not have in mind, as a philosophical pragmatist would, "What results would follow from acceptance of the statement, 'The sun will rise tomorrow'?" It would truly have been strange that Mo-tzu should have suddenly and independently discovered and proposed a solution for the twin problems of truth and meaning without ever explicitly formulating either as a philosophical question.

So this is not pragmatism in the sense of being a pragmatic account of the semantic notions of either truth or meaning. But it is pragmatics in a broader sense, that is, a theory of the effects of language on users and hearers, and a commitment to accept or reject language uses (divisions) depending on their implications for behavior. Thus the third criterion is not a test of truth. It is just an explicit formulation of the Confucian practice, already noted, of arguing from behavioral consequences—with a slight modification for Mo-tzu's utilitarian evaluation of these consequences. The three standards are, in other words, formulations of the common evaluative standards regularly found in intellectual circles in ancient China.

The error in interpreting these standards, as noted above, stems from assuming that the background of Western philosophical tradition lies behind this doctrine as well. If translators render *yen* (language) as "judgments" or "theories" or, as Hu Shih said, "beliefs" or "claims," they make the tests look as if they were crude accounts of what it is to be true, and thus ignore the real insight of the doctrine. The standards are the purported standards of the appropriateness of language use. Viewed in this way, the standards are much more plausible. The tests of the appropriateness of an utterance are its conformity to the tradition of language use, to the reporting practices of the people, and to its functional efficacy in regulating and guiding behavior. It is in assuming that Mo-tzu was talking about sentences and truth as Western epistemologists do that his position is made to seem simple-minded.

Pragmatic Meaning in Mo-tzu

Mo-tzu had a pragmatic sounding doctrine about names as well. Hu Shih translates the following in a discussion of Mo-tzu's allegedly operationalist theory of meaning:

> Now a blind man may say, "That which shines with brilliancy is white, and that which is like soot is black." Even those who can see would not change this. But if you place both white and black things before the blind man and ask him to choose the one from the other, he fails. Therefore I say, "A blind man does not know white and black," not because he cannot name them, but because he cannot choose them.[67]

It is tempting to supply the word *meaning* in the translation and make this look like an appeal for operational definitions—but that would miss the point in almost exactly the way that taking the three standards as tests of truth did. The question is not what the meaning of *black* or of *white* is. The question is what would it be for someone to have mastered the total practices in the use of some distinction—like black-white—in a language, that is, what it is to "know" that distinction. (Recall that "know" is best thought of as "know how.") The linguistic practice involves the ability to make the associated visual discriminations. So the blind man is inherently unable to master (know) all the practices involved in some linguistic color distinctions. Because he cannot divide or discriminate black and white stuff, his mastery of linguistic forms of expression, like "black-white," is incomplete.

Mo-tzu's theories make much more sense and are more interesting as long as we remember that his background assumptions are nominalistic. His conceptual scheme does not involve the mental or semantic apparatus that characterizes Western epistemologists' talk of truth or meaning. The concern is with what is appropriate language use, not what are true mental states, propositions, ideas, or the like.

In general, interpretations of classical Chinese thought for Western audiences have overstressed the concept of mind.[68] Chinese thinkers' philosophical attention is on the more basic view of men engaged in social practices mediated by the social practice of language. A theory of mind does become central with Mencius, who tries to give substance to Confucian moral realism by making the mind the presocial source of all correct regulation of behavior. But even his theory of mind will make more sense against a clear understanding of this philosophical background.

Later Taoism—Chuang-tzu

Being unwilling to make distinctions and evaluations, the Taoists opted out of the dispute over policy that embroiled Confucianism and Mohism—not so much because they had no position, as because they found such wrangling worthless in principle.

The great classical Taoist of the age of the Dialecticians, Chuang-tzu (369–268 B.C.), concentrated on the worthlessness of linguistic distinctions —especially those made by the Dialecticians. He was acquainted with the views of Kung-sun Lung and Hui Shih (380–305 B.C.?), probably through his close personal relationship with the latter. He elaborated and developed Taoist doctrines into a challenge to the Dialecticians' enterprise. Chuang-tzu shares with the tradition a focus on the image of man using language. He blends an interest in regulative and in descriptive language. In using language we make distinctions, dividing the realm about which we talk into evaluatively significant parts. Disputes or disagreements are seen as differing ways of dividing things. The Mohists and Confucians disagree because they carve the world differently and in doing so produce diverging systems of social regulation.

Pien *(Disputes) and Their Resolution*

The linguistic practices of division include forms of dispute between advocates of particular policies. The disputing behavior stems from the different ways they have to divide, evaluate, and regulate. Chuang-tzu's central claim is that such disputes are in principle unresolvable and hence pointless. Once you have a practice of dividing and evaluating in a certain way, arguments from within that practice can never demonstrate that another way of drawing linguistic distinctions is wrong. Chuang-tzu's view is often misleadingly characterized as being about logic, and Chuang-tzu is said to be illogical or to be advocating the abandonment of logic. It should be sufficient to observe that there is no clear conception of logic (except for algebraic inference—see pp. 124–37) in the tradition for him to oppose or criticize. He does know about disputes and argument (in the sense of something you have with someone as opposed to something you give). Nowhere does his criticism of *pien* 辯 'dispute' suggest that he conceives of it as consisting of premises proving a conclusion. The central terms and argument regarding *pien* are found in the second chapter, "On Harmonizing Discussions of Things."[69]

The terms of logical analysis in the *Chuang-tzu* and the Dialecticians attest to the enormous influence of the presuppositions about language outlined above. Some reflect the assumption of the regulative function of language: *ch'ü* 取 'choose', 'select', 'prefer'; *chü* 舉 'pick out', 'select out by means of a name'; *k'o* 可 'permissible' (of actions), 'assertable' or 'admissible' (of utterances or writing strings); and *shih* 是 and *fei* 非, which are the basic approval-disapproval pair. These may be translated as "right-wrong" (with both evaluative and descriptive uses retained), or in verbal uses as "to affirm, agree" "to deny, disagree" and as demonstratives "is this" "is not this." Other terms show the influence of the presupposition that language consists in distinguishing pairs of opposites, for example, *pien* 辯 'to distinguish', 'to discriminate', 'dispute'; *liang* 兩 'the two sides' (of a discrimination or a dispute).

Pien is often translated "argument." And in modern Chinese, the character is used in the compound *pien-lun* meaning "argument." However, such a translation of the ancient term tends to give the misleading impression that Chuang-tzu and his philosophical adversaries were discussing the correctness or validity of arguments, the relation of proof or premise to conclusion. In fact, he never considers such issues.[70]

The dispute between Confucianism and Mohism lies behind much of what Chuang-tzu says about *pien* 'disputes'. As a paradigm, that dispute no doubt contributed to Chuang-tzu's skepticism of the practice. The two schools seldom advanced beyond name calling, holding up to ridicule, and misrepresentation. It could hardly be called an argument because the protagonists were so seldom giving recognizable arguments. Mo-tzu, for example, would criticize the Confucian practice of elaborate funerals because of their great costs; Mencius attacked Mo-tzu's position by caricaturing it as not wanting to bury his parents at all and claiming that such a feeling is unnatural to men. Each criticism would appeal only to someone who had already accepted one perspective or the other. There was no basis of shared assumptions from which agreement could arise. Neither side tended to be reasonable in the sense of constructing arguments or proofs from shared premises or acknowledging and attempting to refute the arguments of the other. So Chuang-tzu's skepticism of the value of argument does not grow from the most charitable example possible.

Chuang-tzu's concern with *pien* 'disputes', consequently, does not stem from his suspicion of reason or of logical argument. It is as if *pien*s were simply immediate, fundamental choices—like matters of taste. Philosophical conflicts are interpreted as initial differences in assigning *shih-fei* to utterances. These initial differences give rise to the different perspectives of the disputants. The opposing distinctions which imply opposing preferences and choices in social and political policy are all made arbitrarily.

The skepticism of *pien* emerges in the *Chuang-tzu* as a negative answer to the question of the correctness or decidability of a *pien* 'dispute'. Chuang-tzu has absorbed the paradigm of intellectual activity as the forming of preferences and the making of choices through language distinctions. For Chuang-tzu this linguistic discriminating activity is the basic intellectual activity—as fundamental to his scheme as sensing or perceiving are to our own. He does not view the making of discriminations as an outcome of some more basic cognitive activity and in particular not the outcome of a reasoning or argumentative process. The opposing discriminations come from naming systems which give rise to differing judgments of *shih* 是 and *fei* 非 —judgments about what a thing is or is not (descriptive distinctions) or about what is right or wrong (evaluative distinctions).[71]

Skepticism and Indexicality of Language

Chuang-tzu's skepticism of language has a different basis from that in the *Tao Te Ching*. His claim is not only that the distinctions in language have no metaphysical base, but that even as conventions they have no stable conventional relation to the world. Chuang-tzu's critique emerges from his concentration on indexical terms and sentences. An indexical is a term whose referent can only be specified relative to the context of utterance, such as *I, here, this, now*. Sentences containing indexicals change their truth value as they are used by different speakers in different contexts. Essentially Chuang-tzu is claiming that all judgment is radically subjective in the way indexical sentences are subjective. His argument trades on some peculiar features of the key judgmental terms in his account of disputes: *shih* 是 'this:right:affirm' and *fei* 非 'not-this:wrong:deny'. All discriminations expressed in language entail *shih* or *fei* judgments and are thus indexical. Utterances of judgments and names thus have no fixed relation to any supposed extralinguistic reality.

Chuang-tzu's conclusion exploits the ambiguity in *shih* and its opposites. *Shih* can be translated either as a factual or evaluative "right," or as a demonstrative "this," "the one in question," or as a verb "to affirm." *Fei* is the opposite of *shih* in each of these uses. It means "wrong" as a moral or factual judgment; as a demonstrative, Graham has argued that *fei* means "not this," "not the one in question"; and as a verb, it means "to deny." Chuang-tzu commonly also uses *pi* 彼 'that' as a demonstrative opposite of *shih*.

Chuang-tzu argues that just as *shih* and *pi* 'this' and 'that' are relative to the speaker's perspective, so are *shih* and *fei* 'this' and 'not this', 'right' and 'wrong'. Everything can be called *pi* from some point of view, and everything can be called *shih*. Thus from *shih*'s use as a demonstrative, Chuang-tzu fashions an argument that all such judgments are perspective-relative. From its use as moral "right" he identifies it with the conflicting moral positions of Confucius and Mo-tzu. Arguing about elaborate funerals is as meaningless as arguing about whether some object is "really" a "this" or a "that."

We should not mistake Chuang-tzu's point as being that of the skeptic of the senses observing that things give different visual effects when viewed from different perspectives. For Chuang-tzu's view is more involved with language. Language is a system of distinguishing and evaluating that is perspective-bound—that is, each person in using the language creates his own conceptual and evaluative perspective. Conflicting judgments or disputes are therefore inevitable and irreconcilable. It is not our sense impressions or the associated ideas that are imbued with subjectivity because of perspective. What is subjective is our employment of a language to express and embody our "position." The language conventionally provides terms that are appropriate only to speaker-relative use. We use the terms in disputes and think because our *shih*ing and *fei*ing are different we have a substantial dispute.

In identifying a *pien* with a *shih-fei*, Chuang-tzu continues the tradition of Taoist skepticism. All *pien* are suspect for the reasons that language is suspect. Language consists of seemingly opposite distinctions that are in fact one. We would realize this if we took the proper point of view, which Chuang-tzu calls "using the light." In making discriminations and using names we both create for ourselves and become subject to a perspective or point of view. There is no naturally correct relation of names to distinctions. All naming is conventional or arbitrary. Being only conventional and lacking any "fixedness," words and speech are ultimately no more significant than the twittering of birds or other noises in nature (the pipes of earth).

Chuang-tzu begins his "On Harmonizing Discussions of Things" with a series of metaphors that illustrate this attitude toward language. Speech is just sound coming out of men the way wind whistling in the trees is sound coming from nature. Then he considers an objection:

> Speech is not just blowing breath. Speech says something. That which it says, however, cannot be determined. Has it really said something then? Or have we never said anything? If you think that saying is different from the tweeting of baby birds, can you make the distinction, or is there no distinction?[72]

"Surely," one might object, "there are some distinctions and preferences that *all* men have in common, that are not perspective-relative."

Chuang-tzu, however, intends his insight to be broader than mere spatial or temporal perspective. Being human is itself a perspective. Even the judgments on which we all agree are relative to our human perspective.

> Moreover let me try a question on you. When a man sleeps in the damp his wais ails him and he dies paralyzed; is that so of the loach? When he sits in a tree he shivers and shakes; is that so of an ape? Which of these three knows the proper place to live? Men eat the flesh of grain-fed beasts, deer eat the sweet grass, centipedes relish snakes, owls and crows savor mice; which of the four has a proper sense of taste? Apes mate with monkeys, deer couple with deer, loaches swim with fishes. Lady Li and Lao Mao were beautiful in the eyes of men, but when the fish saw them they plunged deep, when the deer saw them they broke into a run. Which of these four knows what is truly beautiful in the world? In my judgment the principle of kindness and duty, the road of *shih* and *fei* are inextricably confused; how can I know how to prove the distinctions between them?[73]

Just as Chuang-tzu questions that man can regard his desires and inclinations as the basis for distinctions, he questions that any part of man's nature can claim the arbiter's role in deciding *shih-fei*. Idealist Confucians believe that all men possess a particular faculty that ought to make the discriminations and choices and would make them in the same way—the "evaluating mind" or "heavenly ruler."[74] To this Chuang-tzu has two answers. First, even if there were such a faculty, why should it rule over the other faculties?

> Of the hundred joints, nine openings, six inward organs all present and complete, which should I recognize as more kin to me than another? Are you pleased with them all? or is there a favorite? If so, are all the others its servants? Couldn't the servants also rule each other? Couldn't they take turns as ruler and servant? Is there really such a thing as a true ruler among them?[75]

Second, he denies that there is *any* inborn tendency to choose in these ways. Confucians want the evaluating mind to be innate so its discriminations are "natural" and therefore more authoritative than merely conventional discriminations would be. Chuang-tzu holds that the mind which all men share is not inborn but develops as men acquire "culture," learning, and so forth in a linguistic community. The mind's evaluations are given their particular cast by our being taught distinctions, evaluations, and choices which are embodied in language.

Chuang-tzu feels that in making the discriminations characteristic of philosophical schools' conflicting *shih*s and *fei*s we are doing something analogous to our choices in place to live, mates, food, or the like. We would, however, not incline toward one school or another at all unless we had already been prejudiced toward that choice in some way. The prejudice, according to Chuang-tzu, is due to past discriminations and choices based on them. We develop a prejudiced mind whose content is a language system applied from our perspective. By accepting language distinctions and choices, we incline ourselves to making others and gradually weave the web until we can finally make distinctions in only one way. We then end up with a developed system of *shih*s and *fei*s which we cannot independently evaluate.

> Now if you take the prejudiced minds as the authority, who is without such an authority? Why must it be those who know the period and whose mind selects for itself who have one; the stupid man has one as well. To have *shih-fei* judgments before prejudices form in the mind is like going to Yüeh today and arriving yesterday.[76]

The different systems of discrimination are treated as immediate choices—not essentially different from taste, except that taste evaluations too are only made after the mind has been inclined or prejudiced. Remember, Chuang-tzu doesn't discuss what reasons or evidence might be given for a system of discrimination (logical notions, truth, or semantic notions like meaning are not part of the philosophical idiom), but *if he had*, he could merely observe that reasons or evidence could only be ascertained and evaluated from within some practice of language use. Hence there is no way to arbitrate the differences among the different ways of hooking language up with the world.

> Suppose that I dispute [*pien*] with you, and it is you not I that wins, is it really you who is right [*shih*], I who am wrong [*fei*]? If it is not you who wins, am I really the right one and not you? Are we partly right and partly wrong? If we cannot decide, others are naturally in the dark. Whom shall I call in to judge us? If we call in someone on your side, since he is on your side, how can he judge? If we call in someone on my side how can he judge? If we call in someone who differs from both of us to judge, since he differs from both of us how can he judge? If we call in someone who agrees with both of us, since he already agrees with both of us how can he judge? Consequently, not I nor you nor he can know which of us has won—shall we find another to depend on?[77]

It appears that at no place in this theory does Chuang-tzu consider the relation of presuppositions, premises, or standards to arguments or conclusions. He deals only with the psychological, linguistic, and other conditions of preference or choice behavior. There is a hint of the notion of a standard in one of the other chapters of the *Chuang-tzu*, "The Autumn Waters":

> From the point of view of differences, if we regard a thing as large using that than which it is larger, then all things are large. If we regard a thing as small using that than which it is smaller, then everything is small.[78]

Here too the text deals with conditions for making or drawing a distinction—large-small. He is saying the same thing about large and small that he said about *shih* and *fei*. For all opposites, by changing the point of reference or point of view, one could apply either of the opposing names to any given thing. The point of reference is not a premise or presupposition of an argument leading to that conclusion; it is just a feature of language users that they are conditioned to make the distinction. The process is a kind of immediate perception or judgment—a kind of *wei* (regarding, deeming, or seeing as).

Thus, differing philosophical doctrines or different systems of *shih-fei* judgments are (1) not resolvable, since there is no point of view that will decide between the two alternatives formed by different naming conventions; and (2) not really a disagreement at all, since, like questions of taste, the words used do not have any objective basis so they could as well be reversed—*shih* and *fei* are interchangeable. The conflicting pairs correspond to no real distinction. A *pien* is not to be decided, but dissolved. This is accomplished by viewing it from other perspectives and perhaps from some all-encompassing perspective (the axis of *tao*s). Chuang-tzu also uses the metaphors "opening up to the light" or "reflecting it to heaven" for abandoning perspective (and therefore judgment).

Monism and Mysticism

"The universe and I were created together and all things and I are one."[79] This, Chuang-tzu says, only "comes close" to "it." Chuang-tzu's position is, accordingly, different from, say, Parmenides' monism. For Parmenides, the world really is "one" as contrasted to the perceived world of motion and change. For Chuang-tzu, "the world is one" is itself a judgment from a perspective. It is appropriate not as a correct descriptive assertion about the world, but as a denial of any given distinctions. The "one" is not opposed to the perceived world, but to the language world with its conventional boundaries and divisions.

In Chuang-tzu, then, the *Tao Te Ching* version of Taoist skepticism about any judgments of value became a skepticism that either side of a verbalized dispute *(pien)* could properly be said to be correct. Chuang-tzu's skepticism shares with that of Lao-tzu (and ultimately the Mohist logicians—see pp. 124–37), the basic assumption that language is not fixed. There is no constant relationship between names and the world. The terms he chose to illustrate his view were not names, but indexicals— terms whose applicability varied according to the speaker and the time. In a larger sense, that seems to be Chuang-tzu's point—that all names (language terms) are like indexicals in a crucial way. Chuang-tzu's view of *shih* and *pi*, large and small, useful and useless, and right and wrong (*shih* and *fei*), as shifting their reference depending on who used the term, had monumental significance in China. It undercut the traditional program of Confucianism that was based on the commonsense view that all terms are "names" or rigid, one-to-one markers of things.

The Assumptions about Language in Chuang-tzu

The presuppositions about the nature of language in Chuang-tzu are essentially the same as for the other schools and for early Taoism.

1. Chuang-tzu sees language as regulating behavior, though his attention is riveted on the emotional and attitudinal effects of language through which the behavior is regulated. He sees that our emotions coincide with our *shih-fei* judgments which "shoot out like arrows from a crossbow." Along with the emphasis we have noted in other philosophers on the emotive effects of language, Chuang-tzu adds an emotivist's view of the subjectivity of all our judgments and discriminations.

2. Chuang-tzu's account of subjectivity of judgments does not, however, depend on either a view of emotions warping or distorting our reason or the notion of a private inner cognitive apparatus called a mind. The subjectivity is a natural effect of the nature of language. Language, for Chuang-tzu, still has its essence in dividing things. Chuang-tzu's concentration on examples of opposites—large-small, useful-useless, life-death, this-that—is very much in the

tradition of the *Tao Te Ching*. But the division is always from a unique and complex perspective. All such discriminations and judgments are indexical. The connection of names to things is not fixed.

3. Accordingly, Chuang-tzu's conventionalism shades into pure subjectivism. Our use of language distinctions is not even fixed within a linguistic community but varies for each speaker, and, given the other *shih* and *fei* judgments, for each school and each wing of each school and so on and on. There is no sense in which we can hope to settle disputes that arise at any level because they rest on adopting different arbitrary beginning points.

4. Again, no role has been assigned to abstract or mental objects in explaining Chuang-tzu's philosophical position. We saw that neither his subjectivism nor his skepticism were based on the concept of a private internal "idea" or a representationalist epistemology at all.[80]

So Chuang-tzu is a nominalist. The best interpretation of his view is one assuming that internal mental or knowledge states are linguistic states. He does not view "thinking" as entertaining ideas, images, concepts, classes, or other abstract or mental entities. He nowhere speaks of the meaning of a term as if the meaning were an idea rather than a distinction (in fact, one could not make sense of his view if he did). Although we typically summarize his view as dealing with "judgments" or "beliefs," he is usually speaking of *pien* or *shih-fei*s or *yen* (language). Taoist skepticism in Chuang-tzu as well as in Lao-tzu contrasts with Western skepticisms in its total absence of talk about beliefs, propositions, images, ideas, or concepts. It assumes instead that we operate with language, and since language is not a rigid system of naming then "knowledge"—the "knowing how" expressed in language—is just capricious, arbitrary, and subjective deeming or construing (*i wei* 以爲).

Classical Assumptions about Language in Review

The four presuppositions of language—its regulative function, its connection with dividing or discriminating, its conventional basis, and the name-thing nominalism in theories of language—are central themes in all the classical philosophical schools of China. The different schools and thinkers play variations of those themes.

The regulative function of language is primary and central for Confucianism and *Tao Te Ching* Taoism. Mo-tzu shows more concern with descriptive examples, and both Hsün-tzu and Chuang-tzu incorporate descriptive distinctions and issues in their theories. That the regulation of behavior comes via the inculcation of emotional attitudes and inclinations is probably a common assumption—implicit in the *Tao Te Ching*, dominant in Chuang-tzu, and present in both wings of Confucianism.

The connection between names and divisions or discrimination is a particularly constant assumption of all the schools. Early Confucianism probably did not even worry about divisions other than the role dichotomies of father-son and ruler-minister, which became moral grading dichotomies. Dichotomous division was also the standard *Tao Te Ching* picture, and examples from Mo-tzu, Hsün-tzu, and Chuang-tzu reflect the same focus on pairs of opposites. The only other variation on the division theme is internal to particular thinkers—they may shift from thinking the name corresponds to the division to its corresponding to one hunk of the stuff separated out by the division. The two pictures easily interchange as conceptions of the relation of word and world.

The main source of the basic differences in the pre-Han schools grows out of their differing degree of acceptance of the conventionalism of language. The least accepting would be the Mohists, who thought there were objective standards of value and distinctions (see p. 106 for the Neo-Mohist elaboration) and the Mencius wing of Confucianism, for whom a prelinguistic discriminatory and evaluative mind was a basic assumption. "Realistic" Confucianism, concerned with the rectification of names, entailed (and in the work of Hsün-tzu, openly embraced) the conventionalism of language; the assertability of an utterance (a judgment or distinction) was only a function of community acceptance. Chuang-tzu gleefully pushes the point to complete subjectivism—even a community's language is used by different schools, subschools, and finally even individuals in arbitrary, changeable ways. There is no single function of assertability.

All the philosophical positions are spelled out with no theoretical elements that go beyond the name-thing relation or its equivalent. There is no theory of mediating "ideal types," "meanings," "forms," "universals," "concepts," "ideas," or "essences." There is no abstract or mental theorizing in the philosophical traditions of China.

These philosophical schools set the boundaries and shape the milieu in which the Dialecticians and the school of names developed. The subsequent chapters reveal how the assumptions motivated the semantic theories, the view of logic, and finally the white-horse paradox in Chinese philosophy.

Chapter 4

Neo-Mohist Philosophy of Language

The work credited to the Neo-Mohists is a part of the *Mo-tzu*. It consists of six chapters of the *Mo-tzu*. The Chinese commentary tradition refers to these six chapters as "Mohist Dialectic" (*Mo Pien* 墨辯). The most systematic of the dialectical chapters are four chapters known as the Canon (*ching* 經). The other two, the "picks," are more diverse. The order of the chapters of the Mohist Dialectics are as follows:

1. Canon I 經上 consists of equivalence formulas, such as "Knowledge is Contact" (*chih ch'ieh yeh* 知接也).[1]
2. Canon II 經下 consists mostly of brief assertions with a reference to an explanation via the expression "The Explanation is . . . " (*shuo tsai* ____ 說在 . . .).
3. Canon Explanation I 經說上 contains commentaries of varying length on the formulas of Canon I.
4. Canon Explanation II 經說下 contains commentaries on Canon II.
5. *Ta Ch'ü* 大取 'The Greater Pick' is the most corrupt and obscure chapter in the group.[2]
6. *Hsiao Ch'ü* 小取 'The Lesser Pick' is the only chapter in the dialectical group that reads as a consecutive treatise. It discusses a formal algebralike inference procedure.[3]

The usual practice in discussing the Canon is to pair the formulas of the main canon with the appropriate explanation from the Explanation. I follow this practice and also follow the numbering of the Canon and Explanations used by Tan Chieh-fu.[4]

The *Mo-tzu* is one of the oldest works of philosophy from China. If we judge by the sophistication of its content, the dialectical chapters of the

Mo-tzu appear to have been written later than the main ethical and political chapters. The Canon appears to be a litany of fundamental beliefs more than a point of view of a single author. Some commentators disagree about both points.[5] The present interpretation assumes only that the semantic theories discussed and reconstructed belong to the later Warring States Period of Chinese thought.

The subject matter of the *Mo Pien* is diverse. Hu Shih finds theories of logic, psychology, ethics, economics, politics, grammar, mathematics, mechanics, and optics in the Canon.[6] My concern is mainly with the fragments of the text which can be clearly related to theory of language (semantics and pragmatics), theory of knowledge, and theory of inference. The semantic fragments deal mainly with the functioning of individual and compound names. The theory of knowledge is mainly a classification of various types of and objects of *chih* 知 'knowledge'. The analysis of inference is embedded in the consecutive essay *Hsiao Ch'ü*.

The Mohist Dialectic is a prime example of the need for a coherence theory methodology—both in textual and interpretive theory. Textual corruption is a notorious problem in dealing with all texts of the classical philosophical period in China. The dialectical chapters of the *Mo-tzu* present in one package almost all the examples of the various kinds of corruption. There are two intersecting reasons for the difficulty. The *Mo-tzu* as a whole was not as carefully studied through the Chinese "middle ages," which were dominated by Confucianism, Taoism, and Buddhism. Commentaries, which would have been sources for emendation, were neither collected nor revised as they were for the philosophical texts of Confucianism and Taoism. Further, these chapters' organizational principle is very complex, the content difficult, terse, and fragmented. In centuries of recopying, editorial errors must easily have crept in. To a copyist the fragments would have seemed like a string of unrelated characters. Given the cryptic style, and the lack of a commentary tradition, he was unlikely to have understood the philosophical points being made. Characters were frequently omitted, duplicated, transposed, or mistaken for other characters. Lines were skipped or copied in the wrong order.[7] "Corruption spotting" is complicated by the malleability of Chinese grammar and the absence of punctuation in old texts. One comes to suspect corruption whenever a passage does not yield a coherent reading.

A textual theory tries to reconstruct and reverse the corruption process. It compares all the existing versions of a text, the commentaries from various periods, quotations in other texts, and evidence of systematic substitution of certain character pairs to "reconstruct" a hypothetical "original" text, since, by hypothesis, we have no access to that original. Textual emendation must be judged by the coherence of its theory and of its resultant text. Chinese textual theory uses a wide range of techniques. Accepted practice in emending texts focuses on character substitution based on "loan" characters, varying written forms, ancient phonetic values, and so on. The allowable "moves" in emendation are many. One may (1) transpose or eliminate characters, sentence clauses, paragraphs, and even chapters; (2) substitute characters if *(a)* their written forms at any given time since the original (bronze, pre-Han, printed, simplified, or script) are close enough to have been mistaken by a copyist, *(b)* their sounds are close enough for one character to have been "borrowed" for another, or *(c)* the character was used with that meaning in the same work, by the same author or school or in some other writing from the period, *(d)* one character was taboo during some dynastic period and a mutilated or synonymous character substituted; and finally (3) one may add or subtract characters as necessary to make the sentence "make sense." All these kinds of emendation may be supplemented by such interpretive techniques as revising punctuation, taking statements as ironic, or treating questions as rhetorical negative questions.

The practice of textual reconstruction can be supported by relatively uniform constraints within a general textual theory or it can be virtually unconstrained ad hoc revision. If one were just to make and compound the permitted moves there is no limit (other than imagination) to the magic one could work on a Chinese text. One could make the first paragraph of Confucius's *Analects* read like a transliteration of Ronald Reagan's inaugural address. Because it is a potential source of scientific and logical reasoning in classical China and because it is so hard to interpret, emendation work on the *Mo-tzu* has been particularly unrestrained. A. C. Graham's careful theoretical approach to reconstruction has produced the most plausible emendation of the texts.[8] Kao Heng's emendations are probably the most imaginative and free.[9]

Interpretive theory and textual theory clearly interact in this case. In the first place, text revision is stimulated primarily by semantic problems. We undertake textual revision, punctuation, or employ the use-mention distinction when a text, as it stands, seems not to make sense. We feel satisfied with an emendation, punctuation, or attribution of grammatical structure when the sentence appears to make sense. This makes it difficult to gain new insights from reading a text. Working this way on texts tends to make the object philosopher's work read in ways which the commentator thinks are sensible—ways which are familiar to the commentator. The difficulty of the text and its malleability under all these practices creates a kind of self-reinforcing predicament for an interpretation. We have a hypothesis about what the text says and then can easily mold the text to say it.

The way one can escape from this predicament is by theory-based constraints on interpretation as well as emendation. We should become aware of our own philosophical presuppositions and of how they are likely (given linguistic and other philosophical differences) to differ from those of pre-Han Chinese philosophers. We should entertain as broad a range of assumptions and views as possible to draw on in deciding what would be coherent ways to interpret a text. Emendation, punctuation, and the like ought not to be triggered by a test of what makes sense to the interpreter, but by what would have made sense to the author, given the dominant outlook of his philosophical milieu, the presuppositions, contemporary developments in philosophy, and so on.

Providing that sort of background for interpretive hypotheses has been the purpose of the previous chapters, outlining traditional assumptions in the areas of ontology, semantics, philosophy of mind, and theories of knowledge. I argue that behavioral nominalism with a pragmatic conception of language are background attitudes toward philosophical questions that are explained by the nature of the Chinese language and that help explain the major doctrines of the dominant schools in the pre-Han tradition.

In the discussion that follows, I appeal to these background assumptions and the general interpretive theory of nouns outlined earlier in defending my choice among the conjectures about how to emend the text of the Mohist Dialectic. I have, for the most part, limited myself to choosing from among textual suggestions made by textual scholars. I have relied most heavily on the following commentators for their textual work. The basis of all recent work on the text was laid by Sun Yi-jang. I have also consulted Tan Chieh-fu, Liu Tsun-yan, and Li Yü-shu among recent Chinese commentators.[10] Among Western commentators I have relied primarily on A. C. Graham.[11] His textual reconstruction, as noted, inspires confidence since he emends sparingly and under general theoretical constraints. Graham argues that graph changes must be supported by parallelism, evidence of systematic corruption, and some coherent theory about the structure and development of the text itself.[12]

In this chapter I survey the Neo-Mohist position on the four presuppositions of language used as an explanatory framework for the narrative in chapter 3. Then I develop the Neo-Mohist response to Chuang-tzu's views on *pien* 辯 'dispute'. Finally, I analyze the Mohist study and critique of the formal algebralike inference procedure (sentence-matching)—the closest equivalent to a theory of logic in the period. In viewing the Mohist treatment of that project I speculate on some of the important ways that language can influence the development of logic theories.

The Four Assumptions in the Canon

The dialectical chapters of the *Mo-tzu* are especially important in understanding the classical Chinese attitudes toward language because they mark the emergence of explicit semantic theory in a language with masslike nouns. The semantic theory is limited for the most part to terms and compound terms. The later Mohist writers did not have any theory of sentences except for the minimal and example-dependent analysis in the later *Hsiao Ch'ü* (The Lesser Pick). Specifically, they seemed to have no distinction of functional elements of sentences (predicates and terms) nor of semantic truth and falsity. The semantics of terms is simple mereological nominalism. Names and distinctions are applied to stuffs. Interesting problems come in extending that picture to encompass compound terms. The Mohists characterize the stuffs as interpenetrating. The ontology of this picture produced a famous Chinese controversy about "hard and white" which in turn led directly to the white-horse paradox of Kung-sun Lung.

The explicit development of semantic theory marks some modifications of the four assumptions about language, but the influence of the four assumptions is still evident despite these developments. The most crucial developments concern the last two assumptions—conventionality and nominalism. The dialectical chapters reflect the dominant Taoist attitude toward names as arbitrary tools of a kind of inferior knowledge, but these chapters express a relatively realist theory of reference. The semantic theory is predominantly nominalist. However there are two graphs used frequently throughout these chapters, *i* 'idea' and *lei* 'class', which require analysis because they suggest, respectively, a rudimentary theory of consciousness, and an analysis of semantics focused on something like natural kinds.

To review, the four assumptions outlined earlier are:

1. The chief function of language is regulative; that is, language is a guide to action through its effects on emotions, motives, and evaluative judgments of those who use the language. Conventional distinctions embodied in the use of names create a conventional and shared pattern of evaluation. The Hsün-tzu, "rectification of names," wing of Confucianism and the Taoist critique of Confucianism and Mohism reflect this assumption. The early Mohists were rather more concerned with a descriptive model of language than either of the dominant schools.
2. Semantically corresponding to *ming* 名 'names' were *fen* 分 'divisions' or *pien* 辯 'distinctions'. The distinctions were both descriptive and regulative—they determined what counted as a *wu* 物 'thing-kind' or *shih* 實 'stuff' and accordingly how we ought to respond to what is discriminated.
3. A system of names (*tao* 道 'regulative discourse') is a set of conventional practices of discriminating and responding. The relation of name to thing rests on social practices of discriminating in a purposive context. The social practices have a basis both in history (the founding culture heroes who invented language and *li* [custom]) and in shared agreement. There is no transsocial right or wrong way to set up those practices.
4. In the discussion of names, language, and *tao* 道 'regulative discourse', no appeal is made to abstract or mental entities to explain the functioning or import of names. There were no mediating entities with theoretical roles similar to that of concepts, universals, ideas, meanings, or properties.

The Regulative Function of Language in the Canon

The Neo-Mohist approach continued to diverge into a relatively complete break with the functional assumption which lay behind early Confucian and Taoist writings on language. In the Canon the stock examples—ox, dog, milu deer—reflect less normative interest and more descriptive concern. They speculate relatively rarely on grading terms, role words, and comparative adjectives in their semantic doctrines. Yet the Neo-Mohists remained fundamentally concerned with the ethical issues of early Mohism.[13] The canons do contain definitions and propositions concerning ethics. And even the latest and most logical work, the *Hsiao Ch'ü*, is shaped by a desire to defend the Mohist ethical doctrine of universal love. The utilitarianism of Mo-tzu is developed by the addition of a weighting principle. The basic logical maxim of the Neo-Mohists in the *Hsiao Ch'ü* is one common to ethical and other reasoning—universalization. If you make a judgment in this case on the basis of X, then you must make a similar judgment in other cases of X.

Distinction Marking and Stuff Naming in the Canon

The dialectical chapters develop a theory of naming that brings the stuff-naming version of this assumption into equal or greater prominence than the distinction-marking version. *Fen* 分 'division' is not as central a concept. *Pien* 辯 'dispute', as we shall see later, is still important, but the new theoretical language which includes *t'i* 体 'stuff-substance', *chien* 兼 'compound-stuff', *chü* 舉 'pick-out:denote', *tang* 當 'correspond-to', and *lei* 類 'similar-stuff' suggests a shift toward the stuff-naming view of semantics. The routine examples are seldom contrastive dichotomies but rather natural kinds (ox, dog, sheep) or nonevaluative properties (hot, white, hard), often considered without reference to their opposites.

Conventionalism in the Canon

The Neo-Mohist position on conventionalism, like that of the early Mohists, seems to lie between Taoism and Confucianism. There is little discussion of conventionalism per se. The Neo-Mohist supposedly assumes that specific names are indeed relative to socially accepted symbols and sounds. But he would not hold, with the Taoist, that the apparent distinctions in reality are conventional. The theory presupposes, as does Confucian rectification of names theory, that there is some real basis for the distinctions marked by names.

Rectification of names itself, as an ideal for a language, is rejected on pragmatic grounds. A perfect one-to-one correspondence of name and stuff is not necessary as long as the names "work" fairly adequately and we carefully correct our "name-knowledge" against "contact" knowledge. It is in the nature of language that there might be two names for one stuff[14] or two stuffs with one name.[15]

Knowledge of names is distinct from knowledge of things. While both are valuable, knowledge of things is clearly viewed by the Neo-Mohists as more fundamental. Language is not ultimately reliable as a guide, and in the *Hsiao Ch'ü* rejection of sentence matching, the culprit is language's diverse approaches 多方 , different ways of grouping 殊類 , and opposing purposes 異故. The final judgment is rendered in the fragment *ming shih pu pi ho* 名實不必合 'name and object do not necessarily go together'.[16]

The Mohists directly mention *cheng ming* 正名 'the rectification of names' only once in the Canon.

II 68 彼此彼此與彼此同。說在異。
(彼)。正名者彼此彼此可。彼彼止於彼，此此止於此，彼此不可。彼且此也，彼此亦可。彼此止於彼此，若是而彼此也，則彼亦且此也。

You can "that" this if and only if you both "that" this and "this" that. Explained by: their being different. [Canon II:68]

For those who rectify names, it is admissible to "that" this and to "this" that. "That-ing" that stays confined to that; "this-ing" this stays confined to this [and] "that-ing" this is not admissible. When about to "this" that, it is likewise admissible to "that" this. If "that" and "this" stay confined to that and this, and accepting this condition you "that" this, then "this" is likewise about to be used for that. [Explanation II:68][17]

I do not give the translation here with great confidence, and for present purposes I rely only on the most general point of the passage. The fragment appears to acknowledge the Taoist argument against the rectification of names while denying that it has the drastic consequences the Taoist supposes it to have. Chuang-tzu argued that "names" (actually terms for which he uses demonstrative pronouns as paradigms) are relative to the total circumstances of utterance.[18] Thus, just as nothing was absolutely "that" or "this," so nothing is absolutely ox or horse. X is ox or horse only relative to a classificatory scheme and to the purposes behind that scheme. The Mohist notes that while a reversal of names like *ox* and *horse* can, in principle, take place, the distinctions in the world are independent of language. So even though what was called "that" can be called "this" by a change of perspective, that same change of perspective will make "this" "that."

Chuang-tzu's skepticism was, reflecting his philosophical style, exuberant. Presumably no Confucian and no Dialectician had ever held that "this" and "that" were rigidly linked to particular objects. But Confucians and their Dialectician allies (Kung-sun Lung) did seem committed to an ideal of one-name-one-thing. And the Mohist pointedly observes that there perfectly well could be two names for one thing.[19] This he classifies as a species of *t'ung* 同 'being the same' called *chung t'ung* 重同 'redundance'. The Mohists do not insist on eliminating such redundancies. We need only bear them in mind so we do not draw unwarranted conclusions in judging and acting based solely on names.

The overall thrust of the *Hsiao Ch'ü* is, similarly, best understood as restructuring the "logic" of the rectification of names. Thus while "thief is man" is assertable since both terms are assertable of the same object, "killing thief" is not the same activity (relative to judgement and evaluation) as "killing man." The Canon has a parallel stock example of redundancy—though the moral issue is rather elusive. (Explanation II:54 has been lost.)

II 54 狗犬也，而「殺狗非殺犬也」可。說在重。

Pup is dog; and yet " 'killing pup' is not 'killing dog'" is admissible. The explanation is in "redundant [expressions]." [Canon II:54]

Theoretically, the Mohist position seems to be that there are often exceptions to the dictum of one-name-one-thing and that, furthermore, it is unnecessary to try to eliminate them and rectify language. It is only essential that we beware of drawing inferences for action and judgment from the fact that the two names apply to one thing.

The analysis of epistemological terms also theoretically accepts shifting reference in language. The Mohists assume that a discrimination ability is antecedent to language learning. Our knowledge of the distinctions among things is independent of our use of names. That knowledge of *shih* 'stuff' can always be used as a check on "name-knowledge." The core distinction in the discussion of *chih* 'knowledge' is between conventional, changeable name-knowledge and realist, reliable stuff-knowledge. The later Mohists used the distinction to resolve paradoxes about knowledge.

II 48 知其所不知，說在以名取。
（智）。雜所智與所不智而問之，則必曰，「是所智也，是所不智也」。取去俱能之，是兩智之也。

Know that which he does not know; the explanation is in "using names to choose." [Canon II:48]

If you mix together that which he knows and that which he does not know and then ask about them, then he must say, "this is what I know and this is what I do not know." To be able both to select and reject is to know them in both ways [literally "to pair-know them"]. [Explanation II:48]

The Explanation is an allusion to the black-white choosing test in chapter 47 (Honoring Worthies) of the *Mo-tzu*. One knows the names but cannot divide the things. A blind person can discourse about black and white, but he cannot "choose" them when they are *chien* 'combined' before him. He can be said not to know black-white and can use the names to specify what he does not know.

Finally, the Neo-Mohists implicitly reject the prohibition on creating new names which is so prominent in Hsün-tzu's version of the ideal of rectification of names. The Neo-Mohists coined a great many technical terms of analysis: *tuan* 端 'point', *chü* 舉 'denote: refer', *hsiang chin* 相盡 'mutually exhaust', to name a few. They also discussed such technical constructions as *niu-ma* 牛馬 'ox-horse' and *chien-pai* 堅白 'hard-white'. The Mohists simply do not share the Confucian goal of a language rendered perfect and unchanging for guiding evaluative judgment. They rather view language as a helpful but fallible tool in getting around in the world. And they especially acknowledge a descriptive project as part of the helpful function of language.

Although the dialectical chapters reject the Confucian rectification of names ideal, they do not draw the skeptical conclusions of the Taoists. There *are* real distinctions among things, and people have presocial abilities to make those discriminations. The names are used to *chü* 舉 'pick out' the stuffs that make up the world. That they cannot do it in a way that allows one to obtain knowledge of the world from analysis of names alone is just one of the limitations of language with which we must live. There is a real world to which our language refers, and we have knowledge of it which is independent of our socialization. The conventions of language might well be inherently imperfect, but that is just another of the things we can discover only because we do have independent access to things.

The Mohists are thus simultaneously less skeptical about language-influenced thought than the Taoist, and less sanguine about the reliability of language than a Confucian. Knowledge of names is clearly regarded as inferior to knowledge of things and subject to correction. Names do not, in the Mohist view, rigidly designate stable, unchanging, absolute entities. And the strict ideal of one-name-one-thing is neither possible nor necessary.

This way of dividing knowledge turns several Western perspectives inside out. There is no hint that stuff-knowledge need be of things which do not change. The more valued knowledge is of stuffs, not names. Skepticism in China is, accordingly, not of the resemblance of thought to the world of stuffs, but of the fealty of language to that world. A pragmatic version of that skepticism motivates the Taoist view that no system of linguistic discrimination can be a stable choice and action guide.

Nominalism in the Canon

In the Mohist Dialectic, the formulations of many of the semantic claims are confusing. On the one hand, almost all the sections dealing with semantics apply a nominalistic model—dealing with name and thing only. But the propositions and explanations use two characters which seem part of a semantic scheme reminiscent of traditional European empiricism—*i* 意 (translated as "idea") and *lei* 類 (translated as "class"). If these are part of the semantic model, why are they not incorporated in the general description of the relation of names and things? What semantic role are they playing? The translations of these two characters suggests (1) that the Mohists did indeed think of some mental correlate of words and (2) that they thought of general terms in a framework analogous to the nonmereological notion of members and sets.

I believe that neither conclusion follows. Careful attention to the use of *i* 'idea' and *lei* 'kind: class' reveals that they neither transport empiricist philosophy of mind or semantics nor introduce a class-member or mind-body ontology into Chinese thought. Before examining these questions in detail, let us survey their basically nominalistic accounts of language. The later Mohists, like other Chinese thinkers, discuss semantics exclusively extensionally—in terms of the relations of names and things. This is especially evident in their discussions of kinds of names.

I 78 名。達，類，私。
(名)。「物」，達也。有實，必待之名也。命之「馬」，類也。「若實」也者，必以是名也。命之「臧」，私也。是名也止於是實也。聲出口，俱有名。

Ming ['name']. Unrestricted, similarity-based, private. [Canon I:78]

> *Wu* ['thing'] is an unrestricted name. If there is stuff it necessarily requires this name. To name it horse is to base it on similarities. That of which we would say "it is like the stuff" must use this name. Naming it "Jack" is a private name. This name is confined to this stuff. Whenever sounds issue from the mouth there are names. [Explanation I:78][20]

Notice that the three types of names are distinguished only by how broad a scope they have. In particular, despite the division into three categories, all names are related only to *shih* 實 'stuff'—not to mental or abstract entities.

A similar passage occurs in Hsün-tzu's "Rectification of Names" chapter. It too makes no appeal to meanings, ideas, classes, or forms, but discusses only the different scopes names can have, phrased in terms of the generality or particularity of the thing they name.

故萬物雖衆有時而欲徧舉之故謂之物物也者大共名也推而共之共則有共至於無共然後止有時而欲徧舉之故謂之鳥獸鳥獸也者大別名也推而別之別則有別至於無別然後止

> Although the myriad things are many, we may occasionally want to denote them as a whole, so we call them "thing." "Thing" is the most general term. In proceeding we generalize something and the general then has a more general until we arrive where there is no more general and only then stop. There are times when we desire to denote something partially, so we say of it "It is birds-and-beasts." "Birds-and-beasts" is a great distinguishing term. Proceeding, we can distinguish it; the distinction then has a finer distinction until we arrive where there is no more distinguishing and only then stop.

The initial classification, in the Canon, into three types of names would appear to suggest an analysis on which, for example, *ma* 'horse' denotes a *set* of individuals. This is especially tempting since *ma* 'horse' is characterized as a *lei* 'class' *ming* 'name'. But then the explanation treats this difference between general and particular as mainly a matter of scope of reference, not as different types of reference. Hsün-tzu's treatment is even more explicit. In the place of "individuals" he implicitly has only the final stage of distinguishing or partitioning. It would seem, on balance, that there was not really a clear intuition of the difference between singular and general terms other than their different scopes or ranges of denotation. A *lei-ming* would be only one whose scope is fixed by similarity of the parts of a mereological whole.

Then, despite the fact that this canon marks a seemingly important distinction, these differences in "names" never figure in any subsequent part of the theories of names or knowledge of names. The model of "meaning" is still basically that of the "name" or noun, and the mereological model seems most appropriate for describing the ontology assumed in this theory.

Initially, it seems likely that the troublesome characters *i* 意 'idea' and *lei* 類 'class' must have some important differences in conceptual role from their purported English equivalents. Both the English words are extremely theory-laden terms in British Empiricism and widely used in ordering English talk about words and meaning. The uses of these characters in Chinese may reflect *some* of the normal English uses, but others will be absent. The issue is whether the specific semantic use of the English translations resembles closely the use of *i* and *lei* in the Dialectic. If not, then we can allow the translations as long as we note that they do not pose a counterexample to the analysis of Chinese semantics as nominalistic and based on masslike nouns that are taken as referring to mereological objects.

Let us isolate the technical use of *idea* and *class* in English that is of interest by looking at the abstract genealogy and functions of these terms. *Ideos* was the original Platonic term for the forms. Western nominalists, while denying the metaphysical "ideas," continue to use the term for *mental* counterparts of the forms—their representation in our minds. Ideas are still taken to explain how a general term can signify a plurality of things. They are assimilated to the meanings of the terms and become the building blocks of knowledge.

Class is similarly a nominalist's grouping entity intended to eliminate abstractions such as *property, attribute*, and *essence* from semantic theory. Notoriously, however, classes themselves are abstract entities; they have no spatiotemporal location. (There is one variation on the notion of "class" which *is* purely nominalistic. Russell and Lesniewski's mereological class, to which we have appealed in describing Chinese semantic thought, is viewed as a class which *consists* of the "whole" of all the members, which are its parts.) Classes and sets, like abstract properties and ideas, are designed to explain the one-many relation of a count noun and its multiple denotation.

In analyzing whether or not the use of *i* 意 'idea' and *lei* 類 'class' make them counterexamples to the generalization that the Mohists were nominalists, we must see if their role in Mohist theory is similar in the above ways. In the Neo-Mohist chapters, *i* 意 'idea' does not, in fact, play the semantic role of explaining the meaning of general terms at all. It is used of images of memory or imagination. The eighteenth century view that meanings are images is a separate assumption which we do not need to attribute to the Mohists. The only direct semantic role of *i* 'idea' is in explaining the use of sentences for pragmatic communication—where its translation is "intent" rather than "idea." *Lei* 類, on the other hand, cannot be the technical equivalent of "class" since, in the spirit of the Taoist contrast theory of language, the mathematical notion of class is "born together" with the distinction of subclass and member. Without any such distinction, *lei* could only be regarded as mereological class—using (as we shall see) only the distinction of part-whole. This conclusion, obviously, is reinforced by the masslike grammar of the nouns called *lei*–names and the tendency to explain their semantics in the same way one explains the semantics of proper names. We will notice that the use of *lei* makes it clear that it is mainly used to assert similarity *between* thing-kinds and only derivatively to describe a thing-kind based on similarity of its parts. Neither term, in its use in the dialectical chapters, contradicts the basic nominalist character of the semantic theory.

Let us examine first the fragments of the dialectical chapters which deal with *i* 意. It is used in one canon to explain the notion of a *fa* 法 'standard'.

I 70 法，所若而然也。
(法)。意規員三也，俱可以爲法。

Fa ['standard']: the thing such that, if something is like it, that thing is *jan* ['so']. [Canon I:70]

Idea-images, the compass, circles—all three may serve as standards. [Explanation I:70]

The concern is with how circles may be constructed, and one of the models which may be used is the remembered image of a circle—along with a compass and another circle. The inclusion of *i* 意 'image' along with compass makes clear just how practical the concern is. There is no hint that the images are "abstracted" from particular circles or that they are the meaning of the word *circle*.

A very difficult fragment of the *Ta Ch'ü* also involves the character *i* 意.

意楹非意木也，意是楹之木也。意指之人也非意人也。意獲也乃意禽也。

> Picturing *[yi]* a pillar is not picturing wood, it is picturing the wood of this pillar. Picturing a finger as being man is not picturing man; picturing as being a catch of game is, however, picturing birds.[21]

I am disinclined to be dogmatic about what the point of this corrupt fragment is. It will suffice to note that it does not allege any relation between *i* 意 'ideas-pictures'[22] and *ming* 名 'names'. The first case is easily illuminated by the mass-stuff hypothesis. If we consider a pillar, then the image, though of something wooden, is not the image of wood itself. The finger-man case can be understood in this way as well. The last case has no obvious interpretation. One might suppose that a picture or image must be specific. One can think of the take of game only by thinking of some *particular* kind of game or other. Given its obscurity, this fragment should not count as much evidence for the nominalistic mass noun hypothesis, but it even more certainly does not count as evidence against it.

I 意 'idea-image' occurs in several other places in the Canon in various contexts. Graham has noticed that *i* 意 'idea-image' is used in connection with *hsiang* 想 'image'. In these contexts[23] *i* does seem to be mainly a picture of a remembered or envisioned object. There are other occurrences of a verbal use of *i* (as in the above quotation)—roughly "to imagine a thing." It does have an epistemic use, that is, as envisioning, contemplating, and so on, but it is not used in explaining the meaning of words as such.[24] *I* never functions as an abstraction from concrete images nor as a general idea corresponding to general terms.

Consider, for example, the two Canon fragments in which *i* 意 'image:intention' is used in combination with language and understanding. In these examples, it is natural to connect the use of *i* 意 'intention' with its semantic role in the *Hsiao Ch'ü*, that is, that which is conveyed by *tz'u* 辭 'expressions'.[25] The important fact about this semantic use of *i* is that its role is limited to sentences. *I* never correspond to *ming* 'names' which, as before, simply *chü* 舉 'denote' *shih* 實 'stuff'. Sentences consist of names, but there is no suggestion of the Lockean conclusion that the *i* 意 'intention' of a sentence is a composition of the *i* 意 'image-idea' related to words. Names pick out stuff. Sentences convey intentions.

This restricted interpretation of *i* as "intention" is supported by the definitions of *i* 意 in the earliest Chinese dictionaries. The substitution character offered for *i* in the *Shuo Wen* is *chih* 志 'intent:purpose'. The Mohists' theory is indeed a plausible nominalism. There are only names which are used in more complex expressions to communicate plans, purposes, and projects.

The philosophy of mind suggested by this is also different from that of commonsense conceptualism. The Neo-Mohists usually avoid the word *hsin* 心 'heart-mind' in favor of *chih* 知 'knowledge'. When *hsin* is used, it is in connection with *i*, while *chih* is most common in connection with *ming* 'names'. The division seems to be between the purposive and cognitive processes. The *hsin* 心 'heart-mind' forms the intentions, and decodes the speaker's intention. One *chih* 知 'knows' names and objects. We can draw some interesting conclusions about the use of *i* here. It does have two functions reminiscent of English "idea": as mental image and sentence intention or purpose ("I've got an idea, let's. . . ."). But it is not used to explain word-meaning. In sum, the use of *i* 'image:intention' does not conflict with the basic nominalism of the Mohist and Chinese approach to semantics.

While the Mohist approach is rather more like traditional Western assumptions about semantics in being more descriptive, most of the differences in, for instance, philosophy of mind discussed earlier still apply to later Mohist thought. None of their definitions of knowledge are stated in terms of belief as a mental representation of the meaning of a sentence. They do not use the notion of semantic truth to distinguish knowledge from "mere" belief. The traditional concerns of epistemology do not arise, and the Mohists are instead concerned mainly to elaborate and relate linguistic competencies or skills rather than mind contents. The competence in question is that acquired along with a language, the ability to discriminate and react in accord with that discrimination.

I do not, accordingly, object to the translation of *i* as "idea" except that "idea" is so theory-laden in our philosophical tradition. As long as we remember that the Chinese sense does *not* include word-meaning as a mental content, one need not object to the translation. It is close to our use of *idea* in learning a game or skill: "Now you're getting the idea" does not suggest that you are finally understanding a word. We do have an idea of how to construct a circle, and we have ideas in the sense of remembered images of things. One's ideas (the upshot or point) can be expressed and conveyed in sentences. But none of these uses is parasitic on a philosophical doctrine of abstraction, universals, concepts, or word-meaning.

The term *lei* 類 'class' is more central to the semantic project in the dialectical chapters. Chmielewski is the main proponent of the view that it means "class" in the logical or mathematical sense.[26] If that is true, then it is an abstraction called for by the same problems that generate universals for the Platonic tradition. The suggestion has already been rebutted in part by Graham.[27] He observes that objects are never viewed as members of a class, but as, in his words, of a kind or not of a kind. That is close to my own objection: to suggest there is the notion "mathematical class" without the notion "member" is paradoxical. These are theoretical "brothers" that, like the Taoist opposites, are "born together." The concept of "class" or "species" is generated in a theory which also includes "member" or "specimen" as distinct from "subclass" or "subspecies." Without these companion concepts (which Chmielewski himself claims are absent), it is impossible to understand how *lei* 類 could correspond to the mathematical or semantic term *class*.

Graham's objection points to another curious feature of the use of *lei* in Chinese. The concept seems to stand at least one step above "natural kind." Thus the Mohists say that ox and horse are *t'ung lei* 同類 'same *lei*' but they never say that of white-horse and horse, where we would expect it if *lei* did correspond even to our ordinary nonmathematical use of *kind* or *class*. *T'ung lei* (same *lei*) is used to assert similarity of things in different natural classes, not to represent a relation between objects comprehended by a natural kind term.

It, accordingly, seems most accurate to translate *lei* used nominally as "similar-stuff" and the verbal use as "is similar." This explains why the Mohist avoids saying "white-horse is similar to horse." The Mohist's definitions involving *lei* reinforce the observation that *lei* is a quite general kind of similarity.

I 86 同。重，體，合，類。
(同)。二名一實，重同也。不外於兼，體同也。俱處於室，合同也。有以同，類同也。

T'ung ['same']: redundance, as units, as together, as similar *[lei]*. [Canon I:86]

There being two names but one object is the sameness of redundance. Not being outside the total is sameness as units. Both occupying the room is the sameness of being together. Being the same in some respect is the sameness of being similar *[lei]*. [Explanation I:86]

I 87 異。二，不體，不合，不類。
(異)。二必異，二也。不連屬，不體也。不同所，不合也。不有同，不類也。

Yi ['different']: two, not units, not together, not similar *[lei]*. [Canon I:87]

Their being necessarily different when there are two [of them] is being two. Not connected or belonging is "not units." Not in the same place is "not together." Not having any respect in which they are the same is "not similar." [Explanation I:87]

Judging by its placement and definition, the sameness of *lei* is the least specific of the categories of sameness and difference. *Any* respect in which things are the same could count to make them the same *lei*. Conversely, very few pairs could be considered not-*lei*. Pointing to some differences or other does not rebut the suggestion that two mass-kinds are similar.[28] One naturally wonders just what sorts of things *could* qualify as not-*lei*. The Mohist answer is that mass stuffs are not-*lei* only if comparison between them is illegitimate. The attempt to compare stuffs which are different *lei* is rather like the notion of a category mistake. It yields humorous nonsense. This is made quite clear in the following canon.

II6 異類不吡，說在量。
(異)。木與夜孰長，智與粟孰多，爵親行賈四者孰貴，

Different *lei* ['similarity classes'] are not comparable. The explanation is in measurement. [Canon II:6]

Which is longer, wood or night? Which is more, knowledge or grain? Which is *keui* ['noble, valued, expensive'], rank, one's parents, moral conduct, or a price?[29] [Explanation II:6]

Wood and night are different *lei* because it makes no sense to compare them in point of, say, length. It is not merely an "apples and oranges" problem. For we can compare many features of apples and oranges. Things are different *lei* only when ordinary comparisons do not make sense at all.

As with *i* 'idea' we *could* accept translations of *lei* as "class" as long as we remember the important differences in role. In this case the difference is explained by the mass-stuff hypothesis. Classes have members, and the members are individuals. The Mohist use of *lei* suggests that *lei* are classes of these stuff-kinds which correspond to the nouns of the language. If we remember that difference, the "class" translation need not be misleading. "Similar" or "similarity-group" are safer and would help to illuminate the logical term *t'ui lei* 推類 ("push" a *lei*, i.e., analogy). *T'ui lei* has a very natural interpretation as a principle of moral reasoning on this construction. And since the Mohists (and Mencius) concentrate on the moral use, that is an advantage. If I make some judgment and give as grounds some feature of a situation or person, then I must "extend" that judgment to all cases which are relevantly similar. Neo-Mohists, still focusing on ethical concerns, make this the key kind of consistency in the analysis in the *Hsiao Ch'ü* and in the Canon.

II 1 止類以行人。說在同。
(止)。彼以此其然也說是其然也。我以此其不然也疑是其然也。

Fix the kind in order to "make the man proceed." Explained by sameness. [Canon II:1]

The other, on the grounds that it is so of the instance here, argues that it is so of the thing it is; I, on the grounds that it is not so of the instance here, doubt that it is so of the thing it is. [Explanation II:1]

以類取，以類予。有諸己不非諸人，無諸己不求諸人

Accept using similarity, reject using similarity. What is present in one's own case is not to be rejected in the other man's. What is absent from one's own case is not to be demanded of the other man's. *[Hsiao Ch'ü]*

The use of *lei* in judgments is not, of course, limited to moral judgments. But the moral position in expressing the principle reflects the spirit of early Mohism and its insistence on consistency of moral judgment. One should not hold that killing one man is a crime and at the same time praise and honor the men who exterminate whole cities. When extended to factual judgments, the use of *lei* is similarly a call for consistency relative to stated grounds of judgment—which could produce a use of *lei* in reasoning that traced natural classes. There is no indication in the texts that it is a particular form of argument, such as analogy. And there is especially no reason to suspect that the Mohists had invented a logic of sets or were deeply involved in such matters as scientific issues of classification.

So with regard to both *i* 意 'idea' and *lei* 類 'class' the "idea" and "class" translations can make sense of their uses as long as we remember that the Western notions had semantic and philosophical uses which go beyond the Mohist's purposes and theoretical structure. The only danger in using such translations is that we might try to invoke all the theoretical roles the translations play in Western logic and semantics— especially the abstract ones. There is no evidence of such semantic uses (as explaining the meaning of individual words) in the Mohist semantic theories.

To highlight the difference, look again at a classic Western semantic use of "idea" in the philosophy of Locke.

> Besides articulate sounds, therefore, it was further necessary that he should be able to use these sounds as signs of internal conceptions; and to make them stand as marks for the ideas within his own mind, whereby they might be made known to others, and the thoughts of men's minds be conveyed from one to another.
>
> But neither was it sufficient to make words so useful as they ought to be. It is not enough for the perfection of language, that sounds can be made signs of ideas, unless those signs can be so made use of as to comprehend several particular things; for the multiplication of words would have perplexed their use, had every particular thing need of a distinct name to be signified by. To remedy this inconvenience, language had yet a further improvement in the use of general terms, whereby one word was made to mark a multitude of particular existences; which advantageous use of sounds was obtained only by the differences of the ideas they were made signs of; those names becoming general, which are made to stand for general ideas, and those remaining particular where the ideas they are used for are particular.[30]

Neither *i* 意 'idea' nor *lei* 類 'class' ever figured in Neo-Mohist explanations in even a roughly similar way. They were quite sanguine about a word for every particular thing—since by *thing* they would have meant "stuff-kind." So they never worried about general or abstract as opposed to particular ideas because they did not worry about general as opposed to particular terms. The only classes they worried about were comparison or similarity classes *among* the mass-stuffs (the natural kinds).

The difference from Western concerns and assumptions is important for understanding Neo-Mohist logic. First, we can more easily understand why logic would seem a much less dignified and urgent project if it were originally held to be merely an aspect of the knowledge of names versus knowledge of *shih* 實 'reality'. The twentieth-century philosopher is frequently enough criticized for being interested only in "words." We had two thousand years not only of Platonic protection from this seeming trivialization of philosophizing but of elevation of the subject matter to a more valued reality. Under the Platonic umbrella philosophers could claim to be studying "ideas," the "real world," and "truth." Against the direct and caustic Taoist characterization of their enterprise, Chinese philosophers from the beginning in effect acknowledge that their work is the study of language alone. It is easier to give up in the face of difficulties when one suspects his subject matter is trivial.

Second, the study of inference relationships in China had to go on without the notion of truth. Since most logical concepts—validity, consequence, soundness—are defined in terms of truth this is a serious handicap. The alternative semantic conceptions were relatively unwieldy for logical theory. We shall see how this leads to confusions when we discuss the *Hsiao Ch'ü* later in this chapter.

Third, the Neo-Mohists end up rejecting an intuitively natural and appealing proposal for describing inferences. The rejection is forced by their moral-political concerns, by the suspicion that linguistic distinctions and regularities might warp or distort moral or political institutions or judgments that they deemed important.

In China, the result of the pervasive conventionalist and nominalist assumptions is to draw ridicule of the studies of the dialecticians and analytic thinkers. The first halting and disappointing attempts at a theory of logic were condemned as frivolous. After some initial failures, no one had any stomach to continue trying to find anything stable and reliable in language. The philosophical world, in spirit, accepted the Chuang-tzu critique of language as capricious and arbitrary. Analysis of names and honing of the skills that make up knowledge of names—including the study of logic—were discredited.

On *Pien:* The Refutation of Chuang-tzu

As we have seen, the Mohists took a relatively conventionalist position vis-à-vis fundamental Confucianism. But they did not embrace the absolute skepticism of the Taoists. The Mohists present their attitude toward such Taoist claims in much greater detail, clarity, and directness than they did their attitude toward the rectification of names. There are a number of interesting attacks throughout the Canon on Taoist "anti-language-ism," but the core discussion focuses on the nature of *pien* 辯 'dispute: discrimination'.

We shall note that while the Canon contains a detailed and interesting account of *pien*, it does not contain any evidence to make us alter our earlier conclusion that *pien* is not "argument" in the sense of proof. It is rather the fixing of distinctions for naming and judgment. The Mohists were no more worried than Chuang-tzu about the strings of sentences (the argument) used to support conclusions. They do not, even in this careful analysis of *pien*, formulate any logical rules of reasoning or discuss argument forms. They simply reflect on the implications of *pien* understood as conflicting judgments and pronouncements. Their analysis deals primarily with what would be concluded about such judgments.[31]

Chuang-tzu had argued that in a dispute over a discrimination *(pien)* there was no right or wrong alternative because the conflicting judgments arose from the disputants' differing perspectives. No judge could settle the dispute because his arbitration would be determined by his (the judge's) own perspective. There is no perspective-free bystander (including, one must suppose, Heaven *and tao)*. Therefore there is no perspective-free standard to justify calling one position correct and the other mistaken.

Chuang-tzu's position is, in certain formal ways, similar to that of the Cartesian skeptic of the senses. Descartes was trapped in a circle of representations from which he could never escape. Chuang-tzu maintains that we are trapped by our perspective shaped by linguistic commitments which we can transcend only by refusing to make judgments at all (or at least refusing to make judgments in language). The basis of his conclusion that there are no perspective-free bystanders is that there are no perspective-free judgment sentences. The problem with such sentences is not the proofs of them expressed in other sentences, but that they rest on other ways of distinguishing and dividing which are ultimately arbitrary. *Pien* are not viewed as the conclusions of a process of reasoning, but as skewed immediate judgments—like perceptual judgments. Those skewed in different ways will make the judgment differently. It is therefore impossible in principle to settle a *pien*. So, Chuang-tzu argues, it is meaningless to talk about one party's being right or wrong when engaged in such disputes.

The Mohist reaction to this argument is an example of that same attitude toward *pien*. They ignore the argument and dispute the conclusion. The Canon formulates a principle of excluded middle and uses it in a stipulative definition of what it means to *pien*.

I 37 彼，不可兩不可也。
(彼)。凡牛樞非牛，兩也。無以非也。

Pi [converse]: It is inadmissible to treat both sides as inadmissible. [Canon I:73]

All oxen and non-oxen marked off as a group are the two sides. There is nothing to justify "that is not one." [Explanation I:73]

Pi 彼 literally means "(the) other." It is used as the demonstrative opposite of *shih* 是 'this' in the *Chuang-tzu*. The context of the Canon and Explanation I:73 implies that *pi* means "logical complement or converse."[32] The explanation seems to say, in an ontological mode, that there is nothing outside of a thing and its opposite or complement *(pi)*.

I 74 辯，爭彼也。辯勝，當也。
(辯)。或謂之「牛」，或謂之「非牛」，是爭彼也。是不俱當，不俱當必或不當。(不若當「犬」)。

Pien ['disputation, distinguishing'] is contending over converses. Winning in disputation is mapping onto [it]. [Canon I:74]

One calling it "ox" and the other "non-ox" is contending over converses. Such being the case they do not both map onto [it] and if they do not both map onto [it], necessarily one of them does not map onto it. (Not mapping: like its being dog.) [Explanation I:74]

Thus *pien* is defined in such a way that it applies to a dispute about a distinction only if the disputants take diametrically opposed views about it. From this definition, the refutation of Chuang-tzu is simple.

II 35 謂辯無勝必不當，說在辯。
(謂)。所謂，非同也則異也。同則或謂之狗，其或謂之犬也，異則或謂之牛，其或謂之馬也，俱無勝，是不辯也。辯也者，或謂之是，或謂之非，當者勝也。

To say "There is no winner in disputation" necessarily does not map onto it. Explained by disputation [distinguishing]. [Canon II:35]

If that which is said is not the same, then it is different. If the same, then it is one man's calling it "pup" and the other "dog," or if different it is one's calling it "ox" and the other "horse." Neither's winning is failure to engage in disputation. Disputation is when one says "it is this" and the other "it is not," and the one which maps onto it wins. [Explanation II:35]

The definition of *pien* limits the kinds of disputes to discriminatory judgments expressed in exclusive and complementary pairs. It says nothing about the nature of the reasons or arguments given for them. The Canon really does not address itself to the question of perspectives in language— to how one decides *who* is right. It makes only the logical observation that if you limit the notion of *pien* 'dispute' to truly complementary distinctions, then one description must be satisfied. The "winning" in the Canon apparently does not mean getting the judge's or audience's vote. It is simply being correct—putting the right name on the thing in question.

A Taoist could defend Chuang-tzu against this argument by a slight revision. Chuang-tzu should, they would argue, only have claimed that we can never *know* who is right and that winning, in the sense of outtalking, does not entail that one was right. The Canon used a different notion of "winning" and an implausible one at that—one wins just in case one is correct, whatever one's argument. However, this defense of Chuang-tzu assumes that there is more of an awareness or argument for a *pien* than we have noted in either Chuang-tzu or the Mohist Dialectic. Chuang-tzu proved only the epistemological claim that we cannot *know* who is right.

The other interesting canons dealing with Taoist antilanguage views take the form of semantic paradoxes. These attempt to show that the Taoist position is inconsistent. Ingeniously formulated, they do not depend on any sentences other than the Taoist conclusions to show the contradictions.

II 71 以言爲盡誖，誖。說在其言。
(以)。誖，不可也。之人之言可，是不誖，則是有可也。之人之言不可，以當必不審。

To take all language as perverse is perverse. Explained by: its language. [Canon II:71]

"Perverse" is "inadmissible." If this person's language is admissible, it is not perverse, then there is acceptable [language]. If this person's language is inadmissible; on examination it necessarily does not map. [Explanation II:71]

II 79 非誹者誖，說在弗非。
不(誹)非己之誹也，不非誹。非可非也，不可非也，是不非誹也。

That which denies denials is perverse, the explanation is in "not denying." [Canon II:79]

If he does not deny his own denial, he has not denied denial. Denials can be denied. If denials cannot be denied, then *this* is not denying denials. [Explanation II:79]

The criticism of Taoists made by Neo-Mohists is precisely the one we should like to make of any doctrine of the inherent inadequacy or paradoxical nature of language.

There are some interesting theoretical concepts introduced in the context of the above treatment of Taoist nihilism. The Mohists introduce terms which come very close to the notion of semantic truth: *tang* 當 'mapping:corresponding' and *pei* 誖 'perverse: contradictory: false'. But the exposition continues to rely more on the pragmatic evaluations, namely acceptability or assertability of utterance. And Graham argues convincingly that at this point the Neo-Mohists are concerned not with contradictory judgments but with contrary terms.[33]

These new semantic notions are not taken up and developed in a way which might have illuminated the distinction of sentence and term. In particular, as we shall see, they are not centrally involved in the later Mohist proposals and analysis of formal inference. There, again, the dominant concern is with what would be appropriate to say in certain contexts—not with what is true or false.

We will study in detail the Mohist semantic theories regarding terms and their assertability in the next chapter, where they will emerge as the background theory against which to understand the white-horse paradox. The anti-Taoist fragments above seem to be a quite independent project in the Canon. It might have been an important vehicle for more development if the Mohist school had survived the Confucian orthodoxy of the Han Dynasty.

Algebraic Argument in the *Hsiao Ch'ü*

The final chapter in the dialectical section of the *Mo-tzu*, the *Hsiao Ch'ü*, contains the closest approach found in Chinese classical thought to a discussion of rules of inference—formal logic. The *Hsiao Ch'ü* is also the most easily readable of the Mohist dialectical chapters. It is difficult to sympathize with some of the nonintuitive idiomatic examples used to discredit the proposed rule. That may partly explain why it has been less noticed and translated than the incomplete and much less coherent works of the School of Names—Kung-sun Lung and Hui Shih.

There are a host of examples here which tend to confirm further the mass noun hypothesis. The logical proposal itself is a valuable insight into the nature of reasoning in classical Chinese philosophy. (Some famous Mencian "analogies" are muffed attempts at formal arguments of the form considered here.)[34] More interesting still are (1) the Mohists' rejection of the type of inference suggested; (2) the sophistication of the argument against the proposal; and (3) the feebleness of attempts to repair or improve on the proposal.

The *Hsiao Ch'ü* examines and rejects an inference proposal, a rule for reasoning from one sentence to another. The inferences studied and the semantics offered are not directed at formal relations among premises and conclusion in arguments, nor at logical connectives or other logical constructions. The argument instead focuses on the analysis of complex term and predicate expressions. Sentences are introduced into the analysis to show how complex expressions affect sentences which contain them. Its point is made primarily by several sequences of examples and argument analogies.

The translation that follows is adapted primarily from Graham.[35] I have substituted mass nouns for general nouns when it has seemed relevant to understanding the examples and arguments, and removed abstract translations where they were understandable as either mass-stuffs or mentions.

In the *Hsiao Ch'ü* the province of *pien* 辯 'dispute' seems to have broadened considerably. In the Canon, as we noticed, it was quite narrowly defined (probably for purposes of combating Taoist skepticism). Here it seems to be viewed as a broadly applied intellectual activity. The Neo-Mohists treat *pien* as an activity for resolving questions in morals, politics, semantics, ontology, and science. I have accepted Graham's practice of translating *pien* here as "dialectics," although I think the core sense of "discriminate" still undergirds the analysis.

> The purpose of dialectics *[pien]* is to clarify the distinction between right and wrong *[shih-fei]*, inquire into the successions of good government and misrule, clarify points of sameness and difference and scrutinize the ordering of names and objects. It settles benefit and harm, resolves doubts and difficulties, explores the facts *[jan]* about the myriad things, and considers how various kinds of utterance compare with each other. We refer to objects by means of names, convey ideas by means of phrases, present reasons by means of explanations, and accept and propose by means of similarity. What is present in one's own case is not to be rejected in the other man's; what is absent from one's own case is not to be required of the other man's.

We have already studied some of the issues in this opening section of the *Hsiao Ch'ü*. The progression from *ming* 名 'names' to *ts'u* 辭 'phrases' to *shuo* 説 'explanations' and the pragmatic emphasis signaled by the use of *ch'ü-yü* 取予 'accept-propose' is especially interesting. The first level is the pure or formal semantic level; the relation between name and thing has nothing to do with anyone's intention in uttering the name. The second is the intensional semantic level, the *i* 意 'intention' conveyed by phrases or sentences. The relation at the third level is relatively new in theory, except that all the explanations in the Canon and the tag-on phrases in Canon II are called *shuo* 說 'explanation'. But it is hard to find the common denominator in the two kinds of *shuo* 說 'explanation'. The tag-ons were either terms whose meaning clarified or justified the proposition, or references to more complete theories which did so. The explanation chapters seem mainly to be illustrations or contrasts that help illuminate the main propositions. Neither use can easily be assimilated to a *ku* 故 'cause' or 'reason'. Reasons are relative to the person to whom an explanation is directed and are therefore a pragmatic aspect of language use. The final level, practical choice based on similarity or consistency in *shuo* 'explanations' is the sole logical requirement of classical and later Mohism.

All these language activities are in the province of *pien* 'dialectics-dispute'. There seems a plausible story to connect each kind of activity with a discrimination involving language. *Pien* seems to lie at the base of all these other "linguistic activities." Its arena of operation is strings of language in progressively larger clumps. The introduction of full sentences is consistent with this enlarged focus but still emphasizes the semantics of singular and complex terms; the Mohists do not introduce truth and falsity in their account, and their conclusions are stated as implications for interpreting complex terms.

The second major section is extremely cryptic and affords a host of hooks on which to hang the guess that the Mohists had discovered and defined any commentator's favorite kinds of logical argument. Hu Shih has been the most enthusiastic discoverer of deductive and inductive logic in this section.[36] Others have good alternative explanations. I offer no independent argument, but I am inclined to be conservative in attributing the discovery of various kinds of formal argument structure to anyone until I can be convinced that they had noticed formal argument structure in the first place. The section follows:

"Some" is "not all."
The "so-called" is "in the present case not so."
"Applying" is imposing a certain standard. What is applied is the standard imposed. Therefore, what it fits when applied is the thing in

question, what it does not fit is not. Such is "applying."
"Illustrating" is referring to some other thing for the purpose of clarification.
"Matching" is comparing sentences and developing them together.
"Adducing" is saying "If it is so in your case, why should it not be so in mine too?"
"Inferring" is using what is the same in something which he refuses to accept and in something he does accept, in order to propose the former.
"This is like saying . . ." implies sameness; "How can I say . . ." implies difference.

T'ang Chün-i treats this series of definitions as a running account of some typical argument.[37] Graham's analysis takes the series of definitions to explain the use of terms which function in the argument which follows these introductory sections. Both interpretations can be compatibly combined by treating the whole chapter as the detailed map of more or less typical stages in a dispute about the use of terms. These are ways to keep one's opponent dealing fairly in argument. As we will see, they are not plausibly treated as deductive forms since the Mohist is at pains to show that they can "go wrong."

The following section contains just such a warning about these rhetorical devices.

When things are the same in some respects, it does not follow that they are altogether the same. The matching of phrases is valid only within limits. If matters are so, there are reasons why they are so; but although they are the same in being so, they are not necessarily so for the same reasons. If claims are accepted there are reasons why they are accepted; but they are not necessarily accepted for the same reasons.

Graham has noticed an interesting structural feature of the opening sections of the *Hsiao Ch'ü*. The first paragraph contained, as we noted, a four-step progression of language function. Graham suggests that these four steps are replicated in three sequences. The first is the language function—semantics and pragmatics. The second is the technique for *pien* 'disputing' about the things. The third lists the limitations of the arguments. The third sequence is ultimately the main theme of the rest of the body of the *Hsiao Ch'ü*—not the efficacy of the rhetorical argumentative devices but their limited justification (especially when applied against the Mohists' own favorite arguments!). Graham organizes these sections as follows to bring out the parallels:

A	B	C
It *refers* to objects by means of names;	"Illustrating" is *refering* to some other *thing* for the purpose of clarification.	When *things* are the same in some respects, it does not follow that they are altogether the same.
expresses ideas by means of *phrases;*	"Matching" is comparing *phrases* and developing them together.	The *matching* of *phrases* is valid only within limits.
expresses ideas by means of *phrases;*	"Adducing" is saying, "If it is *so* in your case, why should it not be so in mine too?"	If matters are so, there are *reasons* why they are so; but although they are the same in being so they are not necessarily so for the same reasons.
and *accepts* and *proposes* by means of similarity.	"Inferring" is using what is the same in something which he refuses to *accept* and in something which he does accept, in order to *propose* the former.	If claims are *accepted* there are reasons why they are accepted, but although they are the same in being accepted they are not necessarily accepted for the same reason.[38]

Of these four levels, techniques, and limitations, the focus of the following analysis is mainly on the second—the matching of phrases (sentences). And of the three points made about the technique the last one, its limited reliability, is the point of the piece as a whole. This is confirmed by an internal summary which stresses again a warning not to take any of the techniques too far.

> Therefore phrases which illustrate, match, adduce and infer become different as they develop, become dangerous when they change direction, become fallacious when carried too far, become detached from their base

when we let them drift, so that we must on no account be careless with them, and cannot use them in all cases. Hence language discourse has many aspects, divergent kinds, different explanations, which must not be looked at only from one side.

This final warning before the sections of examples underlines the direction of argument. The point of the Mohist analysis will not be to prove that these techniques and forms of inference are correct, but to show their limits—to deny their universal validity. And the cause of the restricted applicability of these techniques is that they rest on the functions of language which are subject to vagaries. The examples quite painstakingly establish this skeptical conclusion with regard to the most formal of the techniques—the matching of phrases or sentences.

"Sentence matching" may be understood intuitively as a form of one-step inference. One begins with a basic sentence (typically an equation, i.e., X is Y—Chinese "X Y yeh"). Then, as in algebra, one adds the same element to both sides of the equation.[39] The new equation should preserve "assertability." So given the equation, for example, "Horse is animal," we should be able to assert "head of horse is head of animal."[40]

I have translated the proposal into the main Chinese term for evaluating expressions—*k'o* 可 'assertability'. But assertability is not actually appealed to in the examples. Instead, a syntactic characterization *which seems to assume assertability* is the basis of analysis. That is, instead of asking if the sentence resulting from the algebraic addition (or subtraction) is assertable, the examples just give an "appropriate" sentence and the analysis turns on whether *that* sentence is affirmative or negative—contains a *fei* 非 'is-not' or not. Call this syntactic negation element a sign. If a sentence has a *fei* 非 'is-not' call it "signed," if not, "un-signed." Call the original equational sentences the "base" sentences, and the *acceptable* versions of sentences produced by the algebraic techniques the "resultant" sentences. Now we can describe the analysis in the *Hsiao Ch'ü* as follows: The Mohists call an unsigned base sentence a *shih* 是 'this: thus' sentence and a signed base sentence a *fei* 非 'not-thus' sentence. An unsigned resultant sentence is called a *jan* 然 'so' sentence, and a signed resultant sentence is called *pu-jan* 不然 'not-so'. The inference rule being tested is: does the algebraic technique always produce *jan* sentences from *shih* sentences and *pu-jan* from *fei* sentences? The (correct) answer given in the analysis is "no." The introduction to the long example section makes the Mohists' position quite explicit.

> Things are partly thus *(shih)* and so *(jan)*, partly thus and not-so, partly not thus and yet so, partly general and partly not, partly "one thus and one not."

In other words, the inference works sometimes, and fails sometimes. Then some other anomalies are also offered that illustrate other vagaries in language. Notice that the explanation of these failures of consistency is that "things" are thus and so. That is, the Mohists' explanation of the problems in this technique rests on the semantics of *term* expressions.

The analysis begins with examples of the inference rule working properly:

> White horse is horse; ride white horse is ride horse. Black horse is horse, ride black horse is ride horse. *Huo* is man; to love *huo* is to love man. *Tsang* is man; to love *tsang* is to love man. These are *shih* ['thus'] and then *jan* ['so'].

For the Mohists, the logical proposal to be tested was: can you generate sentences by matching them in the sense of adding the same character to both sides of a base sentence and getting a resultant sentence which would be assertable and have the same "sign"? This paragraph illustrates the proposal to be tested. The Mohists now rebut the rule by counterexample. There are cases that follow the algebraic rule, yet do not preserve the sign. The first and most important counterexamples are unsigned *(shih)* base sentences which yield signed *(pu-jan)* resultant sentences.

> Huo's parents are man, Huo's serving parents is not serving man. Her younger brother is handsome man, her loving her younger brother is not loving handsome man.

It is tempting to try to supply a rationale for explaining what goes wrong from our own as well as the Mohist point of view. Unfortunately, the Mohist's own account does not expound on the nature of the problem. It merely gives the counterexample together with the broad charge of the introduction that the technique "becomes dangerous when it changes direction" and that we cannot use it in all cases. The only culprit identified is the instability of language—its "many aspects, divergent kinds, different explanations."

We might find the choice of acceptable resultant sentences incredible. Accepting the argument seems to require some faith that the Mohist is accurately reporting pre-Han moral attitudes. The moral position can be understood as the result of the traditional rectification of names pattern of moral reasoning with fixed rules. Rectification of names may be seen as an attempt to preserve the rule-based moral judgments *and* the algebraic inference rule (which indicates that both are regarded as intuitively correct). The rectification of names solution would be to preserve the rule by altering the semantics of the terms: a king is not an ordinary fellow, a thief is not a man, a brother is not a handsome man (see p. 130). The dialectically inclined Mohists thought that one-name-one-thing was not the way language actually worked and was unattainable as a goal of language. As long as someone could imagine a moral counterexample, the theory could in principle force the denial of any conceivable "X is Y" (X Y *yeh*) sentence. The ideal rectification of names goal leads to problems in cases where the terms in the equational sentence are analytically related, as we shall see in discussing the white-horse issue. In any case, the redrawing of semantic boundaries was not necessary. The Mohist instead rejected the inference rule.

For these cases, there is a way to locate the trouble in the different levels of language use. *Handsome man* and *brother* are the names of *shih* 實 'stuffs' which at the purely formal level might be the same stuffs. But the phrase *love handsome man* is used to convey a different *i* 意 intention than *love brother*.

So now the question shifts from denotation of names to verb-object expressions of actions (intents). What kind of behavior counts as being in accord with and as violating certain rules? "Serving parents" and "serving man" are distinct kinds of obligations, and different patterns of behavior count as fulfilling each rule. Just fulfilling the rule "serve parents" does not satisfy the rule "serve men."[41] Similarly, there are two different "acts" of loving—loving someone romantically (because he is handsome) versus loving as a brother. This example fits more easily into our own moral consciousness, but we would be likely to express it in causal or motivational terms—loving someone *because* he is handsome or *because* he is a brother. The moral point in China must be understood as being that loving handsome men was a different act-intention from that of loving a brother. This is the most plausible motivation for these exceptions to the algebraic inference rule.

Other examples of the breakdown of algebraic inference involve the denotation versus action-purpose use of language as well as the part-whole problems implicit in the mass-stuff semantics.

> Carriage is wood; riding carriage is not riding wood. Boat is wood; entering boat is not entering wood.

Why can we not say that riding a wooden carriage is riding some wood, that entering a wooden boat is entering some wood? It may be that there is nothing more here than the strangeness of the idiom. Part of the explanation may be the same as for the previous examples: the intentions conveyed by the *phrases* are not fixed or determined by the stuffs the *terms* used in the phrases denote. Intending to ride wood is distinct from intending to ride a carriage. Intending to enter a boat is different from intending to enter wood (whatever that intention might be!).

The next examples, the most famous, bring the point of the exercise home in the defense of the Mohists' moral theory.

> A robber-man is a man, but abounding in robbers is not abounding in men; being without robbers is not being without men. How shall we make this clear? Hating its abounding in robbers is not hating its abounding in men. Wishing to be without robbers is not wishing to be without men.

The end purpose of the attack on the reliability of "sentence matching" is apparently to defuse attacks on the Mohist view that "to kill a thief is not to kill a man." They saw their opponents' attack on this view as being based on the application of the inference rule in question to the identity sentence, "Thief is man," which Mohists accepted. We have a way of formulating their view that has been common to the earlier examples. "Thief is man" is based on the *ming* 名 'name' *shih* 實 'stuff' level of semantics. *Kill thief* and *kill man* are phrases conveying actions (intents or purposes). The identity of the formal designation of a term in such a phrase does not make the intentions expressed by the phrases identical. This way of explaining the failure of the inference is confirmed by the last two examples, which overtly introduce propositional attitudes (hating and wishing). One must note in passing that if the Mohist did indeed have some notion of the intension, sense, or idea of a term as opposed to its extension or denotation, this would have been a natural place for it to have been employed. But the Mohist does not offer any such analysis. The first example in this segment is a classic fallacy of division. It seemingly has nothing to do with purposive *i* 意 'intent'. The exposition does not give any specific diagnosis of the breakdown of the inference, it simply observes that the inference fails in such cases. Sentence matching is, accordingly, not a totally reliable rule, and Mohists should not be criticized for violating it in asserting that "kill thief" is not "kill man" while accepting "thief is man."

> The whole world agrees that these are right; but if such is the case there is no longer any difficulty in allowing that, although a robber-man is a man, loving robbers is not loving men. Not loving robbers is not not loving men. Killing robber-men is not killing men. The latter claims are analogous to the former; the world does not think itself wrong to hold the former, but thinks the Mohist wrong for holding the latter. Is there any reason for it but being, as the saying goes, "clogged within and closed without"? (Gloss: having no empty space within the heart; it is indissolubly clogged.)
> These then are *shih* ['thus'] and yet not so *['pu-jan']*.

The issue probably is related to the Mohist goal of universal love. This is apparently different enough from Christian love to exclude thieves. This seems to be a Mohist concession in defense of the ideal to the following, intolerant question, "Well, you say we should love all men equally; should we love thieves too?" Should a Christian love Charles Manson and Hitler? We think a Christian is consistent to answer "yes." The Mohist argues, in effect, that it is not inconsistent to answer "no!"

What about a stronger issue, based on the assumed justifiability of the practice of punishment? It is certainly permissible to punish thieves. If killing a thief is permissible, and a thief is a man, then killing a man is permissible. But the inference rule that justifies that conclusion is, the analysis argues, not reliable. So the Mohist is not unreasonable to hold that killing thieves is permissible and killing men is not.

Who was the Mohist answering? What school in China might have attacked his position? Conceivably the attack could have come from two opposite directions. On the one side the Confucian fundamentalists and their formal dialectical allies (like Kung-sun Lung), committed to the ideal one-name-one-thing language, would, in principle, have agreed with the conclusion. Mencius held that killing King Chou was not killing a ruler, but killing a common fellow. He consistently should have held that killing Chieh was not killing a man, but killing a thief. But the Confucians (or at least their Dialectician allies) would have used rectification of names to make this judgment consistent with the inference principle. They would then be forced to conclude that thief is not man.

On the other hand, the attack could have come from the other direction—from someone who really rejected the permissibility of killing thieves and who advocated instead that we ought to love them. Perhaps at some level of argument the Taoists or their Dialectician allies, like Hui Shih, might have been even more extreme than the Mohists in advocating universal love. And the Taoist objection to government and society could easily have translated into opposition to punishment—which is by definition a social sanction. Graham suggests that the attack came from the Taoist side; I think it came from the Confucian. But there is no evidence in this text itself to settle the issue. Conceivably it could have come from either quarter.

The next group of examples are cases of the opposite breakdown, cases where the base sentence is signed (is *fei*) and the resultant sentence is unsigned. These are cases where things are "not thus" and yet "so."

> Moreover, reading a book is not a book, but to like reading books is to like books. Cockfights are not cocks, but to like cockfights is to like cocks. Being about to fall into a well is not falling into a well, but to stop someone from being about to fall into a well is to stop someone from falling into a well. Being about to go out of doors is not going out of doors, but to stop someone from being about to go out of doors is to stop someone from going out of doors.
>
> If such is the case, there is no longer any difficulty in allowing that: Being about to die prematurely is not dying prematurely, but to stop someone from being about to die prematurely is to stop someone from dying prematurely. Acknowledging the existence of *ming* 命 ['destiny'] is not destiny, but not to acknowledge the existence of destiny is to deny destiny.
>
> The latter claims are the same as the former; the world does not think it wrong to hold the former, yet condemns the Mohists as wrong for holding the latter. Is there any reason for it but being, as the saying goes, "clogged within and closed without"? [Gloss as on p. 133.]
>
> Here what is so *[jan]* comes even though they are not thus *[shih]*.

The shift to destiny or fate as an issue and to a formally different argument suggests that the Mohists are attributing the argument form to their opponents and using it to organize their defense of a number of their key doctrines against attacks of whatever logical form. The first examples, the books and cockfights, fall into the pattern we noticed earlier; they are explainable via the distinction between phrases conveying attitudes and intentions and terms denoting objects. But a quite different explanation is necessary for the "stopping someone from being about to . . ." cases. And there is again no hint in this text that the authors had a specific analysis of the cases in mind. They turn on facts about causation. An earlier causal stage is not identical to a later one, but stopping an earlier causal stage is (explains)[42] stopping the later one.

The defense here is of the key classical example in the Mohist opposition to fatalism. Accidental or early death is a paradigm candidate for a fated happening. The Mohist argument against this would presumably resemble our own—that one's death by accident was not fated since any number of things could have prevented the accident. "If he only hadn't stopped to buy cigarettes, he would not have been there when the bomb exploded." It is conceivable that someone countered with the argument, "Well, in that case, you have not prevented his death by accident, you have only prevented his being about to die." But as a defense of a fatalist point of view, such a response is implausibly feeble. We would then conclude that a thing is fated only at the precise moment it is happening. Since the appeal to fate is designed to make us feel less guilty for not preventing certain occurrences, it is hard to imagine a fatalist gaining any comfort from the argument. Most likely, as suggested earlier, the Mohist is attributing this argument structure to his opponents who are fatalists for no better reason than that the Mohist has this refutation available.

The acknowledging and denying destiny argument is an anomalous puzzle among these examples. I offer the following ad hoc conjecture which turns on one of the classic ambiguities of Chinese syntax. *Fei* 非 'is not' can be used as a transitive verb, "to deny." So "*fei* x" might be read either as "is not x" or "denies x." Now either a person affirms "there is destiny" or not. We cannot all be fated to affirm destiny since some do not. And not to affirm destiny is to deny destiny. But in this conclusion the ambiguity of *fei ming* is exploited to yield the reading "is not destiny." Thus neither attitude is destined.

The next set of examples does not fall in the formal sentence-matching pattern but is a set of other, seemingly inconstant, language relations. They still turn on both the distinction between a term's denotation and its use in phrases conveying intention and on the part-whole ambiguities inherent in the mass-stuff semantics. The central question is when a phrase should be interpreted as applying to all the stuff denoted by one of its terms or only part. The text calls these examples where one is *chou* (universal) and one not.

> "Love mankind" requires completely loving mankind before it can constitute loving mankind. Not loving mankind does not depend on

completely not loving mankind. Not completely loving mankind thus constitutes not loving mankind. "Riding horse" does not require completely riding horse [i.e., riding all horses] before it can constitute riding horse, to have ridden on horse [for there to be a horse on which one has ridden] thus constitutes riding horse. On the other hand, "not riding horse" depends on completely not riding horse before it can constitute not riding horse.

These are cases of one being universal and one not.

In order to understand how this could seem to the Mohist to be a puzzle, we have to assume, consistent with the explanatory hypothesis of chapter 2, that the term *jen* 人 'man:mankind' as well as *ma* 馬 'horse' are taken to be singular referring expressions. So the Mohist is puzzled about why one seems to refer to only part of the stuff and the other to all of the stuff. He seems equally puzzled over why negating a sentence should reverse the universality of reference—making a universal reference to a stuff becomes a partitive reference to a stuff and vice versa.

Again, the Mohist only expresses the puzzle (as evidence of his claim that language is inconstant and unreliable) without trying to diagnose it. There seems to be no part of the Mohist program that yields a diagnosis. Certain verbs in certain uses impose quantifiers on mass nouns in the object position. *Water* in "he abhors water" is implicitly universally quantified—it refers to the all water, the substance itself. In "he drank water" the term is implicitly existentially quantified—it refers to some water, a quantified portion of the substance. The effects of the negative in reversing quantification would not be as problematic if we knew how to formalize quantification for mass terms.

The next section, dealing with things of which one is this *(shih)* and one is not *(fei)*, also contains a number of problems connected with cumulative and noncumulative reference of mass nouns. Others seem to have no more basis than the apparent assertability of peculiar idioms in Mohist Chinese.

> If you inhabit somewhere in a state, you are deemed to inhabit the state; if you own one house in the state, you are not deemed to own the state. The fruit of a peach [tree] is the peach; but the fruit of the bramble is not the bramble [i.e., the thorn]. Inquiring about a man's illness is inquiring about the man; disliking a man's illness is not disliking the man. [The ghost of a man is not a man]; the ghost of your elder brother is your elder brother. Sacrificing to a man's ghost is not sacrificing to a man; sacrificing to your eldest brother's ghost is sacrificing to your elder

brother. If this horse's eyes are blind, we deem this horse blind; if this horse's eyes are big, we do not say that this horse is big. If these oxen's hairs are yellow, we say that these oxen are yellow; if these oxen's hairs are many, we do not say that these oxen are many. One horse is horse, two horses are horse. "Horse four feet" is one horse and four feet, not two horses and four feet. "Horse some white" is two horses and part [i.e., one] white, not one horse and partly white.

These are cases of one being thus and one not. . . .

We will not conjecture more explanations for the various examples. The important historical point, again, is that the authors do not diagnose the problems, only offer them to undermine the view of language as a stable, reliable inference tool.

The last example is interesting in showing how the mass-stuff semantics led to philosophical puzzles which may strike us as peculiar. The grammar of "horse" in "horse four feet" and "horse some white" seems identical, but the logical structure is quite different. The first is "every (standard unit of) horse has four feet" and the second is "some horse(s) are white."[43] We could adapt this analysis more to mass substances by reading the first as "horse stuff is four-footed-stuff" and the second as "some horse stuff is white." The text's setting of the problem underlines the character of mass nouns: any sum of parts which are mass-x is itself the mass-x. Hence one horse is horse, two horses are horse. The Mohists seem to have no point in all these examples except to reinforce the underlying skepticism of the reliability of language as a form of knowledge.

Finale: Words, Ideas, and Logic

The later Mohists shared to a large degree the presuppositions about language found in the Confucian and Taoist schools. They can be distinguished from each of the traditional schools by their relatively more descriptive analysis of the function of language, their relative stress on stuff denotation versus distinction marking in semantics, and their moderate position on conventionality. The later Mohist philosophical puzzles and semantic theory provide the greatest detail of any work of the pre-Han period in confirming the hypothesis that the intuitive semantics associated with the language and behind the explicit semantics is that of mass-stuffs.

The technical uses of i 意 'intention:image' and lei 類 'similar' have been shown to include none of the abstract roles of the common

English translations. The details of their use in the dialectical works confirm the negative side of the hypothesis—the nominalist presupposition. *I* makes most sense in the Neo-Mohist theory as "intention" sometimes and as "image" other times. It is seemingly never taken to be the semantic counterpart of words as opposed to phrases or sentences. *Lei* functions as "class" only in the senses which do not require the companion notions of subclass and member, that is, as mereological classes and thus equivalent to mass-stuffs. It is mostly used to assert similarity between these mass-stuffs.

The Mohists both rejected the ideal of a perfectly rectified language for moral judgment based on one-name-one-thing and refuted the absolute Taoist skepticism about the decidability of *pien* 'dispute' with concise and careful arguments. Several interesting semantic paradoxes are formulated in rejecting dogmatic Taoist skepticism.

The key semantic paradox used against the Taoists showed that one could not claim that all *yen* 言 'language' was perverse. But the school itself tended to regard language as ultimately unreliable as a form of knowledge. The most extended argument in the corpus had precisely that moral. The *Hsiao Ch'ü* examines what was a seemingly natural theory of inference based on the algebraic use of terms in Chinese. It rejects the inference rule by giving a host of counterexamples. The formulation of the proposal uses syntactic rather than semantic characterizations of the premises and conclusions. And the Mohists give no deeper diagnosis of the failures of the logical proposal than to observe that language is unreliable. A great many of the examples turn on the difference between a term's denotation and its use in phrases to convey intentions. A great many of the examples seem to be puzzling because of the part-whole ambiguity of the masslike features of nouns used as referring expressions.

If one is a nominalist and tempted to applaud the Mohist approach, it is interesting to consider the possibility that their being right about that issue may be part of the reason for their failure to persevere in trying to construct logical theories. A belief in abstract entities might have motivated more persistence in diagnosing the problems in the inference procedure studied and also in proposing others. It is more satisfying to devote oneself to such studies if one can represent one's activity as the study of "a deeper reality" or of ideas rather than mere words. The Mohists openly saw their study as the study of words, which they themselves regarded as an inferior kind of knowledge.

In Western philosophy, at least prior to the twentieth century, the sense of the triviality of words was ameliorated by the comfort that beyond and behind the words stood ideas—common to all men and rationally ordered. Words were capricious and arbitrary.

> Thus we may conceive how words, which were by nature so well adapted to that purpose, came to be made use of by men as the signs of their ideas; not by any natural connection that there is between particular articulate sounds and certain ideas, for then there would be but one language amongst all men; but by a voluntary imposition, whereby such a word is made arbitrarily the mark of such an idea.[44]

I have assumed that the *Hsiao Ch'ü* is the final word on logic in ancient China. We have no record of other attempts until the introduction of Buddhist logic after the Han Dynasty. Conceivably this school might have continued to study logic right up to the time the school was wiped out during the Ch'in and Han dynasties. However, I read the tone of the *Hsiao Ch'ü* as being defeatist. In spirit, the Mohists seem to have joined hands with Chuang-tzu. Language is capricious, arbitrary, and merely conventional. So it was declared, even by those philosophers who specialized most in the study of language, to be ultimately useless as a tool to discover an absolute way.

Chapter 5

Kung-sun Lung and the White-Horse Paradox

Indeterminacy and Paradox

The white-horse paradox is stated in the opening line of the second chapter of the work titled the *Kung-sun Lung-tzu*. The paradox is stated in a simple four-character sentence: *pai ma fei ma* 白馬非馬 'white horse is-not horse'. There follows an argument in dialogue form about the assertability of the paradoxical sentence. Interpreting and explaining the paradox has become a source of fascination to scholars. There have been numerous interpretive theories in modern times (see p. 143), nearly all of which employ metaphysical, mental, abstract, or semantic concepts borrowed from the Western philosophical tradition. The challenge is to explain why Kung-sun Lung would consider the sentence assertable. This chapter is an argument from the philosophical perspective laid down in chapter 2 for a nominalistic interpretation of both the paradox and the dialogue which follows it. I contend that we do not need to treat *ma* as "horseness" nor *pai* as "whiteness" to explain Kung-sun Lung's view that "white-horse not horse" is assertable.

It is notoriously the case that one *can* translate a language in a number of radically different ways. The indeterminacy of translation is one of the "axioms" of post-Quinian philosophy of language (although the interpretation of the claim that translation is indeterminate is indeterminate).[1] Given a sentence, a chapter, or even a dialogue, there could be a variety of "manuals" for translating and interpreting which would all "work." The grammar and content of the corpus would not strictly dictate which one of the interpretations was the correct one. No facts about usage could conclusively disprove all the radically different translations of such a corpus.

Thus, to switch to the favored Chinese example, *ma* 馬 could be in a dictionary as "horse," "horse-stages," "collection-of-horse-parts," "bit-of-horse-stuff," "instance of horseness," "concrete horse-essence," and so on. Each such radical translation is possible in the sense that it would lead one to use the term correctly in all "ordinary" contexts. However strange it may seem to Sally to think of herself riding on a collection of horse parts, she does indeed do so whenever she rides a horse.

So the different translations make no obvious difference in our patterns of use, but they are nonetheless different. They each presuppose a different framework, a different conceptual structure, a different set of background beliefs and modes of dividing up the world. These differences are problematic primarily to philosophers—those analyzing or rationalizing conceptual frameworks and those trying to interpret the frameworks generated by other philosophers. By and large, practicing linguists seldom need worry about translation indeterminacy.[2]

So the concern with the alternative dictionaries which embody different conceptual schemes or background beliefs is a live one primarily when translating philosophy. In philosophical analysis the translations do make a difference; Kung-sun Lung's philosophical theories will seem to be more reasonable, more understandable, if we attribute one set of background beliefs and conceptual assumptions than if we attribute another set.

That, at least, is what I argue in this chapter. In particular, I argue that of two alternative dictionaries or "translation manuals," one that translates *ma* as "horseness" and one that translates it as "horse-stuff," the latter provides a more coherent interpretation of the *Kung-sun Lung-tzu* text in its context.[3] The context suggests that the text in question is motivated by semantic problems generated in the Neo-Mohist Dialectic and by the assumptions of language common to Taoist skepticism and Confucian rectification of names tradition in China.

The white-horse dialogue of Kung-sun Lung has usually been interpreted by attributing to Kung-sun Lung a peculiarly Western philosophical set of beliefs, namely, that individuals are a combination of particular substances and properties. The paradoxical conclusion *pai ma fei ma* 白馬非馬 (literally "white-horse is-not horse") might be rendered in any number of such schemes. For example, white-horse stages are not horse-stages. One need not, however, despair that no interpretation is possible or that all are equally arbitrary. The explanation we can give for Kung-sun

Lung's advocating the paradox will be better on some interpretations than on others. I will not try to compare all possible interpretations. Only two will be studied here: the traditional abstract interpretation (and equivalent ones using abstract mental ideas with the same role) and the mereological or mass-stuff proposal of chapter 2.

The conclusion of such an approach deserves modest statement. All that can emerge is that one interpretation is the more plausible of two available interpretations. This is the effect of treating interpretations as theory. I can make no claims to have access to Kung-sun Lung's internal subjectivity—only to propose a coherent and plausible theory about the text attributed to him.[4]

The first part of this chapter deals with an argument for the comparative advantages of a nominalistic interpretation and spells out the background conditions that motivated the text on this interpretation. The nominalist interpretation offered here is based on the hypothesis that the ontology and semantics of Chinese common sense is that of mass-stuffs. I argue that the mass-stuff based interpretation is more plausible, in the above sense, than any of the interpretations which attribute to Kung-sun Lung the discovery of theories about abstract or mental objects. The second section of the chapter is the translation and exposition of the dialogue using the mass-stuff hypothesis.

The Chinese Language and Abstractions

A central part of the argument against the interpretive hypothesis that "white-horse is-not horse" refers to abstract objects is that it would not have been reasonable for Kung-sun Lung to propose such a theory. That, I have argued in chapter 2 (pp. 42–53), comes from a hypothesis about what role abstractions play in theories from various branches of philosophy. To review, for example, theories of abstraction serve an important function in semantics. They provide a solution to the perennial Western philosophical problem of the-one-and-the-many in language. General terms are "true of" (denote) a multitude of objects. Various kinds of abstract theories explain how this is possible by giving *two* semantic relata of common nouns: ordinary objects and the abstraction. The abstract entity, functioning as a repeatable object "realized" in each ordinary object in some way, gives a metaphysical explanation of the relation between the single "name" and its multiple denotation.

Abstract entities, accordingly, are individuals that are outside the physical realm.⁵ The semantic role of these entities suggests ontological roles for them as a transcendental reality. They may, as noted earlier (pp. 63–65), be employed to deal with related problems in epistemology and in philosophy of mind. However, this entire set of patterns of thought is superfluous to interpreting the paradox if Chinese philosophy is not based on the assumption that the semantic relation of names to things is a one-many relationship. Given the features of grammar discussed above, it is highly plausible that one-many is not the basis; all the background theories involving language in the period show no signs of any such assumption (chap. 3). The overt semantic theories discussed in chapter 4 similarly undercut any rationale for attributing theories of abstract or mental objects as background assumptions in interpreting any philosophy of the period.

Paradoxically, the key feature of Chinese language that is usually appealed to in postulating Kung-sun Lung's discovery of abstractions is the *lack* of the grammatical features which motivated such a discovery in the West, namely, the lack of plural and abstract inflections for Chinese nouns. This lack is treated as evidence that Chinese nouns ambiguously correspond to English singular, plural, and abstract terms, and that Kung-sun Lung discovered this fact (supposedly without discovering English). On the contrary, as argued earlier, those grammatical features are precisely what would explain a radically nominalistic Chinese approach to semantics and ontology.⁶ Accordingly, they are evidence that the passage is best interpreted nominalistically.

The Standard Interpretations

Probably the classic interpretation of the Kung-sun Lung philosophical view stems from Fung Yu-lan in his influential *History of Chinese Philosophy*.⁷ He claims that Kung-sun Lung's writings are best understood as dealing with Platonic "Ideas" or universals. A rather more recent interpretation is that of Janusz Chmielewski, who claims that the most plausible explanation has Kung-sun Lung dealing with logical or mathematical classes or sets. These interpretive proposals by Fung and Chmielewski do have a significant insight behind them. Chinese nouns are different from English (and presumably Slavic) nouns. The differences allow the use of singular, plural, and abstract forms of English nouns at different times in translating Chinese nouns. The more elegant explanation of Chinese nouns, as argued on pages 77–78, is that they are masslike nouns. We can focus the contrast between the abstract and nominalist approaches by noting the considerations that seem to justify the use of abstractions in interpreting this troublesome passage.

Let us see how the abstract interpretations function grammatically. Fung suggests that the words *pai-ma* and *ma* in the formula *pai ma fei ma* do not mean "white-horse" and "horse," but, as used by Kung-sun Lung, refer to the abstract universals "white-horseness" and "horseness." They thus make each term logically singular and consequently make the *fei* 'is-not' function as "is nonidentical with." The proposal makes Kung-sun Lung's conclusion seem reasonable because, indeed, white-horseness is *not* horseness. On this interpretation, the seemingly paradoxical formula is true.

Fung's explanation of Kung-sun Lung's paradox requires attributing to Lung the more or less conscious "discovery" of the theory of unchanging abstract universals. Similar arguments have been offered which allege that Kung-sun Lung discovered, for example, qualities,[8] properties,[9] concepts,[10] general ideas,[11] attributes,[12] classes,[13] and meanings.[14] All these alternatives share three characteristics. They attribute to Kung-sun Lung the invention of theories involving entities that (1) perform the semantic work of classical abstract entities; (2) are relatively important mainstream notions in the development or elaboration of Western logic, ontology, philosophy of mind, or semantics—hard, "respectable" philosophy; and (3) are all otherwise rare or absent from Chinese thought.

All these interpretations are, from the point of view of radical translation, possible accounts of the text. They are, however, less plausible as stories about how the paradox emerged than interpretations which generate the paradox from philosophical and semantic concerns reflecting more sensitively the grammar of nouns in Chinese language. Still, the argument for supplanting the abstract with the mass-stuff interpretation must be able to explain the appeal of the *pai ma fei ma* formula to Kung-sun Lung at least as well as these abstract alternatives do.

The objection to an abstract interpretation can be summarized in the following points:

1. There is no historical background that would explain the invention of theories postulating abstract entities. Nothing in the history of Chinese philosophy prior to Kung-sun Lung, as we have seen, shows any problems, doctrines, approaches to issues, or the like that might have eventuated in the development of such a conceptual revolution. This claim is not contested by most of the proponents of abstract interpretations. These

accounts themselves often implicitly assume that Kung-sun Lung is a unique exception to the general character of Chinese thought:

> The important fact that Kung-sun Lung . . . was unable to establish his abstract concepts (such as the concept of the horse, or of whiteness) in a coherent and systematic fashion is sufficient evidence that ancient China was entirely unaware of a closed system of concepts, each of which represents an abstract and exclusive whole, entirely organized around the very clear notion of inclusion and exclusion.[15]

Some (see paragraph 7 following) even assert that Kung-sun Lung discovered abstractions despite the fact that they cannot be expressed in Chinese.[16]

2. It is acknowledged by even the proponents of the abstract interpretation that Kung-sun Lung was not understood by any of his contemporaries nor by any subsequent Chinese philosopher *until* the contact with Western philosophy. Contemporary and subsequent accounts of Kung-sun Lung's views usually explain his error as resulting from his being confused about the scope or extension of compound terms. They tend to view his paradox as generated by an erroneous account of the effects on the scope or extension resulting from adding "white" to "horse." Hsün-tzu (fl. 298–238 B.C.) discusses Kung-sun Lung's paradox after a section in which he explains the relation of particular and general terms and claims that compounding has *no fixed consequences* in making more particular or more general the scope of the original term. He then dismisses the white-horse paradox as resulting from confusing the reality by names, that is, taking rigid naming relationships so seriously as to assert "unreal," or counterintuitive, conclusions.[17] K'ung Ch'uan, who debated Kung-sun Lung, seems to have taken Lung's argument as entailing that "white-horse" was more general than "horse."[18] At best we should have to conclude that Kung-sun Lung was an abominable expositor of philosophical views or that he did not even try if he could not even begin to convey his new theory about nonphysical entities to his contemporary philosophers.

3. Kung-sun Lung's abstract interpreters have him making a use of paradox that must be considered, at best, deviant. Normally a paradox is used to discredit some *received* and widely held theory which the paradox maker believes false; for example, Zeno's paradoxes are intended to show that motion and change are impossible. Alternately, the paradox may be offered to provoke a necessary revision of fondly held views; consider Hume's paradox of induction and Russell's paradox. Here, by contrast, we

are asked to believe that Kung-sun Lung invented a novel abstract doctrine and then without saying anything to motivate or explain the doctrine derived a relatively silly paradox from it. Lung's sole method of motivating and presenting this philosophical invention was to derive this counterintuitive paradox. He is arguing, in effect, that *his own theory* entails something that those he is trying to persuade of the theory must consider false.

4. On these various abstract interpretations, as I noted above, the paradox is rendered true. But the truth is purchased at the price of making the whole enterprise seem rather silly. There are many interesting features of classes, universals, or properties on which Kung-sun Lung might have remarked to elucidate, expand, or defend his view. Why should he focus on a paradoxical formulation of the rather trivial claim that distinct entities of this sort are not identical? That has all the philosophical excitement of the observation that Pegasus is not Zeus. If these interpretations of Kung-sun Lung are correct, then he is hardly worth philosophical attention.

5. Following Graham,[19] I do not regard the "hard-white" dialogue or the "name and things" dialogue as authentic Kung-sun Lung writings. But most of the abstract interpreters do, and this makes their interpretations internally incoherent because these contain even more evidence against abstract interpretation of Chinese terms. If Kung-sun Lung had, as they suggest, arrived at some sophisticated theory of properties, attributes, classes, forms, or the like, one could reasonably expect that it would have had some role in his theories about the relation of name and thing. But the dialogue on names and things is as thoroughly nominalistic as the Neo-Mohist Canon (from which Graham argues it was copied). There is not the slightest hint of any abstract doctrine in that explicitly semantic chapter. The dialogue on hard-white, on the other hand, contains the assertion that white is necessarily white—even when not in combination with things. This is precisely what abstract theories would normally deny. An object's being white is explained as its having some sort of relation to whiteness. It cannot coherently be taken to be the relation whiteness has to itself. The idea 'whiteness' is not itself white, nor is the class of white things a white class. Hardness is not itself hard. But white-stuff, taken as a concrete mass substantive, *is* white and hard-stuff is hard.

6. While the conclusion can be understood by translating it so that it contains the terms *white horseness* and *horseness*, the occurrences of *ma*

and *pai ma* in the body of the discourse and in the arguments given by the Chinese sophist can only be understood if both are taken as concrete; for example, the "ask for a horse" argument (J/6, p. 259) has (supposedly Kung-sun Lung) asserting, "If you ask for a horse a yellow horse will 'answer'." But if one asks for *horseness*, yellow-horseness surely would *not* "answer." To say that it would, apart from being false, is inconsistent with the insight attributed to Kung-sun Lung by the interpretive hypothesis in the first place—that distinct abstract entities are not identical.

7. The exposition of the various abstract interpretations all seem essentially[20] to entail an implausible "museum" account of the relation of language and thought, i.e., of thought as a collection of interculturally identical mental items in the mind which are labeled differently by the words of different languages.[21] A rather bald expression of this "myth of the museum" with regard to Kung-sun Lung graces the introduction to one of the abstract translations of the *Kung-sun Lung-tzu:*

> [Ancient Chinese] had no means of rendering the scientific transformations of the concrete into the abstract. Our mind passes from an individual horse whether black or white or any other color, to the *equus caballus* which in our modern translation we invariably render as "horsehood"; but Kung-sun Lung after performing *the same mental operation* had to fall back upon the same identical character: *ma*.[22]

Bodde's statement of a similar point is a bit more refined. (He at least does not assume that we think in Latin and "render" those thoughts in "Modern.")

> Kung-sun Lung's difficulty in proving this thesis [Platonism] is heightened by the nature of the Chinese written language, which, because it is pictographic and ideographic, and at the same time non-inflected, can express the difference between singular and plural objects, the concrete and the abstract, etc., only with difficulty.[23]

This very account of the difficulties of Chinese language provides an insoluble puzzle for the abstract interpretations. The evidence for what Kung-sun Lung thought is what is written in Archaic Chinese written style. If it is impossible (or "difficult") for that language to express or distinguish abstractions, then it is impossible (or "difficult") to prove from the text that the author had such beliefs!

The Comparative Advantage Case for the Mass-Stuff Interpretation

The present hypothesis is that Kung-sun Lung treats terms such as *ma* in a way that is natural to treat mass nouns: as singular terms naming "stuffs." Such a concrete interpretation, by contrast, has the corresponding strengths that

1. It can be understood as challenging semantic assumptions of the Neo-Mohists and defending the formal equivalent of the influential Confucian theory of rectification of names.
2. It explains contemporary judgments of Kung-sun Lung which imply that he was confusing the scope of names when compounded.
3. It makes Kung-sun Lung a reasonable proposer of paradoxes. He is not the inventor of the very doctrine that the paradox undermines.
4. We can agree with Chinese common sense that the paradoxical conclusion is false, yet still represent it as a philosophically motivated mistake with a rationale stemming from widely held views in the philosophy of language (indeed, in a sense, we can regard Kung-sun Lung as the David Hume of one-name-one-thing-ism).
5. Although I regard the evidence against the authenticity of the "hard-white" dialogue and "name and things" dialogue as very nearly conclusive, they can be shown to be consistent with the mass noun interpretation in crucial ways where the idealist interpretation cannot. The interpretation in conjunction with the Neo-Mohist background also provides an account of what Kung-sun Lung's having separated "hard" and "white" would have amounted to in relation to the rest of the tradition.
6. We can translate all the text on the same hypothesis on which we translate the conclusion. All the concrete nouns in the text are to be read either as mass terms or as mentions of mass terms.
7. On the present view, Kung-sun Lung was not a "prisoner" of his language—thinking the unspeakable. The only language difficulties he faced were the logical difficulties of his theory of language.

The Neo-Mohist Semantics of Compound Terms

A program for semantics that starts from a Mohist account of the semantics of simple "names" (term and predicate expressions) naturally encounters next the problem of characterizing modification. A modifier in semantics takes a term into a new term (a compound term) which has a different scope or range of extension. How do we explain the connection between, say, "white-horse" and the world in terms of the originally given relation between "white" and "horse" and the world? Traditional abstract semantics provides a simple neat answer. Words (nouns and adjectives) correspond to properties that are instantiated in individuals or particular substances that those words have as their extension or scope. Modified nouns denote those individuals who have both the properties corresponding to the component words. "White-horse" denotes individuals who have both the properties "whiteness" and "horseness."

Modern semantics provides a different answer. It would associate a class of objects with each word and would explain the denotation of a compound like "white-horse" as the intersection of those classes—the set of members that fall into both the original classes {white objects} and {horses}.

Those are solutions to standard "extensional" modification in languages like English with count nouns and an ontology of individuals. There are other thorny nonextensional problems about modification, for instance, explaining "big flea" and "small elephant." Does a big flea share some independent property, bigness, with big elephants but not small ones? Or does a small elephant belong to a class that includes small fleas but not big ones? Some modifications rule out *any* relation with the original noun semantics; a phony priest does not belong to the class of priests nor does he have the property 'priesthood'. A potential heavyweight champion is not the heavyweight champion. A potential person is not a person. Some of Chuang-tzu's skepticism of semantics stems from concerns with the relativity of modifying expressions like *ta* 'large' and *hsiao* 'small', but Mohist semantics seems not to have given much attention to either of these puzzles in nonstandard modification.

The Mohist has, however, another puzzle about extensional modification that is rather more peculiar to Chinese. Chinese modifiers are not inflected, and terms may be modified by other terms or by predicates (adjectives). Standard extensional modification has two varieties because of the masslike lack of pluralization in Chinese grammar. One of the compounds is like our own "white horse" and the other like our "cats 'n' dogs." The later Mohist must accordingly produce two different accounts of the "stuffs" that figure in the different compound terms. The paradigm for the former was "hard-white" and for the latter "ox-horse."

Kung-sun Lung's paradox results from rejecting one of the accounts of the semantics of compound terms (the mass-product hard-white model discussed on pages 155–59) which was a cornerstone in the semantic program of the Neo-Mohist Canon. He rejects the view on the ground of the one-name-one-thing rule of rectification of names. The Neo-Mohists' views grow out of their attempt to account for the functioning of ''names'' in compounds—combinations of two characters. That attempt gives rise to interesting reflections on an ontology of ''stuffs.''

I offer here a brief preview of the whole argument outlining the Mohists' semantic theories and the way they fit into Kung-sun Lung's motivation for his assertion of the paradox. The details and quotations will follow.

The Mohist view is that names designate stuffs but not with absolute consistency. In particular, names may designate stuffs of varying generality (Canon I:78).[24] The referring or designating relation is a basic unexplained primitive of their theory. It is nowhere buttressed by further theories of a medium of ideas, meanings, or concepts. That names ''pick out'' the stuffs they do is a matter, presumably, of convention—it has no further explanation. In principle, to take a recurrent example, what we now call ''ox'' could be called ''horse,'' hence it is possible that ''horse'' and ''nonhorse'' might exchange denotation.[25]

The straightforward, nominalistic simplicity of the basic semantic account of names forces the Neo-Mohists to wrestle with the problem of compound names in the Canon. The Canon is deeply involved in explaining how various kinds of name compounding can be interpreted. There are several technical concepts developed for dealing with compounding: *fu* 復 'adding name to name'; *ch'ü* 傴 'separating into collections'; *t'i* 体 'corporeal stuff taken as a unit'; *chien* 堅 'compounds of *t'i*'; *niuma* 牛馬 (ox-horse) 'paradigm example of compounds which do not interpenetrate'; *chienpai* 堅白 (hard-white) 'paradigm example of compounds which do interpenetrate'.

T'i are more or less natural kinds in the sense that they correspond to single words (names). They combine to form *chien* or compounds. The Mohist uses *chien* for the ontological compound and *fu* for the syntactic compound.[26] The *t'i-chien* relationship, like the part-whole relation, is relative to the level of analysis and interest. What is a part for one purpose may be treated as a whole for some other purpose. A *chien* accordingly may be regarded as one or as two.

Kung-sun Lung and the White-Horse Paradox

The "hard-white" *fu*–name is semantically different from the *fu*–name which denotes a *chien*. "Ox-horse" is the stock example to contrast with "hard-white." The theory can best be put schematically.

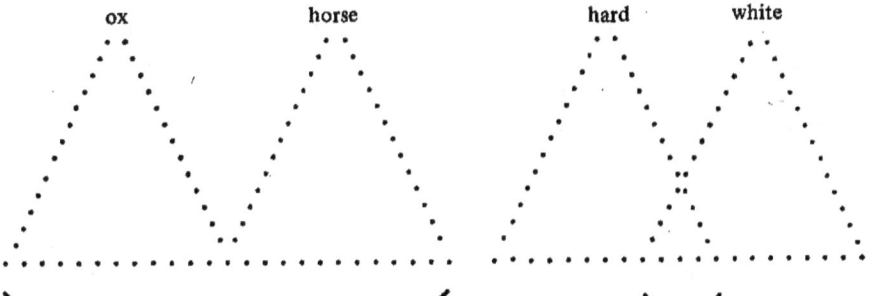

The Mohist theory is that the *fu*–name "ox-horse" (and others of that type) "name" all the stuff *added together*. The *fu*–name "hard-white" (and others of that type) name only part of the stuff that the components name individually—the bracketed segment. This theory is presented via arguments about what kinds of sentences involving "ox-horse" are *k'o* 'assertable', and by talk about the "interpenetration" and "inseparability" of "hard-white." Kung-sun Lung, committed to a rigid view of naming, rejects the "hard-white" model (i.e., he separates "hard-white") and argues that "white-horse" should function as "ox-horse" does—that it is *k'o* 'assertable' in the same way that "ox-horse" is. The Mohists hold that because some of the stuff named by "ox-horse" is not ox, "ox-horse not ox" is assertable. Kung-sun Lung holds that if we interpret compounds by the model which preserves the rigid relationship of names and things, then by parity of reasoning, some of the stuff named by "white-horse" is not horse so "white-horse is not horse" is *k'o* 'assertable'. Now the details.

Chien *and* T'i

The Neo-Mohist analysis of compound terms involves two operations on a mass-stuff structure: mass sum and mass product. A mass sum is the sum of two (or more) mass-stuffs. It corresponds to the union of sets. A mass product corresponds to the intersection of sets. Mass products depend on the possibility of mass-stuff's "overlapping." The mass product is that stuff which is *both* masses. The mass sum is the members of the union class taken as a whole; the mass product is the members of the intersection taken as a whole. The mass sum of X and Y is everything that is either X *or* Y. The mass product of X and Y is everything that is *both* X *and* Y. We will talk of the scope or range of denotation of a term as the "stuff" it denotes. So a single term will have a mass-stuff (*t'i*) as its scope; a compound will have either a mass product or a mass sum as its scope.

T'i 'units:mass-stuffs' introduced in the Canon are defined as divisions in a *chien*—like one in two (Canon I:2). What the divisions are in a *chien* (mass-sum) depends on (is relative to) what *chien* we are considering. This relativity of the use of *t'i* is underscored by the definitions of *t'i*–sameness and *t'i*–difference in Canon II:86–87 (see pp. 106–10). *T'i*–sameness applies when "not outside a *chien*," that is, when *t'i* are taken as parts of some total, and *t'i*–difference when "not connected or belonging to," when not taken in some whole. The *t'i-chien* relation is essentially, then, a part-whole relation.[27]

In the discussion of compounding, *t'i* is the stuff denoted by the component terms and *chien* that denoted by the compound expression. Since *t'i*'s nontechnical use is usually translated by "body," "body parts," or "substance," the use of *t'i* in semantic analysis of compound terms reflects an assumption that sum compounding is performed only on corporeal stuffs. The Mohists do discuss another kind of compounding in which the component terms denote noncorporeal stuff, like "hard" and "white." Thus the theory has two models to explain the semantics of compound terms. They will turn out to be mass sum and mass product. The Mohist characterizes them, however, not by their scope, but by the interaction of the stuffs. So he describes the two models as those where the component stuffs cannot interpenetrate, and those in which the component stuffs do interpenetrate. The latter do not involve *t'i* and are not called *chien*.

A *chien* or compound is, paradigmatically, a mass sum. In Chinese a particularly large number of *fu*–names (those composed of two characters) name *chien* or mass sum compounds; examples include "heaven-earth" (the world), "mountain-water" (scenery or nature), "elder-brother-younger-brother" (brother), and "ox-horse" (draft animal). The abundance of mass sum compounds in Chinese is a seemingly natural consequence of the masslike grammar of nouns. Some theories of mass nouns stress that plurals often behave like mass nouns. Plurals are suggestively like mass nouns in their compounding behavior. Notice that English compounding replicates the mass sum behavior when the grammatical terms of the compound are plurals: "woods 'n' waters," "brothers 'n' sisters," "cats 'n' dogs." By contrast, where English compounds consist of grammatically singular forms of count nouns, such as "man-wolf," we "sum" the meanings or ideas instead of the scopes.

A central question posed in the Neo-Mohist account is whether a mass sum compound should be regarded as one or two. The question is a live one in the tradition because of the background model of an ideal language as one with the names rectified, that is, in a one-to-one relation with things. The Mohist's answer, which a more rigid "rectifying" semanticist like Kung-sun Lung must abhor, is that the mass sum may be regarded as either one or two—depending on the circumstances.

II 11　合與一，或復或否。說在樞。

Together or one thing, in the former case one adds name to name, in the latter not. Explained by marking off as a group. [Canon II:11]

II 12　歐物一體也。說在俱一，惟是。
　　（俱）。「俱一」，若牛馬四足。「惟是」，當「牛」「馬」。數牛數馬，則牛馬二。數牛馬，則牛馬一。（若數指，指五而五一。）

Things marked off as a group are one *t'i* ['mass-substance']. Explained by all as individual, being just this [stuff]. [Canon II:12]

"All as individual," for example, "ox-horse has four feet." "Being just this," it maps onto ox-horse. If you count oxen and count horses, then ox-horse is two. If you count ox-horse, then ox-horse is one. (For example, counting the fingers. The fingers are five but the five are one.) [Explanation II:12]

The first kind of *chien* is discussed in terms of the assertability of the stock term for mass-sum compounding, *niu-ma* 牛馬 'ox-horse'. The Mohist's way of putting the question is to ask whether or not the sentence "ox-horse non-ox" is assertable. To understand the Mohist approach we must think not only of *ox* and *horse* and even *ox-horse* as mass terms, but we must think of *non-ox* as a mass term.

II 67　不可牛馬之非牛與可之同，說在兼。
　　（不）或　非牛而非牛也可，則或非牛或牛也可。故曰「牛馬非牛也」未可，「牛馬牛也」可，則或可或不可，而曰「牛馬牛也未可」亦不可。且牛不二，馬不二，而牛馬二，則牛不非牛，馬不非馬，而「牛馬非牛非馬」無難。

There are the same grounds for treating "ox-horse non-ox" as either inadmissible or as admissible. Explained by: *chien* ['compounding']. [Canon II:67]

If, when part is non-ox, "is non-ox" is admissible. Then, since part is ox though part is not, "is ox" is also admissible. Therefore, if we say "'Ox-horse is non-ox' is inadmissible" and "'Ox-horse is ox' is admissible" then we treat [it] as partially admissible and partially inadmissible. And it is, further, inadmissible to say "'Ox-horse is ox' is *in*admissible." Moreover, ox is not two; horse is not two, yet ox-horse is two, thus ox is not non-ox, horse is not non-horse yet there is no difficulty with "ox-horse is non-ox-non-horse." [Explanation II:67][28]

The Mohist analysis treats the term *ox-horse* as we would treat "oxen 'n' horses" or "ox-stuff-horse-stuff." *Ox-horse* names the sum of the stuffs "named" by the terms *ox* and *horse*. The various allowable conclusions—some of ox-horse is not ox; some is ox; some is not horse; some is horse; ox-horse is non-ox-non-horse—all confirm that ox-horse is taken as a sum.[29] The observation that ox-horse is two while ox is one and horse is one reminds us of the *t'i-chien* formula—"like one in two." The *t'i* are natural kinds, denotations of noncomplex terms, taken as units (mass stuffs). The *chien*, the thing named by a compound name, is the sum of the *t'i* named by the components of the compound.

There are two important keys to the white-horse dialogue in this canon.

1. The central semantic property used for analysis is "acceptability" or "assertability" *(k'o)*. This pragmatic property can do much of the work of semantic truth, but it is clearly not equivalent to "true." It has some of the character of "logically possible"—no contradictory phrases are jointly assertable. In the ox-horse canon, it appears to mean something like "semantically possible"; that is, we can give a reading to or understand a sentence called "admissible." There could conceivably be situations in which it would be appropriate to utter it.
2. The reading we give to the sentence "ox-horse non-ox" is that some of it (ox-horse) is non-ox (the horse part). Accordingly, this reading even makes the sentence "ox-horse is (non-ox)-(non-horse)" assertable. (The grouping is necessary to see that the predicate is not an expansion of "is non-(ox-horse)." "Ox-horse non-(ox-horse)," on the model of "ox non-ox," would presumably *not* be assertable.)

The Mohists, as we have noted in chapter 4 (p. 106), abjure strict one-name-one-thing-ism. And the classification of t'i and *chien* is relative. Thus, in another context (Canon II:12) the Mohists say that ox-horse can be regarded as one. In talking about the mass sum compounding structure they claim that ox-horse is two. This abandonment of the rectification of names ideal for languages is apparently what distinguishes the Neo-Mohists' semantic program from that of Kung-sun Lung. The Mohists have no objection to saying that for certain purposes, we may regard ox-horse as one—as the stuff named by that compound name—and as two—making "ox-horse non-ox" an admissible *(k'o)* sentence.

Thus, even though "ox-horse" can be regarded as a name, and the thing it names as a mass-kind which may be taken as an individual, there is an important sense in which it is two *t'i*s. The concept of *t'i* appears to be a way of dividing "stuffs" corresponding roughly to the "natural" distinctions—those embodied in language as single characters. There is nothing wrong with coining compound terms to demarcate stuff in collections other than those conventionally recognized, but the stuff so named is still, in a deeper sense, dual. This basic sense of the duality of *chien* compounds appears to motivate a Mohist claim that the *chien* is "separable." It has real parts. So a *chien*, even if regarded as an individual, is still ontologically complex.

This interpretation is consistent with what appears to be the Mohist's moderate view on conventionality (see chap. 4, p. 106). People may intelligibly (acceptably) coin new names that divide things in the world in slightly different ways. The existing divisions in the language, however, are roughly those in "reality." It might be that the *word* (sound and symbol) used for "ox" is conventionally arrived at, but the *t'i*, the kind of thing, is a natural portion of the world which our conventional names pick out. The portioning of reality, in other words, is antecedent to the naming. Names "recognize" but do not create the different stuffs that make up reality.

Hard and White

The Canons dealing with hard-white form the other side of the Mohist semantic program for analyzing dual or compound names. The components of hard-white compounds are concrete but noncorporeal. Hard and white, that is, are distinguished from, say, ox and horse, not because of how they segment in reality, but because the segments can interpenetrate. Hard stuff and white stuff thus behave differently from *t'i* stuffs. Two bodies (corporeal stuffs) cannot occupy the same space at the same time. Hard and white can. This ontological difference gives rise to a semantic difference. The compound name for the interpenetrating stuffs does not name the sum (union) of the stuffs, but names their product (intersection)—the area of interpenetration.

The discussion of hard-white is one of the more thoroughly studied arguments in the Neo-Mohist Canon (especially by Luan Tiao-fu and A. C. Graham).[30] One of the cornerstones of all the studies is the assumption that the Neo-Mohists and Kung-sun Lung had different theories of how to treat hard-white. That dispute was couched in an argument about the "separability" of hard-white.[31]

Briefly, the Mohist position is that, unlike ox-horse, which, being a *chien* consisting of *t'i*, is two and therefore separable, hard-white ought to be regarded as an inseparable compound. This ontological point could be expressed semantically by saying that, by contrast with ox-horse, "hard-white not hard" is *not* assertable. The spatial metaphor used to illustrate the essential unity of hard-white is "wherever you go [in the compound mass] you get two" (Canon I:65). To make a parallel metaphor, one could say that with ox-horse, you could "go" to certain parts of the compound mass and "find" non-ox; at other parts you could "find" non-horse. There is no place where the two are inseparably together, that is, no mass product (the intersection of the sets is empty).

Let us now turn to those sections of the Neo-Mohist Canon dealing with hard and white. They are also relevant to the understanding of *t'i*. First some definitions:

I 65 盈，莫不有也。
　　（盈）。無盈無厚。於尺無所往而不得二。

To fill out is to be nowhere absent. [Canon I:65]

What does not fill anything is dimensionless; along a measurement, wherever you go you find two. [Explanation I:65]

I 66 堅白，不相外也。
　　（堅）。異處不相盈。相非是相外也。

Chien pai [as hard to white:mutually pervasive] is not excluding each other. [Canon I:66]

Different positions do not fill each other. Not being each other is excluding each other. [Explanation I:66]

I 67 攖，相得也。
(攖)。尺與尺俱不盡，端與端俱盡，尺與端或盡或不盡。堅白之攖相盡，體攖不相盡。

Ying ['touching:coinciding'] is occupying each other. [Canon I:67]

Of measured feet, neither wholly exhausts the other. Of starting points, each wholly exhausts the other. Of the measured foot and the starting point, one is wholly exhausted and the other is not. The coincidings of hard-white wholly exhaust each other. *T'i* ['units'] do not wholly exhaust each other. [Explanation I:67]

Explanation I:67 entails that the "stuff" named by "hard-white" is not made up of *t'i*. *T'i* are masses which, in combination *(chien)*, do not "wholly exhaust" or interpenetrate—while hard and white do. Hard and white are still viewed as located and extended in space (thus concrete rather than abstract) but they are not corporeal in the sense that they can (unlike *t'i)* occupy the same space, that is, interpenetrate.

I 46 損，偏去也。
(損)。偏也者：兼之體也。其體或去或存，謂其存者損。

Sun ['reduction'] is partial removal. [Canon I:46]

The partial is a *t'i* ['unit'] of a *ch'ien* ['compound' or 'sum']. Of its *t'i* (units) some are removed some remain. Call the remainder reduced. [Explanation I:46]

Notice that "reducing" can only involve *t'i*. Reducing, accordingly, is not an abstraction operation—not, that is, a mental "taking away," say, of properties, or characteristics. The notion described here is more akin to physical "breaking off." (Similarly, the inseparability of hard-white is not a mental inseparability but a physical coinciding so that any part contains both.[32] A *chien* which is made up of *t'i* can be separated—taking one away (ox) and leaving the other (horse). But in, for example, a rock, anything you physically take away removes both the hard and the white.

Thus, in spite of the occasional appropriateness of regarding ox-horse as the single mass named by the compound "ox-horse," it is two in a sense that justifies distinguishing compounds as separable and inseparable. Ox-horse is a *chien* (mass sum) made of *t'i*s (unit stuffs). There is no mass product of ox-horse—which seems to be the point of the Neo-Mohist's claim that ox and horse do not "exhaust" or "occupy" each other. They do not, that is, interpenetrate (Canon I:67).

The stuff named by *hard-white*, by contrast, is both white throughout and hard throughout. The two *shih*s (stuffs) are viewed as interpenetrating to form a compound stuff—but in this case, a mass product. That mass which is the intersection of hard-stuff and white-stuff is what is named by the term *hard-white*.

These contrasting accounts of the semantic effects of compounding count as an example of a danger the Neo-Mohists frequently warn against—the danger of assuming that compounding names will always have consistent consequences. Such a rigid view of language would "lead one astray."[33]

The Neo-Mohist semantics seems based on an ontology of stuffs. The ontological substances are all of the same logical type, as contrasted with a substance-attribute ontology or an individual-property ontology. The key elements in the Neo-Mohist ontology are:

1. *T'i:* The fundamental constituent. *T'i* resembles substances (in the commonsense meaning of the term as opposed to the Aristotelian sense). *T'i* are the stuff-kinds of which the world is made. They are corporeal, natural (as opposed to linguistic, social, or conventional), and concrete. Any part of a *t'i* is a *t'i* down to the "starting point" (Canons II:7, I:2). Any sum of parts of a *t'i* is a *t'i* ranging up to the natural kind itself taken as a mereological whole or unit.
2. *Chien:* These are compounds of *t'i* that are ontologically complex. They may, however, be regarded as one. The *t'i* in *chien* exclude each other and are separate in an elementary physical sense.
3. Noncorporeal stuffs that have no specific name: Hard and white are the stock examples. They are however, concrete in the sense that they have a spatiotemporal location.
4. Compounds of (3): These are mass products in which the stuffs interpenetrate. These are also ontologically complex, but not separable. The (3) and (4) should be relative in the same way the *t'i-chien* relation is; hard-white may be a unit in, for instance, hard-white-cold-damp. Are the unnamed (3) and (4) prelinguistic natural kinds as *t'i* are? We have no hint. However, these noncorporeal stuffs seem dependent in a way on *t'i* with which they interpenetrate, or whose space they fill. Intuitively, the pattern of distribution of, say, white depends on the shape, location, and so on of *t'i*—stones, horses, or whatever.[34]

The ox-horse and hard-white semantic doctrines in the Neo-Mohist Canon continue to reflect a "mass-stuff" background ontology. The passages are more intelligible when the ordinary nouns and adjectives used in them are interpreted as singular names of stuffs, as names (individual constants) with scattered, aggregate objects *(shih)* either corporeal or noncorporeal, as the referents.

The White-Horse Paradox

Kung-sun Lung initiates his dialogue with the question, "Is [the sentence] *pai ma fei ma* 白馬非馬 'white-horse not horse' *k'o* 可 'assertable'?" The question is followed by the answer that it is. The dialogue then goes on to a series of objections and answers to the paradoxical thesis. We identify the objector as an opponent from either a commonsense or Neo-Mohist point of view and the answerer as Kung-sun Lung (given the independent evidence that Kung-sun Lung did advocate the position). I will follow Graham[35] in marking the answers and objections by *S* for *sophist* and *O* for *objector* respectively.

The interpretive theory for the text is that Kung-sun Lung, committed to the rigid principle of rectification of names, objected to the two different semantic accounts of modification given by the Neo-Mohists. The sophist states his objection in a logical form, which indicates that he is more inclined to accept the ox-horse than the hard-white analysis of compounding. His choice of one term from each paradigm signals that he advocates a single, strict semantic model of compounding. The model he prefers is the "separable" one—the ox-horse (mass sum) semantics for compounds. The mass sum model preserves the relation of name and thing in a way the mass product model does not. His reported advocacy of separating hard and white is most plausibly his attempt to treat hard-white on the ox-horse model. This interpretation thus explicates the traditional view that Kung-sun Lung was separating white from horse as he was separating hard from white, and also his own reported claim that he was defending a Confucian doctrine—the one-name-one-thing rule of rectification of names. The issue between the Neo-Mohist semantic program and Kung-sun Lung's centers on what is the proper account of the scope, the extension, of compound names.

The motivation for Kung-sun Lung's approach is that compound terms should be explained in ways which do not violate the strict naming relation. If a name has two component terms, the compound name should preserve the relation of the names to their stuffs. Compound terms must *always* be more general (or they must be treated as something other than compound terms). All true compound terms name the sum of the stuffs named by each component term. Hence, white-horse, the example that calls for a decision between the semantic models, should be understood as the mass sum of white-stuff and horse-stuff. The argument for the admissibility of "ox-horse not ox" then carries over to the white-horse case.

The Mohist argument for "ox-horse not ox" concluded only that it was admissible or assertable. Similarly, Kung-sun Lung only insists that "white-horse not horse" is assertable *(k'o)*. One modern analogue that might be helpful in understanding the paradox is to say that for Kung-sun Lung "white-horse not horse" is not analytically false, that is, "white-horse horse" is not analytically true.

The sophist's argument as it emerges from the dialogue takes the form of a dilemma. We must either interpret "white-horse" in a strict sense as a compound conforming to the strict standard for right use of names, or in its ordinary sense. Either way, the argument will yield the conclusion that "white-horse not horse" is admissible.

Suppose we view the problem example according to the paradigm appropriate to the "horse" part. Then white-horse works the same way as ox-horse. That is consistent with the one-name-one-thing rule, but it is different from the ordinary use of the term, and it allows the conclusion that white-horse is not horse by the same argument as that given by the Neo-Mohists (see pp. 151–55).

The other horn of the dilemma is the more complicated one (and the one which is more prominent in the dialogue). It turns on the rigid interpretation of the nature of a name. A name must always pick out the same object. Suppose, then, the other alternative, that "white-horse" has its "commonsense" denotation. What then does "white" name? White-stuff in general? Then "white-horse" must include in its denotation the piece of chalk on my desk. Perhaps "white" in "white-horse" only names the white-stuff that is also horse, and similarly, "horse" as used in the compound "white-horse" only names the horse-stuff that is white. In that case, "horse" in "white-horse" is not *the same name* as "horse" *simpliciter* because it does not name *the same stuff*. Since the names used in the compound are not identifiable with those names used individually, the claim "white-horse not horse" is not necessarily false—it is *k'o* 'assertable'. On Lung's analysis of this second view, white-horse is not ontologically complex—not a compound object made up of two components—but a unique entity with a unique name.

This dilemma seems to structure most of the sophist's replies in the dialogue, but some problems remain. The presentation is often confused by the failure of the sophist to make clear when he has shifted from one to the other horn of the dilemma. Further, specious arguments are scattered among the theoretically illuminating ones. One such argument suggests that since "horse" and "white-horse" can be regarded as "ones" (individuals) and since they are different, they are not identical. This is the argument which lends plausibility to the abstract interpretation. However, as noted above, it can as easily be adapted to a claim about the nonidentity of singular stuffs.

Another well-known argument from the dialogue is also of little help in analyzing the theory behind the paradox. It is a simple and common deductive fallacy. The formal structure of the argument is: A is B; A is not-C; therefore B is not-C. (Yellow-horse is horse; yellow-horse is not white-horse; therefore white-horse is not horse.)[36] I have placed the argument at the end of the dialogue since it contributes nothing to developing the theory behind the dialogue.

Translation and Commentary

In the following translation and commentary, I am essentially following the order proposed by Graham.[37] The sentences are numbered and lettered. The letters represent Graham's order and the numbers the traditional order.

白馬非馬可乎。
曰可
曰何哉
曰馬者所以命形也。白者所以命色也。命色者非命形也。故曰白馬非馬

O. Is it admissible that white-horse is not-horse?
S. It is admissible.
O. Why?
S. "Horse" is used to name shape; "white" is used to name color. What names color is not what names shape. Therefore, I say white-horse is not horse. [A–D/1–4]

This first argument has had considerable attention and analysis. Graham noted that the argument proves only that the white is not horse.

Chmielewski has defended the argument as deductively valid with "white-horse not horse" as the conclusion.[38] Chmielewski assumed that Kung-sun Lung was employing a logic based on the language of mathematical classes. That is to attribute to the sophist a neat and flexible ontology (classes, subclasses, and members) that would normally be taken as a coherent account of the proposition that a white horse *is* a horse. The problems with that interpretation were discussed in chapter 2 (pp. 42–53): Kung-sun Lung seemingly does not distinguish between subclasses and members, nor, on Chmielewski's view, does he allow classes to intersect.[39] Chmielewski does acknowledge that it is a strange logic of classes which does not allow for class intersection. The point ought to be that a theory which does not distinguish between classes and members nor allow intersection of classes is not a logic of mathematical classes at all.[40]

As a consequence of the seeming inadequacy of the first argument, many commentators amend the penultimate sentence on the authority of a Sung Dynasty version of the text to "What names the color *and the shape* is not what names the shape" by adding or substituting the character *hsing* 'shape'. T'an Chieh-fu argues that this makes more sense of the argument.

> To say "that which names the color is not that which names the shape" is to say "that which names white is not that which names horses"—but this hardly needs saying and, having said it, it is neither to the point at issue, nor is it sufficient to support what follows. Therefore, I suspect that *che* 者 is a mistake and here I have corrected it to *hsing* 形 'shape'.[41]

But Graham finds the textual variant on which the suggestion is based of questionable authenticity given contemporary quotations of the same argument:

> But although the variant is very attractive, the standard reading is supported by the summary in the first chapter and its *Hsin Lun* parallel as well as by the quotations of Chang Chan (fl. 370) and Liu Chun (462–521).[42]

The emendation of *che* 者 'that which' to *hsing* 形 'shape' does not render the argument more convincing. It merely makes the third sentence instead of the fourth out of place and implausible. The first two sentences would be irrelevant to the third instead of the first three irrelevant to the fourth.

Something is missing that fills the gap between this first argument and the supposed conclusion. I suggest that it is an argument a semanticist might take as already given, namely, the "ox-horse not ox is acceptable" argument mentioned earlier. A–D/1–4 is the argument for extending that result to the white-horse example. Kung-sun Lung proves, as Graham insisted, only that "some white things are not horses." But that premise triggers the rest of the argument to the conclusion "white-horse not horse." Some white things are not horses, so "white-horse not horse" is assertable.

This is the argument from the first horn of the dilemma. Since *white* names some non-horse, then it does so in the compound name as well. The compound name, on the ox-horse, mass sum model, names all the stuff which is either white-stuff *or* horse-stuff. *White-horse* is, on this analysis, a more "general" term than either *white* or *horse*. It is, accordingly, admissible that white-horse is non-horse because some of the stuff named by the compound is non-horse. The first argument is to the triggering premise in an argument which was already available in ancient Chinese semantic theory.[43]

The argument given by Kung-sun Lung proves only that white is not horse, but that is conceivably all that Kung-sun Lung may have intended. He can now appeal to the analysis of ox-horse. Since white is not horse, then "white-horse not horse" is, in the Mohists' words, "without difficulty." This follows if we accept the first alternative in the dilemma and think of both *white* and *horse* as names with the same reference before and after forming the compound. Then, the sophist insists, we must treat *white-horse* as naming the mass sum of white-stuff and horse-stuff. This is the apparent semantic translation of the claim that "white-horse" is a separable compound. Separable compounds are those which are mass sums.

In the next exchange the objector uses the algebraic inference discussed in chapter 4 to attack the apparently general conclusion that colored horse is non-horse. The sophist's answer seems still to be in the mass sum model. Horses are colored and there is white-horse, and there is horse, but white is not horse and so one may assert of the combination of white and horse that it is non-horse.

曰以馬之有色爲非馬天下非有無色之馬也。天下無馬可乎
曰馬固有色故有白馬。使馬無色有馬如巳耳。安取白馬。故白者非馬也。白馬者馬與白也。馬與白馬也。故曰白馬非馬也

164   *Language and Logic in Ancient China*

> O. If we take horse's having color as non-horse, since there is no colorless horse in the world, is it admissible that there is no horse in the world?
>
> S. Horse certainly has color, which is why there is white-horse. Suppose horse without color, then there would be just horse and where would you find white-horse? The white is not horse. White-horse is white and horse combined. Horse and white is horse, therefore, I say white-horse is non-horse. [E–F/7–8]

In the final sentence, "horse and white is horse" appears to contradict the sophist's intended conclusion, but not if we suppose he is using the mass sum model of compounding. Again, like the Mohists he can accept both "ox-horse is ox" and "ox-horse is non-ox." If Kung-sun Lung is building on that doctrine, then the troublesome phrase is totally consistent with his view. He is not saying "white-horse is horse" is inadmissible, only that "white-horse is non-horse" is equally admissible.

The objector, defending the commonsense view, chooses the other horn of the dilemma. He wants to read "white-horse" in the alternate Mohist model, the "hard-white" model, as naming a mass product. The objector has argued that horse is invariably connected with some color. Similarly, he will argue that white cannot exist independently but always interpenetrating something else, that is, white interpenetrates (is not a *t'i*) and is an "inseparable" part of any compound which contains it.

The mass product model is the one to which Kung-sun Lung must object. It raises problems for someone attracted to the strict view of names implied by the rectification of names—one-name-one-thing. The "hard-white" model generates the other horn of the dilemma. The sophist apparently feels that if hard-white is inseparable, interpenetrates, and has a smaller scope than either component term, then there are two names for what seems to be one stuff. Ox-horse is not one stuff in this sense at all, but two. If we regard hard-white as ontologically complex, its components are not coextensional with the hard and the white. So since "white" in "hard-white" just does not have the same scope as does "white" by itself, it could not be the same name. *Hard-white* must be a name which is, in this sense, independent of *hard* and *white*.

This horn of the dilemma exposes the difficulty of assuming that all words are names. Kung-sun Lung views naming as the sole semantic relation *and* sticks to a rigid version of the account of the naming relation. Those in his tradition had difficulty refuting him, supposedly, because the name-thing paradigm was so well entrenched. The strict account of names seemed plausible *and* in accord with the Confucian doctrine of rectification of names.[44]

The Mohists, not overly concerned with the strict requirements of the rectification of names, were not bothered by different kinds of compounds. Kung-sun Lung was, and thus tried to separate hard and white, to show that they were not a unity but ultimately two things even when combined.

The objector notes that Kung-sun Lung's answer mixed the two models by talking about white horses with the "commonsense" mass product extension while arguing that the words should have the mass sum extension. So his argument for the paradox is incoherent. The sophist's answer seems to shift to the second horn of the dilemma.

曰馬未與白爲白馬。白未與馬爲白。合「馬」與「白」復名「白馬」是相與以不相與爲名未可。故曰「白馬非馬」未可

曰「白」者不定所白。忘之而可也。「白馬」者言白定所白也。定所白者非「白」也。「馬」者無去取於色。故黃黑皆所以應。「白馬」者有去取於色。黃黑馬皆所以色去。故唯白馬獨可以應耳。無去者非有去也。故曰「白馬非馬」

O. If it is horse not yet combined with white which you deem horse, and white not yet combined with horse which you deem white, to compound the name "white-horse" for horse and white joined together is to give them when combined their names when uncombined, which is inadmissible. Therefore I say: it is inadmissible that white-horse is not horse.

S. "White" does not fix anything as white; that may be left out of account. "White-horse" says "white" fixes something as white. What fixes something as white is not white. "Horse" neither selects nor excludes any colors and, therefore, it can be answered with either yellow or black. "White-horse" selects some color and excludes others, and the yellow and black are both excluded on grounds of color; therefore, one may answer it only with white-horse. What excludes none is not what excludes some. Therefore I say: white-horse is not horse. [G-H/9-14]

In allowing there is white-horse, the sophist, according to the objector, has violated his own principle. He has used the name *white* (in the compound *white-horse*) to name white in combination with something. The sophist replies that, in effect, the compound *white-horse* does not contain the name *white* or the name *horse*. The name *white* in the compound *white-horse* "fixes" something as white, that is, has only horses in its range, and what "fixes" something as white is not the name *white*. A similar argument is suggested for the name *horse* in *white-horse*; since *horse* in *white-horse* "selects and excludes colors," that is, includes in its range only white horses, it is not identical with the uncombined name *horse*.

Kung-sun Lung's name-centered position is that the name *white-horse* cannot be regarded as consisting of the names *white* and *horse*. It is, like *palomino*, an independent name for only that thing. The only way available for talking about names is via the object referred to, and since the referents of the "names" are different, they cannot be the same names.

The objector uses a phrase, *combined with*, which is the term used in the Neo-Mohist Canon for interpenetrating compounds (相與). Whether the objector is using the Mohist view or just formulating a commonsense view, he continues to hold that the combination is one of the interpenetration, mass product type. In the next exchange, the objector again uses algebraic inference against Kung-sun Lung, adding *yu* 有 'have' to his equation.

> 曰「有白馬」不可謂「無馬」也。不可謂「無馬」者有馬也。「有白馬」爲「有馬」白之非馬何也。

O. Having white-horse cannot be called "not having horse." What cannot be called "not having horse" is having horse. Since having white-horse is deemed having horse, why claim that if white it is not horse? [I/5]

> 曰以「有白馬」爲「有馬」謂「有白馬」爲「有黃馬」可乎
> 曰未可
> 曰以「有馬」爲異「有黃馬」是異黃馬於馬也。異黃馬於馬是以黃馬爲非馬也。以黃馬爲非馬而以白馬爲有馬此飛者入池棺槨異。處此天下之悖言亂辭也。

S. If you deem having white-horse as having horse, is it admissible to say that having white-horse is deemed having yellow-horse?
O. No.
S. To deem having horse as different from having yellow-horse is to distinguish yellow-horse from horse. To distinguish yellow-horse from horse is to deem yellow-horse as non-horse. To deem yellow-horse as non-horse and yet claim that white-horse is having horse, this is like flying underwater and saying the two parts of a coffin are in different places—it is the most perverse doctrine and confused phrase under heaven. [L-N/10-12]

The sophist's response to the objector looks frivolous. There might be a serious point at issue here, however. Perhaps the objector really is a skilled Mohist dialectician, and the sophist is taking a veiled dig at one of the Mohist positions—the "killing thieves is not killing men" argument. The progression of question and answer is too imprecise to be sure. As it stands, the sophist's first question has nothing to do with his subsequent accusation. The objector "distinguishes," reasonably enough on his grounds, white-horse and yellow-horse. Kung-sun Lung assumes that he has admitted that having yellow-horse is different from having horse. Thus he presents the identity argument discussed above: because yellow-horse (or white-horse) can be distinguished from horse, it is not horse.

The objector seems here to turn back to the first horn of Kung-sun Lung's dilemma, seemingly to argue that the dilemma faces the sophist as well. He cannot consistently formulate either horn of the dilemma without shifting between the two accounts of how names work. He addresses Kung-sun Lung as a *li che* 離者 'one who separates' (supposedly, hard and white). *Li che* are those who hold that all compound names represent combinations of the ox-horse type and are, therefore, separable. But as we saw in the Canon and in the sophist's own earlier answer (pp. 163–64), one can still say that white-horse is horse. It must therfore be assertable that he has horse if he has white-horse. It is, to be sure, also assertable that he has non-horse, but it is not assertable that he does *not* have horse.

> 曰有白馬不可謂無馬者離白之謂也。不離者有白馬不可謂有馬也。故所以為有馬者獨馬為有馬耳。非有白馬為有馬。故其為有馬也不可以謂馬馬也。

> O. Even those who hold that white is separable [i.e., like ox-horse in combinations] say "having white horse" is "having horse," [since having the sum is having the parts]. If you do not separate white, you say that "having white horse" cannot be called "having horse." So what is used to constitute "having horse" is exclusively deeming horse as "having horse" and he denies that "having white horse" is "having horse." So in his use of "having horse," he cannot call horse "horse." [K/13]

The objection does seem to assume a lot of common ground with Neo-Mohist semantic theory. The Mohists directed their arguments about hard-white against a doctrine of separation. Kung-sun Lung was known as one who separated hard and white. The Mohist doctrine is that hard-white is different from ox-horse in that no matter where you go in the combination you will find both—they cease to have separate identity. Ox-horse, on the other hand, is "separable," and in part of the mass named by the compound you will come upon non-horse and non-ox. Thus one can say "Ox-horse is not horse." But even for ox-horse, you must also say that if there is ox-horse there is horse (because part of it is horse). You can also say there is non-horse, but that does not deny that there is horse. The objector has made the sophist contradict one of his principles in the separation thesis and deny that there being white-horse, there is horse—which, he justifiably argues, should be true even for those who hold the doctrine of *li pai* 'separation of white'. But this advocate of separation denies even that. So he must deny that having anything but pure (i.e., uncolored) horse can be called "having horse." Since by his earlier admission (F/8, pp. 163–64) that there is no uncolored horse, he cannot even call horse "horse."

Kung-sun Lung's second argument, based as it is on the assumption that all words are strict names, has forced him to an untenable ontology. White-horse must be treated as ontologically simple, and he must deny that the world contains horse at all—since he acknowledges that all horse is colored. This is potentially disastrous for him since he would be forced by a similar argument (adding another adjective like, e.g., *wild*) to deny that there is white-horse or yellow-horse either, and so on ad infinitum. Kung-sun Lung is open to the objector's last criticism because of his use of the second horn of the dilemma, according to which compounds like *white-horse* are to be understood as names of unique entities—having no relations to entities named by the parts of the compound. That account would make learning a language take forever. Every modified noun would have to be separately learned by ostension.

The sophist's final reply does not really attempt to salvage his position. It seems designed merely to confuse his opponent. This is the deductive fallacy discussed on page 161 and is most charitably regarded as an act of desperation.

> 曰求馬黃黑馬皆可致。求白馬黃黑馬不可致。使白馬乃馬也是所求一也。所求一者白者不異馬也。所求不異如黃黑馬有可有不可何也。可與不可其相非明。故黃黑馬一也。而可以應有馬而不可以應有白馬。是白馬之非馬審矣
>
> S. If someone seeks horse, yellow- or black-horse will suffice. In seeking white-horse, yellow- or black-horse will not suffice. If one makes white-horse horse this is to make what is sought identical. If

what was sought was identical then white (stuff) would not be different from horse (stuff). If what is sought is not different then such as yellow and black are both admissible and not admissible—how can this be? Admissible and not admissible are clearly mutually incompatible. So yellow- or black-horse is one and it can correspond to having horse but it cannot correspond to having white horse. This is the explication of white-horse's being non-horse. [J/6]

Probably the nicest thing we can say about this argument is that it may be taken as an attempt to justify the relatively trivial "identity" interpretation of the paradox: "white-horse" is not identical with "horse." As I note on page 161, this argument is the most often quoted one from the dialogue, and it seems to me the least helpful in understanding the theoretical position.

Ignoring the desperate final shot, the dialogue leaves us with two positions for Kung-sun Lung. The first arguments and the objector's later response indicate that Kung-sun Lung wants to "separate" white and horse in a way that changes the ordinary "scope" of the name *white-horse*, that is, to make it the sum of the masses named by *white* and *horse*. This makes the position one which explains the criticism by other philosophers from pre-Han times (e.g., Hsün-tzu and K'ung Ch'uan) who took the issue to be one of the generality of names in combination. It also explains Kung-sun Lung's reputation as one who separates hard-white.

But the sophist is pushed to other arguments that suggest a different theory. They indicate that he wanted not so much to separate "white-horse" as to insist that it had no semantic relations to "white" or "horse" used alone. These "names" used alone could name nothing at all, as the objector notes. The sophist's position commits him to an ontology that excludes horses and a semantics that makes learning a language unmanageable.

Kung-sun Lung correctly senses that there is a problem with the Neo-Mohist account of compounding, but he is even more committed than the Mohists to the key error, namely, regarding all terms as names. The Neo-Mohists were pushed by their accounts of commonsense use of language to deny that there was any strict relation between language and world—and to affirm, rather, that it shifted and changed with context. Kung-sun Lung wanted to make what the Mohists regarded as unreliable names into strict names which followed the one-name-one-thing formula.

Both the sophist's proposals are designed to satisfy that formula. The problem is that on the first proposal, we may only intelligibly talk about the things for which there are characters (names), and compound terms (including modified nouns) can denote only sums of those things. On the second proposal, as the objector points out, the character *ma* 馬 'horse' will name nothing at all since all actual horse is colored.

Overview of the Theoretical Interpretation of White-Horse

This account was not, as the abstract accounts usually are, intended as a vindication of Kung-sun Lung. Indeed the perspective of the interpretation given here is that his argument for the paradox is faulty. Further, there was a more adequate treatment of the questions which motivated the paradox in the Neo-Mohist semantic program. Still the interpretation does provide an account of a line of thought which could reasonably have shaped a rationale for the strange conclusion. That line of thought is both linked to other major approaches to the philosophy of language and reflected in the dialogue itself. We can understand why no one was convinced and also why it was so hard to refute Kung-sun Lung, given Chinese assumptions about language. The assumption that all words are names was very well entrenched, and the strict rectification of names model seemed vitally important to, at least, the Confucian moral-political theory.

There is no appeal in the dialogue to considerations that reflect any interest in abstract repeatable entities or in a theory of meaning that links meaning to abstract ideas in the mind. There is, finally, no reason from consideration of this paradox and the dialogue that accompanies it to suppose that any philosophical system of China postulated the existence of abstract or mental objects of the sort characteristic of the Western tradition in philosophy.

The inverted pyramid of argument for the view that there is no abstraction in classical Chinese philosophy has reached its apex. We saw in chapter 1 that a radically nominalist interpretation had promise as an explanation of the differences between Chinese and Western thought, and further that the hypothesis could itself be explained by a fundamental difference in the logic of Chinese nouns. The application of this and related assumptions to the various schools of traditional Chinese thought did produce more philosophically satisfying and coherent interpretations of the general direction of Chinese philosophy. Then the extensive nonabstract semantic theory of the Neo-Mohists was outlined and used as a background to yield the motivation for the white-horse dialogue. That framework produced a more coherent and intelligible account of the most commonly cited counterexample to the claim that Chinese thought did not generate theories about abstract or mental entities.

The absence of such theories does not imply that there was any inadequacy in the Chinese language which made expressing such theories either difficult or impossible. Later, in fact, similar theories as part of Buddhism were introduced into China. Predictably, their appeal was not very strong, and the more phenomenal schools did not fare as well in China as did those whose doctrines could fit better into the mold of the Taoist presuppositions of language.

Things are changed to a degree by the introduction of Buddhism. A different model of mind and knowledge is introduced and with that a conflicting account of the relation of both with language. This alters even the way in which one would talk about the conventionality of language. But Chinese philosophy continues to be holistic in ways that reflect the mass-noun-like grammar of Chinese. That language has a regulative or practical role and that mind is conditioned by language remain crucial presuppositions in all of Chinese philosophy up to and including the thought of Mao Tse-tung.

Notes

Chapter 1

1. Richard Grandy, "Reference, Meaning, and Belief," *Journal of Philosophy* 70, no. 14 (August 16, 1973):443. Credit is due my colleague, Philip Kitcher, for bringing to my attention and vigorously championing this principle of translation.
2. Derk Bodde, *China's First Unifier* (Hong Kong: Hong Kong University Press, 1967), p. 228. I do not mean to suggest that Bodde has used the special logic retort in making these observations, only that they are the kinds of observations to which the retort might appeal.
3. Plato, *The Republic*, b. 2, pp. 514*A*–521*B*.
4. René Descartes, *Meditations* III.
5. Hajime Nakamura, *The Ways of Thinking of Eastern Peoples* (Tokyo: Japanese National Commission for UNESCO, Tokyo Japanese Government Publications, 1960), p. 177.
6. Classical Chinese, if formalized, has elements which would trigger a full tense logic despite the absence of a system of an inflection based on time.
7. The failure of the inferences does show that the translation is, to that degree, wrong. In effect any inconsistency arising from these kinds of divergences is an inconsistency in the translating theory, not in the text being translated.
8. Chang Tung-sun, "A Chinese Philosopher's Theory of Knowledge," in *Our Language and Our World*, ed. S. I. Hayakawa (New York: Harper and Bros., 1959), p. 304.
9. See Y. R. Chao, "How Chinese Logic Operates," *Anthropological Linguistics* 1, no. 1 (1959):1–8, and "Notes on Chinese Grammar and Logic," *Philosophy East and West* 5, no. 2 (July, 1955):167–68. Graham notes that Luan Tiao-fu has proposed a particularly natural way to translate the propositional forms.
10. It is notorious that syllogism does not account for mathematical reasoning and that the model of the latter produced the modern revolution in logic. But long

before that it was recognized that there are many more "ordinary" inferences that could not be cast in syllogistic form. Interestingly enough, the most common example, "A horse is an animal therefore the head of a horse is the head of an animal," is very close in structure to the type of argument that the Neo-Mohist logic *could* countenance (see chap. 5, pp. 170–71).

11. There is an idiomatic use of implication that allows the falsity of the consequence to imply the falsity of the antecedent, such as "If . . . then I'm a monkey's uncle."

12. Anyone familiar with the work of W. V. O. Quine will, of course, recognize this argument. Quine holds that in any translation manual of a language, classical propositional logical truths (tautologies) must be preserved. I am after a broader point. It is not that I object to nonclassical logics or even deviant logics as possibilities for interpretation. But I regard as absurd the claim that we can engage in translation with *no* prior logical commitment or with a commitment to some "Chinese logic" that remains undefined except for being inconsistent. (I do think classical logics work perfectly well for Chinese despite Chuang-tzu's toying with denying the law of excluded middle.) Standard negation is required to compensate for the absence of an overt and distinctly disjunctive sentential connective. Disjunction is usually accomplished by implication plus negation—including double negation.

13. Janusz Chmielewski, "Notes on Early Chinese Logic I," *Rocznik Orientalistyczny* 26, no. 1 (1962):8.

14. Ibid., p. 7.

15. Chmielewski, "Notes on Early Chinese Logic II," *Rocznik Orientalistyczny* 26, no. 2 (1963):103.

16. Chmielewski, "Notes I."

17. A. C. Graham, "Two Dialogues in the *Kung-sun Lung-tzu*," *Asia Major*, n.s., 11, pt. 2 (1965):142–43.

18. Chung-ying Cheng, "Inquiries into Classical Chinese Logic," *Philosophy East and West* 15 (July–October, 1965):200.

19. Ibid., p. 21.

20. Chung-ying Cheng, "Logic and Language in Chinese Thought," in *Contemporary Philosophy*, ed. Raymond Klibansky, vol. 3 (Florence: La Nuova Italia, 1969), p. 338 n.

21. Notice that I am not claiming that such considerations are illegitimate, but that there is no reason for them simply to override considerations of coherence and intelligibility when these are in conflict. Ultimately which ought to override depends on a higher level theory of the text. If we hold that it is a text of poetry, then the poetic consideration can dominate, but if we hold that the texts are philosophical, then the *ceteris paribus* coherence considerations should dominate.

22. The interpretive conflict over lines 3–6 in chapter 1 of the Wang-Pi edition of the *Tao Te Ching* has been argued in such terms. Peter Boodberg, "Philosophical Notes on Chapter I of the *Lao-tzu*" (*Harvard Journal of Asiatic Studies* 20:598–618) has argued that one punctuation yields a more philosophically interesting and coherent reading of the chapter; the other makes the sentences more "balanced" or more "natural." What the latter really does is to render

the chapter internally incoherent and in some conflict with the work's opposition to desires. Among English translators, only Duyvendak and Bodde's translation of Fung Yu-lan's *History of Chinese Philosophy* (Princeton: Princeton University Press, 1952) have followed the "philosophically interesting" punctuation, while contemporary Chinese commentators seem about evenly split between the two punctuations. The dispute is now complicated by the discovery of a Legalist version of the text from the Han Dynasty, which cuts the traditional text, burying the first chapter in the middle, and adds grammatical particles that impose still a third punctuation. The methodological presumptions of scholars can be exposed quite neatly by observing what conclusion they draw when forced to choose between a stylistically balanced and a philosophically interesting version of the same lines.
23. Hurlee G. Creel, *Sinicism* (Chicago: Open Court, 1929), p. 2. Professor Creel informs me that he has repudiated this work, but I do not know if it is for this expression of attitude or because of other more mundane errors.
24. Ibid., p. 21. I am quite sure Professor Creel would repudiate this part.

Chapter 2

1. I borrow this term from Wilfrid Sellars, *Science, Perception, and Reality* (London: Routledge and Kegan Paul, 1963), especially his essay, "Empiricism and the Philosophy of Mind." Other well-known modern nominalists include W. V. O. Quine, especially in *Word and Object* (Cambridge, Mass.: MIT Press, 1960), and Nelson Goodman, *The Structure of Appearance* (Cambridge, Mass.: Harvard University Press, 1951). I am tempted to find strong similarities between modern nominalism and the Chinese version, but of course the ways of expressing the view differ radically. This is because Western nominalism can be much more explicit and clear about its orientation. It has a large and influential abstract and mentalistic tradition against which it is reacting and against which it can highlight its disagreements. It also has a powerful logical and formal apparatus to argue for and detail its perspective. Chinese nominalism, if I am right, was not a philosophical position against abstractions and mentalism, but just a tradition that never was even grammatically tempted to conceive of a world of abstract objects.
2. Mei Tsu-lin, "Chinese Grammar and the Linguistic Movement," *Review of Metaphysics* 14 (1961):459, made a similar observation regarding modern Chinese nouns. He was not arguing for an interpretive hypothesis about Chinese thought but criticizing Western analytic philosophy of language for overgeneralizing its own grammar.
3. This suggests that demonstratives "localize" the stuff enough to require dividing the stuff into units, while the free-standing noun can be viewed as the name of an aggregate, scattered object. In modern Mandarin a noun with no modifiers functions roughly like a definite description, while in Cantonese the measure alone precedes the noun for definite description.
4. See page 137 for puzzles involving "*erh* 'two' *ma* 'horse' *ma* 'horse' *yeh* (particle)."

5. Nouns regularly functioned alone or with only generic modification as terms. But there must have been a rudimentary individuating principle in such nouns to allow number modification. This individuating principle functions when modified by numbers and perhaps when modified by demonstratives (although cases of 'demonstrative + noun' where the context indicates the noun could be plural are fairly common). We may consider them mass nouns in that they could be associated with a range of individuating or counting conventions though perhaps with a default principle built in. Some linguists have suggested that even English nouns may be so construed. See Richard Garvey, "Does English have only Mass Nouns?" (Paper presented at Western Division American Philosophical Association, Chicago, Ill., December, 1978).

6. W. A. C. H. Dobson, *Late Archaic Chinese* (Toronto: University of Toronto Press, 1959), pp. 21–22. This is as complete a treatment of the problem of the logic of nouns as I have found in any grammar—and it is in a footnote! I think failure to understand the logic of Chinese nouns is one of the fundamental reasons for the difficulty in explaining the conceptual scheme behind Chinese philosophy.

7. *Ming* in fact includes all words including quantifiers. Chinese semantics distinguishes between *shih* 'reality' *ming* 'names' 實名 and *hsü* 'empty' *ming* 'names' 虛名. The former seemingly include adjectives and verbs and the latter grammatical particles. Adjectives can be seen as names, because like nouns they have a range of denotation which could be thought of as a stuff of which the adjective were the name. There were grammatical differences between nouns and adjectives (e.g., the use of *yeh* [particle] and *fei* [negative] 非, but the differences are not as pronounced as in English, and the term-predicate structure is not as forcefully imposed on users of the language. The upshot is that the differences were ignored and semantic problems were discussed on the assumption that all terms that introduce mapping onto the world in a sentence are considered stuff-names.

8. Note that *substance* is not being used in the sense of substratum, but roughly like *stuff*. Even that is a little strong. *Ma* 'horse' functions in ways which are close to, for instance, livestock. "Stuff" is, however, the broadest way of characterizing the reality element of this picture, and I use it throughout the exposition with only slight reservations.

9. Unlike count nouns, mass nouns do not require a principle of individuation across possible worlds, but like count nouns and unlike adjectives, they do carry a principle of identity across worlds. Adjectives in Chinese can stand alone as sentences. Mass nouns (nouns in general) must minimally be followed by the particle *yeh* 也.

10. The modal fallacy is deliberate. I think it underlies both the Western and Indian versions of skepticism and ontological aversion to change. See also chapter 3, pages 66–72 for more detail on this topic.

11. Classic statements of this view can be found in F. S. C. Northrop, *The Meeting of East and West* (New York: Macmillan Co., 1953), e.g., p. 340; and in Liou Kia-hway, "The Configuration of Chinese Reasoning," *Diogenes* (Montreal), no. 49 (Spring, 1965):75, and Nakamura, *Eastern Peoples*, p. 185.

12. If one's semantic theory involves a commitment to abstract objects, no doubt sometimes that theory would assign such objects to certain uses of Chinese graphs.
13. The character *hsing* 'nature', which is used for translation of abstract inflections in modern Chinese, was used (though probably without graphic variation from *sheng* 'life') in classical Chinese. It was not, however, a grammatical inflection, but a theoretical term used mainly in psychological theories. Of course, one could argue that the psychological theories were about abstract entities, but that would not follow merely from the use of that graph after nouns denoting animal species.
14. *Kung-sun Lung-tzu,* "Dialogue on Hard-White."
15. It can, of course, be objected that the Chinese philosopher might not have seen this mistake. But unless there is independent evidence that the philosopher is talking about abstract objects, we must conclude that this is the translator's mistake—especially in cases like this example, where this sentence is cited as the key evidence that there was theoretical talk about abstract objects. If the best evidence available that a philosopher was talking about abstract objects is a sentence that turns out to be false when interpreted as being about abstract objects, then there is no reason to saddle the philosopher with being mistaken about the nature of abstract objects (or, in the case of Kung-sun Lung, about the nature of sets, properties, etc.).
16. This argument is limited to denying the plausibility of interpreting single terms of predicate graphs as referring to abstract objects. I am not committed to any conclusion about how to interpret such constructions as "*ta* 'great'-*hsiao* 'small'" or "*yu* 'have'-*wu* 'lacks'" nor to the correct interpretation of numbers, or normative qualities like *te* 'virtue' or *jen* 'benevolence'. I am denying that ordinary descriptive terms and predicates ever require abstract interpretation. I do allow that translation into English abstract terms is often the more stylistically satisfactory rendering. But in such cases I would argue that since the semantics of abstract terms in English is far from being settled, we can regard the English translation itself as equivalent to one of the other alternatives discussed above.
17. Henry Rosemont, Jr., "On Representing Abstraction in Archaic Chinese," *Philosophy East and West* 24, no. 1 (January, 1970):71–89, argues against basing any claims about the inability of Chinese to represent abstractions on features of classical literary Chinese. The literary or written language, he argued, was probably *never* a natural spoken language. The natural language may have had grammatical forms not reflected in the abbreviated analytic literary structure. Since the present account is not that Chinese were unable to represent abstractions (whatever that could mean) but that, in the Wittgensteinian spirit, they were not puzzled by their grammar in ways that would have motivated philosophical theorizing about abstractions, Rosemont's hypothesis does not count against this argument. In fact, one plausible reading of his "uniqueness" thesis would add support to the present account. Assuming that literary Chinese began as esoteric religious symbolism and evolved into a general secularized means of communication, it is plausible to suggest that the

grammatical features it picks up in its historical development reflect grammatical possibilities of the natural language. Thus the gradual addition of measures or sortals to the literary language plausibly reflects a feature of natural Chinese languages in ancient as in modern times. I do not mean to endorse Rosemont's uniqueness hypothesis (I do not know how the claim that any particular language is not a "natural" language could be tested), but to note that the hypothesis that Chinese nouns are assimilable to mass nouns is helped rather than contradicted by his thesis if true.

18. This philosophical difference is related to the frequent observation that there was no mind-body dualism in Chinese philosophy. That is true, but the issue is much more subtle and the implications more far-reaching than that simple observation suggests. This is a case in point where one feels that we need to move from mere cataloguing of differences to explanations, from descriptive to explanatory accounts. Given the pervasiveness of the mind-body problem in Western thought and its centrality to a wide range of philosophical issues, if the Western student of philosophy is merely told that there is no such concern—period—his response is likely to be to dismiss Chinese thought as uninteresting. What is required is some account of how the rationales leading to a particular formulation of a mind-body dualism fail to get off the ground given the conceptual framework of Chinese. That is part of the goal of this analysis.

19. This is a classic explanation of Platonism, but there is some legitimate doubt about whether or not Plato actually appealed primarily to such an argument in his own theory. See Alexander Nehamas, "Confusing Universals and Particulars in Plato's Early Dialogues," *Review of Metaphysics* 29 (December, 1975):287–306.

20. We should remember that Chinese philosophers, lacking a clear use-mention convention, are likely to regard such nominal uses as very general names—referring respectively to what exists and what does not exist. There is no hint that they thought of such terms as referring to entities in some transcendental abstract realm.

21. The particle *yeh* 也, an assertion marker, functions to distinguish this relation from genuine predicate use of what are normally nominal graphs. The role of *yeh* 也 was easily ignored by Chinese theorists since it was also optional after predicate expression, in which case the translation convention seems to be to identify it with the idle modal operator "It is the case that." *Yeh* 也 has a host of other functions (which are still not well understood). Graham has noted that the semantic theorists seemed totally to overlook its functional role and thus to ignore the distinction between terms and predicates (including adjectives).

22. *Mo-tzu*, "Hsiao Ch'ü."

23. Later tradition (but apparently not the Neo-Mohists) distinguished between "empty names" (虛名) and "stuff names" (實名). But even that did not separate nouns from adjectives. In that scheme *yeh* 也 would be an empty name, and *white*, *hard*, and *horse* would be stuff names.

24. In what seems like their later, more mature works they focused a good deal more on relational sentences (*ts'u* 辭). But they never produced any theory of the structure of a sentence as they did for the structure of a compound term.

25. The characterization of Chinese as pictographic or ideographic is under nearly constant attack from Chinese linguists who seem to prefer the term *logographic*. It is hard to understand the passion and intensity of their arguments on the choice of a word to denote a range of languages that includes exactly one! In any case, we need not find any way to resolve the issue. What is important for the present argument is that Chinese themselves view their own written language as conventional representations of the semantic content, that is, pictures or diagrams. The written forms of the pre-Han period were even more "picturelike" than is the regularized modern (post-Han) script. In fact, the vast majority of Chinese characters have phonetic components. But Chinese etymologies tend to interpret these ideographically too, and with some justification. There is usually a range of choices of phonetics available for a particular use, and the choice of the phonetic component probably does reflect semantic concerns as well as phonetic ones.
26. Actually, a great many characters have a range of alternate one-syllable pronunciations depending on the characters' use. This (and other phenomena like rhyme schemes, character borrowing, and phonetic character construction) has led to speculation that in the very early history of the language some characters might have been bisyllabic or at least have involved consonant clusters of much greater complexity than in dialects of modern Chinese.
27. Chinese languages in archaic times, as at present, differed not only in pronunciation but in grammar and idiom. These differences tended to show up as discernible differences in written style.
28. Aristotle, *De Interpretatione*, 1:16,3,3.
29. John Locke, *An Essay Concerning Human Understanding*, bk. 3, chap. 1, sec. 3.
30. *I* 意 'ideas' are present in other contexts in Chinese thought, such as in the explanation of invention, creation, and action. This present disclaimer is limited to denying only the representationalist semantic role of ideas. For a more detailed discussion see pages 110–20.
31. See pages 106–10.
32. Jowlett, B., trans., *Dialogues of Plato*, vol. 1 (New York: Random House, 1937), pp. 179–80.
33. Locke, *Essay Concerning Human Understanding*, bk. 3, chap. 2, sec. 6.
34. Illiterate Chinese speakers can use the latter method and may also employ other techniques to specify which word (character) they mean—they use the phrase "the X of XY."
35. In fact, the puzzle about learning is identical in both stories. Our ability to acquire discriminatory skills adequate to learn a language is what needs to be explained. What is hard for us to acknowledge, given our commonsense commitment to mental abstract ideas, is that the detour through ideas doesn't explain that ability at all. It merely pushes the puzzle to a different level. See Wittgenstein's *The Blue and Brown Books* (New York: Harper and Row, 1958) and Jonathan Bennett, *Locke, Berkeley, Hume: Some Common Themes* (London: Oxford University Press, 1971), for discussions of the problem of learning how to discriminate and classify.
36. Nakamura, *Eastern Peoples*, pp. 178–79.

37. Notice that none of this argument is based on an East-West dichotomy in thought. For my purposes it is significant that Indian philosophy is almost exactly like Western philosophy in its universal acceptance of a representationalist and antiphysical mind, ideas, meanings, and so on.

Chapter 3

1. Graham suggests that the closest counterpart of genus-species form for a definition is an analogy-difference structure. A. C. Graham, *Later Mohist Logic, Ethics, and Science* (Hong Kong: Chinese University Press, 1978).
2. David Nivison, "'Knowledge' and 'Action' in Chinese Thought Since Wang Yang-ming," in *Studies in Chinese Thought*, ed. A. F. Wright (Chicago: University of Chicago Press, 1953), p. 115.
3. Herbert Fingarette, *Confucius—The Secular As Sacred* (New York: Harper and Row, 1972).
4. Chang Tung-sun, "A Chinese Philosopher's Theory of Knowledge," *Etc.* 9 (1952):208.
5. Fingarette, *Confucius*, p. vii.
6. Donald Munro, *The Concept of Man in Early China* (Stanford: Stanford University Press, 1969), p. 55.
7. D. C. Lau, *Lao-tzu: The Tao Te Ching* (London: Penguin, 1963), chap. 32.
8. Wing-tsit Chan, ed., *A Source Book in Chinese Philosophy* (Princeton: Princeton University Press, 1963), p. 156.
9. In anticipation of the views of the Taoists, one should perhaps refer to a name-world or name-reality distinction since the *Tao* includes *wu* 'what there is not' as well as *yu* 'what there is'. Having acknowledged the possibility of misunderstanding here, I shall continue to speak of the world, the universe, or reality so as not to overmystify what I say at this point.
10. Hsün-tzu is, I believe, more the influenced than the influencer relative to the Neo-Mohist semantic theories. I shall, therefore, consider him in the Confucian section and only those of his views that I regard as continuous with the Confucian outlook. I do not place the *Tao Te Ching* first to imply that it is chronologically earliest (which I doubt), but because I believe it exemplifies the presuppositions of language in something close to a classical sense. It is illuminating, therefore, to view Taoism and Taoist skepticism-nihilism as the impetus for Chinese philosophizing, though of course the *Tao Te Ching* might not directly have influenced, for example, Confucius or Mencius.
11. For convenience here, I shall speak of Lao-tzu as if there were such a person and he wrote the *Tao Te Ching*.
12. The syntax of classical Chinese knowledge claims does not suggest that knowledge has a proposition as an object, but rather the assignment of a language division to an object: that is, X knows S's being P rather than X knows *that* S is P. See pages 63–65.
13. *Chuang-tzu*, chap. 33 (Ssu Pu Pei Yao edition [SPPY] 10:17B) (reporting the view of the early Taoist Shen Tao). One of the notable differences between the

Lao-tzu and the *Chuang-tzu* is that *Chuang-tzu* is more explicit about the application of relativism to the self-other distinction than is the *Lao-tzu*.

14. *Tao Te Ching*, chap. 64. In *A Source Book in Chinese Philosophy*, ed. Wing-tsit Chan (Princeton: Princeton University Press, 1963). For the convenience of those using translations I shall give chapters of Chinese classics rather than SPPY locations. Where I have taken over a translation without change, I shall name the translator in parentheses.
15. Ibid., chap. 71.
16. Ibid., chap. 81 (Chan).
17. In fact, negative knowledge is a variety of conventional knowledge. We become aware that there are *tao*s—systems of naming, discrimination, desiring, acting—only by learning to speak the Taoist's language, that is, learning to distinguish name-induced desires from "natural" ones in an appropriate way. We thus learn to disvalue the conventional systems.
18. *Tao Te Ching*, chap. 56 (Chan).
19. Ibid., chap. 20 (Chan).
20. Ibid., chap. 2.
21. Ibid., chap. 14 (Chan).
22. Ibid., chap. 32 (Lau).
23. Ibid., chap. 1.
24. Ibid., chaps. 18–19 (Chan).
25. Ibid., chap. 12 (Chan).
26. Ibid., chap. 37 (Lau).
27. Sometimes "rectification of names" means no more than "tell the truth" or "promise only what you can deliver."
28. This anomaly has led some to doubt the authenticity of the doctrine. See Hurlee Creel, *Confucius, The Man and the Myth* (New York: John Day, 1949) and Joseph Needham, *Science and Civilization in China*, vol. 2 (London: Cambridge University Press, 1956), p. 9. Professor David Nivison has remarked to me that the idiom in the passage is distinctly pre-Mencian. My own view is that the rectification of names can be regarded as a genuine Confucian teaching *in the sense that* without it, the ethical system of Confucius would be considerably less coherent. (See my "Freedom and Moral Responsibility in Confucian Ethics," *Philosophy East and West* 22, no. 2 [April, 1972]:169–86.) Thus the theory of language in the doctrine is coherent with the larger ethical-political doctrines of Confucius, and the passage may be taken as a reliable account of the underlying or actual theory of names of the school whether or not Confucius was astute enough to have formulated it.
29. *Analects*, 13:3 (Chan).
30. Ibid., 12:17 (Chan).
31. Ibid., 12:11. There is an interpretation of this passage that could make it an example of rectification of names in the primary sense. It involves the hypothesis that Duke Ching misunderstands (deliberately or subconsciously) Confucius's proposal that the duke should rectify names. Then the series of noun-noun sentences Confucius utters should be read as verb-object (with a "mention-verb," see pp. 43–44) rather than subject-verb sentences; for exam-

ple, *fu-fu* 父父 'father-father' should be read as "apply the name *father* to fathers (and treat them as such)."
32. Few scholars take this tradition, which stems from Mencius, seriously as history, but it does illustrate the philosophical presuppositions of rectification of names.
33. Hu Shih, *History of Ancient Chinese Philosophy* (Taipei: Commercial Press, 1968), pp. 97-98.
34. *Kung Yang Commentary*, SPPY 1:4B-3-5A-8.
35. *Luxurious Gems of the Spring and Autumn Annals*, chap. 3 (Chan).
36. *Mencius*, 1B:8 (Chan).
37. *Analects*, 13:18.
38. *Mencius*, 4A:17.
39. *Mo-tzu*, SPPY 11:6B-10-12.
40. For more detail on the Mohist solution see pages 124-37. Briefly, they, by contrast, free names for their normal descriptive use, but build evaluation into the phrases and then drive a wedge between term meaning and phrase meaning.
41. Hu Shih, *The Development of Logical Method in Ancient China* (New York: Paragon Press, 1969), p. 27.
42. *Analects*, 12:13 (Chan).
43. Ibid., 13:3.
44. *Hsün-tzu*, chapter 22, "On Rectification of Names" (Chan).
45. Ibid. (Chan).
46. Objective or absolute justifications of "realist" traditionalism are available by making maximizing survival and effectiveness the test of *the correct* system of names *(tao)*.
47. The Mencian version of Confucianism, of course, has quite the opposite characteristics. It is absolutist and potentially revolutionary.
48. *Hsün-tzu*, chap. 22 (Chan).
49. Ibid. (Chan). Hsün-tzu goes on here to say that names do have a certain pragmatic appropriateness (*shan* 'good at'), that is, they may be easy to learn, suggestive, or nice sounding or appearing.
50. Hu, *Development*, p. 52.
51. Fung, *History*, p. 60.
52. Clarence Burton Day, *The Philosophers of China* (New York: Philosophical Library, 1962), p. 33.
53. Grading criteria may be regarded as definitional, but grading can go on without any explicit formal definitions so that definitional ways of "fleshing out" the doctrine are not necessary.
54. *Analects*, 7:1.
55. *Mo-tzu*, SPPY 3:1A-4-10. Translation follows *Mo-tzu, Basic Writings*, ed. Burton Watson (New York: Columbia University Press, 1963), p. 34.
56. This tendency to pursue social control and efficiency by control of evaluative attitudes rather than force is, of course, a common element in Chinese political thought from Confucianism to Chinese communism.

57. This human authority was the "viscount of Heaven" who agreed with Heaven's judgments, and Heaven's judgments were, according to Mohism, purely utilitarian.
58. *Mo-tzu*, 7:9A-2–4 (Watson, p. 92).
59. Ibid., 9:1B-8–12.
60. Ibid., Canon II:53.
61. Needham, *Science and Civilization*, vol. 2, p. 169; Y. P. Mei, *Motse: Neglected Rival of Confucius* (London: Arthur Brobstein, 1934), p. 68; Hu, *Development*, p. 78.
62. Hu, *Development*, p. 78.
63. Needham, *Science and Civilization*, p. 170.
64. Mei, *Motse*, p. 68.
65. Hu, *Development*, p. 78.
66. Mei, *Motse*, p. 73.
67. Hu, *Development*, p. 66.
68. Of course, for Buddhism and Neo-Confucianism it is much more important than in the classical period. And I do not mean to suggest that it is unimportant in the classical period. But the concept is quite different from the Western cognitive, knowing mind.
69. A. C. Graham, "Chuang-tzu's Essay on Seeing Things as Equal," *History of Religions* 9 (November, 1969–January, 1970):139.
70. The character *pien* 辯 'dispute' consists of *pien* 辨 'divide:distinguish' with a "speech" radical. Both have a core meaning of "distinguish" or "discriminate." The *Shuo-wen*, the oldest Chinese dictionary, gives *pan* 判 as a synonym for *pien* 辨. The structure of *pan* is suggestive; it consists of two elements, one meaning "half" and the other meaning "knife." The *Shuo-wen* synonym for *pan* is *fen* 分 'to divide'. *Pan* is used in compounds meaning to "judge" or to "decide."
71. *Shih* and *fei* have both descriptive and evaluative uses, and the equivocation is central to Chuang-tzu's exposition—see pages 91–92.
72. *Chuang-tzu*, 2:5 (Graham).
73. Ibid., 2:17 (Graham).
74. Munro, *Concept of Man*, p. 12.
75. *Chuang-tzu*, 2:3 (Graham).
76. Ibid., 2:4 (Graham).
77. Ibid., 2:13 (Graham).
78. Ibid., 17:13.
79. Ibid., 2:11.
80. The frequent use of the "butterfly dream" to introduce Chuang-tzu's skeptical philosophy is, as offered to a Western audience, horribly misleading because it suggests wrongly that the skepticism is just like that of some Western Cartesian or classical Empiricist—based on skepticism of sense presentations. Not only is such a view absent from Chuang-tzu's own arguments, but the intrusion of that view muddles and distorts the much more interesting and different basis for that skepticism.

Chapter 4

1. Canon I:5.
2. Graham's monumental study of Neo-Mohism has reconstructed this chapter. He renames it "Expounding the Canon." A. C. Graham, *Later Mohist Logic, Ethics, and Science* (Hong Kong: Chinese University Press, 1978).
3. Graham's reconstruction leaves most of this chapter intact. He calls it "Names and Objects." Graham, *Logic*.
4. Tan Chieh-fu, *Mo-Pien Fa-wei* (Taipei: World Book Co., 1961). All quotations from the Canons will be identified by their numbers from Tan. Quotations from the *Ta Ch'ü* and *Hsiao Ch'ü* will be identified by the SPPY location in the *Mo-tzu*.
5. Li Yü-shu is the most extreme in this regard, giving Mo-tzu credit for the entire Canon. Liang Ch'i-ch'ao credits Mo-tzu with at most only the first two books but not the "explanation" chapters. I am still most inclined, considering the level of sophistication compared to that in the rest of the *Mo-tzu*, and in that time in China, to follow Hu Shih and Graham in treating the whole semantic dialectical corpus as being a late development—considerably after Mo-tzu.
6. Hu, *Development*, p. 85.
7. This kind of corruption was also due to the practice of writing texts on bamboo strips that became dislocated and were reassembled. See Graham, *Logic*.
8. Ibid.
9. Kao Heng, *Mo Ching Chiao-ch'üan* (reprint ed., Taipei: World Book Co., 1967).
10. Tan Chieh-fu, *Mo-Pien Fa-wei* (Taipei: World Book Co., 1961); Liu Tsun-yan, "A New Interpretation of the Canon of the Moists," *New Asia Journal*, vols. 6–7, 1964–65; Li Yü-shu, *Mo-pien Hsin-chu* (Taipei: Commercial Press, 1968).
11. Graham's massive and impressive reconstruction work was available to me mostly in several of his published papers during most of the work on this book. I had access to his manuscript and used it to check and correct many of my translations. I have not tried to incorporate all of his important insights into my study of semantics, but I believe that my interpretation is consistent with the textual arguments and evidence adduced in that work. But at many crucial points the interpretations differ. I have not attempted a detailed analysis and refutation of Graham's more mentalistic approach, but I submit the following observations: (1) Graham's evidence for his more mentalistic conclusions comes mainly from passages that depend most heavily on accepting emendations to get the key mentalistic terms in, for example, *hsien* 'a priori' for *wu* 'lack'. These passages were originally among the least intelligible in the corpus. On a coherent theory approach they would be reconstructed, if at all, in ways consistent with the parts of the text that are clear and not so corrupt. (2) There is no direct evidence that the Mohists thought that definition captures the "ideas" conveyed by words, nor even that words and ideas are linked in any relevantly semantic way. (3) All the concrete examples of "a priori knowledge" that Graham cites are synthetic, factual statements that have no

obvious connection to definitions and which even the Mohists claim have some experiential basis and import, for example, that the color inside is white—given that it is the same as here and it is white here. (4) There are places where mentalism should certainly be in evidence if it were as central to the Mohist project as Graham assumes, such as in the frequent discussions of knowledge of names. But these are never explained as involving ideas, and not even as specifically involving definition. (5) Graham himself does not seem to see the conflict between his own frequent claims that Mohists are nominalist to whom the problem of the meaning of general terms never arose and attributing to them a mentalistic Platonism which would have to have been motivated only by precisely the same linguistic puzzles about meaning of general terms.

12. Most important and valuable has been Graham's discovery of the use of stock technical examples and terminology and his proposal to use emendation to recover rather than remove strange technical graphs. Other commentators have usually treated many of those terms as unintelligible and removed or changed them wherever possible. Graham's constraints include a prohibition on the appeal to meaning (semantic or interpretive grounds) in emendation. His reason appears to be that such grounds tend toward self-fulfilling circularity. But given suitable constraints on interpretive theory, there is no reason to exclude semantic evidence for a textual theory. In fact, such criteria are ultimately unavoidable, and I would submit that Graham tacitly appeals to interpretive grounds for emendations; for instance, he does not change *every* *wu* 'lack' to *hsien* 'a priori'—only those in contexts where the interpretation fits better his own recovery of mentalism in the text.

13. Graham's reconstruction of the *Ta Ch'ü* is based on evidence that it was the *first* of the canonlike chapters and was concerned with ethics. It came before and was presupposed by the scientific and semantic canons. See Graham, *Logic*.

14. Canons II:40 and I:86.

15. This possibility is broached in only one canon, in which the point depends on Graham's reconstruction. Canon II:72.

16. *Mo-tzu*, SPPY 11:3B:7. Graham takes this to be the opening stanza in his reconstruction of this chapter.

17. I have followed Graham's analysis of this passage mainly out of respect. I cannot endorse the reasoning he gives for it. He analyzes the structure *ABAB* as an extremely rare verb-object structure (*V1 V2 O2 O1*). He also analyzes the structure *x yü y t'ung* (x 與 y 同) as an asymmetric relation. I have changed that in my translation. Graham's translation is as follows:

[II:68] You cannot use 'that' for this without using both 'that' for this and 'this' for that. Explained by: their being different.

E. It is admissible for the man who uses names rightly to use 'that' for this and 'this' for that. As long as his use of 'that' for that stays confined to that and his use of 'this' for this stays confined to this, it is inadmissible to use 'that' for this. When 'this' is about to be used for that, it is likewise admissible to use 'that' for this. If 'that' and

'this' stay confined to that and this, and accepting this condition you use 'that' for this, then 'this' is likewise about to be used for that. His "use *x* for *y*" is, of course, the verbal "mention" construction discussed in chapter 2, pages 43–44.
18. *Chuang-tzu*, chap. II, "Essay on Seeing Things as Equal."
19. Canon I:86.
20. Again I have followed Graham. Nothing of philosophical import rides on the grammatical issue here. The more common reading among commentators on this passage takes the sentence break to come after *ming-chih* 名之 'name it'. Graham breaks earlier, citing a generalization that the Mohist never uses *yeh* 也 (assertion marker) in such a way. The internal evidence of this passage seems to indicate that, in fact, the Mohists did at least once use *yeh* 也 (assertion marker) in this way. (One counterexample is usually sufficient to disprove that kind of generalization.) What we need and lack, of course, is a plausible generative semantic-syntax for Chinese. Otherwise no such generalization can have the force necessary to overrule such apparent counterexamples.
21. SPPY 11:3a 10–11.
22. I have shifted translations here to follow Graham's rendering. I suppose one could have said "imaging." I do agree that this is a verbal use of *i* 意 'image' so even more unlikely to correspond to the English "idea."
23. Canon II: 38, 41, 57, and 58.
24. Graham disagrees here. He suggests that the Mohist philosophy is indeed like our own slightly modified commonsense conceptualism. The definitions, he argues, are implicitly embodied in *i* and connected with *hsien chih* 先知 'a priori knowledge'. I find the first claim unsupported in the text, and the second misleading in its use of "a priori knowledge" instead of, say, "knowing beforehand" to translate *hsien chih* 先知. The difference is that we can know by inference, before actually seeing them, many a posteriori truths—including all those used as examples in the Canon.
25. SPPY 11:5b:6. Graham has suggested that these canons accordingly belong to that later phase of Mohist thought.
26. Chmielewski, "Logic I."
27. A. C. Graham, "Two Dialogues in the Kung-sun Lung-tzu," p. 143.
28. See Canon II:66.
29. I have ignored the rest of this fragment. The interpretation is very difficult.
30. Locke, *Essay Concerning Human Understanding*, bk. 3, chap. 1, sec. 2.
31. Hu Shih and others take Canon I:1 to be a discussion of premises and proof in argument. Canon I:1 says, "A cause [故] is that which when it is present the thing is accomplished [成]." The explanation says, "lesser cause: it may exist and not necessarily be thus, but if it does not exist necessarily it is not thus; greater cause: one which, when it exists the thing is necessarily thus." One could, of course, claim that the causes were reasons and greater and lesser causes were "necessary and sufficient conditions," but I cannot see any reasons for doing so other than an abiding desire to prove that Mohists were investigating arguments and logic. The canon in question does seem to be dealing with actual causation, not justification. It further makes no reference to

pien, to language or sentences, and it is far removed from the section of the canon which discusses *pien*.

32. Graham's manuscript argues that *pi* 彼 is a corruption of *fan* 反, which literally means "opposite." That is a plausible emendation but, since the philosophical point is not altered by it, I have followed the unemended text.
33. Graham, *Logic*.
34. *Mencius* 6:A1–4. See the analysis by D. C. Lau in *Mencius* (Middlesex: Penguin, 1963). David S. Nivison also has a most interesting interpretation of Mencius's "analogies."
35. A. C. Graham, "The Logic of the Mohist *Hsiao Ch'ü*," *T'oung Pao* 51, no. 1 (1964):2–11. The translation follows the traditional order. SPPY 11:5b:3–7b:11. Graham has incorporated this chapter in his overall reconstruction of the dialectical works. He has removed and reordered part of the beginning and inserted fragments from the *Ta Ch'ü* among them. I have not followed him in this reconstruction, though not out of any textual or historical objection to it. I could not sense that the additions illuminated the rest of the chapter beyond his earlier analysis. I have accordingly relied on his earlier analysis of just this chapter. Graham suggests that his reconstruction proves that the Mohist Dialecticians "discovered the sentence." In fact, most of the issues he introduces in the beginning of the chapter, like the chapter itself, concern only the effects of modification on expressions (terms or predicates) and show no awareness of the sentence as a combination of functionally interrelated and interdependent semantic elements and especially not of the sentence as denoting truth values. Nothing of theoretical interest seems to be added to this chapter by the reconstruction.
36. Hu, *Development*, pp. 93–98.
37. T'ang Chun-i, *Chung-kuo Che-hsüe Yuan-lun* (Hong Kong: Life Publishing Co., 1966), pp. 135–59.
38. Graham, *Hsiao Ch'ü*, pp. 21–22.
39. I know of no hint of a historical connection, but it is certainly a fascinating coincidence that, as Joseph Needham has noted, Chinese mathematics was relatively stronger in the development of algebra and weaker in geometry than was the case in the West. See Needham, *Science and Civilization*, vol. 3.
40. I use *equation* as a grammatical form. But it could be argued that sentences of this type are indeed equations and not classic subject-predicate assertions. The second term would be regarded as implicitly quantified existentially so that the logical form would be "horse is identical with some animal." Or, to capture the part-whole structure of the mass-stuff ontology, "horse is identical with part of animal." I suspect that, contrary to Frege, English nominal predications are also equations. See the dissertation by Anil Gupta, "The Logic of Common Nouns: An Investigation in Quantified Model Logic" (Ph.D. diss., University of Pittsburgh, 1977).
41. This example seems like a kind of concession to Confucian moral consciousness as opposed to Mohist universalism. But it seems to be a modified position that is spelled out in fragments of the *Ta Ch'ü*. See "Expounding the Canon" fragments 3–10 in Graham, *Logic*. These sections seem concerned with

making these kinds of ethical distinctions. Mencius, in a debate with I Chih, seems to read I Chih's point in this way.
42. Causal explanation is one of the uses of the "X Y *yeh*" sentence, especially when the terms are nominalized or embedded sentences.
43. Quantifiers ranging over the subject variable follow the subject expression in Chinese. Unless the context indicates a definite description reading, no quantifier is equivalent to a universal quantifier.
44. Locke, *Essay Concerning Human Understanding*, bk. 2, chap. 2, sec. 8.

Chapter 5

1. W. V. O. Quine, *Word and Object*, chap. 2. The indeterminacy of translation is an "axiom" only in that all seem to agree that there is *some* sense in which it is true. Quine's own claims about the implications and significance of the principle are controversial.
2. This observation about the limited practical import of the indeterminacy of translation is due to Richmond Thomason.
3. The translation "horse-stuff" provides a more coherent interpretation in the sense of explaining his speculations more reasonably and consistency with the tradition. That clearly rests on two possibly false assumptions: that Kung-sun Lung is a serious reasonable philosopher, and that he fits rationally into the tradition as it has been interpreted here. These are the methodological assumptions treated in chapter 1 that are corollaries to treating the *Kung-sun Lung-tzu* as a work of philosophy.
4. The "text" should be read as "text under a particular textual theory" to account for my reliance on Graham's reordering of the sequences of argument.
5. That is, abstract entities do not need the same technique to explain how they are denoted. They are "named" by proper names not common nouns.
6. A. C. Graham has consistently maintained that the semantics of both the Neo-Mohist works and of the white-horse dialogue is nominalistic. Instead of arguing that the grammar of nouns supports a nominalistic rather than abstract semantics, he argues that lack of singular and plural inflection is unimportant. ("The Logic of the Mohist *Hsiao Ch'ü*," pp. 46–48.) His strategy is to deny what seemed to be a premise in the abstract argument, when one ought to have noted that the premise does not support the conclusion. He says that the lack of singular and plural is essentially "just a translator's" problem. (See also his *Logic*, pp. 28–29.) He would, of course, be right if it were only that there is no inflection for *plural* marking. Then we could say merely that Chinese nouns, like English *fish*, *deer*, and *sheep*, have plural forms that are identical with their singular forms. The masslike features of nouns in Chinese suggest that the difference is much deeper than that. It is not just that Chinese do not have plural *inflections*, but that they do not undergo pluralization at all in the way *fish* and *sheep* do. The significant point is that Chinese lacks the grammatical operation of pluralization.

   Even that by itself might not be significant, but it is coupled with other grammatical and semantic features that mark Chinese nouns as belonging to a different logical class than common nouns. The philosophical significance of these syntactical observations is that Chinese lacks general terms—the very terms which motivated abstract theorizing in the West.

Thus Graham is surely correct that the dialectical thinkers' use of nominals is always concrete. But in saying that the reference is always to concrete *particulars* he unconsciously assimilates Chinese nominalism to Western *traditional* nominalism. And that form of nominalism could only occur in a tradition that had Platonism. That tradition still appeals to "abstract ideas" or "general ideas" in semantic explanations. General ideas still correspond to general terms (common nouns). The traditional Western nominalist differs from the Platonist in refusing to reify the semantic notions (except as mental entities). Abstract ideas are held to exist only in the mind. This leads to private language and solipsism problems in that tradition. Chinese nominalism is of a much more radical sort (as Graham, in fact, repeatedly notes) in that the thinkers not only do not reify such notions, but never even seem to consider them. Simply put, the argument to this point is that Chinese philosophers do not appeal to any of the counterparts of general ideas because there are no general terms.

7. Fung, *History*, pp. 203–5.
8. Hu, *Development*.
9. Tu Kuo-hsiang, *Hsien-Ch'in Chu-tzu Jo-kan Yen-chiu* (Hong Kong: Hong Kong Modern Day Press, 1958).
10. Wang Tien-chi, *Chung-kuo Lo-chi Ssu-hsiang Shih-lian Fen-hsi* (Peking: Commercial Press, 1955).
11. Tu Kuo-hsiang, *Hsien-Ch'in*.
12. Y. P. Mei, "The Kung-sun Lung-tzu," *Harvard Journal of Asiatic Studies* 16 (December, 1953): 424.
13. Chmielewski, "Logic I," p. 19.
14. A. C. Graham, "Kung-sun Lung's Essay on Meaning and Things," *Journal of Oriental Studies* 2, no. 2 (1955):290.
15. Liou Kia-hway, "The Configuration of Chinese Reasoning," p. 68.
16. Please note here and again (see chap. 2, pp. 37–53) that the claim that Chinese *cannot* express abstractions is *not* my view.
17. *Hsün-tzu*, chapter 22, "On Rectification of Names."
18. See Graham, "Two Dialogues in the *Kung-sun Lung-tzu*," p. 139. Graham comes close to this interpretation when he speculates that somehow it must be less obvious to Chinese that "white-horse" is less general than "horse."
19. A. C. Graham, "The Composition of the Gongsuen Long Tzyy," *Asia Major*, n.s., 5, no. 2 (1957):147–83.
20. I do not know if the position can be put in other ways that avoid the myth of the museum or not. All amount to saying, in effect, that Kung-sun Lung was "thinking" Plato or Locke, and struggling to "talk" them in poor impoverished Chinese.
21. Both modern and Chinese philosophy reject the "museum" account; see pages 63–65.

22. Rev. Brother Cassian, Introduction to Max Perleberg, *The Works of Kung-sun Lung-tzu* (Hong Kong: Local Printing Press, 1952), p. xvi.
23. Fung, *History*, p. 203. I do not understand what Bodde means by "with difficulty" here. Does he think that there are abstract expressions but they are complicated to write? That there are contexts where it is clear that the reference is abstract? It is not easy to distinguish his "difficult" from "impossible."
24. Canon and explication numbers, here as in the previous chapter, follow T'an Chieh-fu, *Mo Pien Fa-wei* (World Book Co., 1961).
25. The relation of *horse* and *non-horse* to reality could be other than it is. However, there is a kind of necessity that remains despite that. No matter how the use of *horse* varies, if the language contains *ox* as a distinct name then whatever it designates will be non-horse (Canon I:50).
26. This is presumably purposeful, because some *fu*–names (e.g., "hard-white") do not denote ontological compounds, and perhaps also because, if Graham is right, the theory distinguishes between relations of names and of objects. Hsün-tzu uses the ontological term *chien* for all compounding because he is not committed to prelinguistic natural kinds that would force a theory of ontological compounds—antecedent natural kinds or categories. For Hsün-tzu, compounding simply alters (in different ways) the conventional scope of names over a single variegated reality. Hsün-tzu (see chap. 3, pp. 97–99) is actually a more radical conventionalist than the Neo-Mohists despite his much-noticed "empiricism."
27. The "scope" variability of *t'i* is reflected in nontechnical Chinese usage, where it is typically taken to refer to either the body or parts of the body. It is also frequently translated as "substance," which is suggestively close to mass-stuff, and it has a verbal translation that parallels this technical use, "to identify with."
28. My reading of this passage is considerably different from Graham's. I will reproduce his here for comparison.

> B67 [II.67]. There are the same grounds for denying that oxen-and-horses are not oxen as for admitting it. Explain by: the total of the two.
>
> E. If it is admissible that since some are not oxen they are not oxen, then, since some are oxen though some are not, it is equally admissible that they are oxen. Therefore, if it is inadmissible to say either "oxen-and-horses are not oxen" or "oxen-and-horses are oxen," then, it being admissible of some but not the others, it is likewise inadmissible to say "'oxen-and-horses are oxen' is inadmissible."
>
> Moreover, if neither oxen nor horses are two, but oxen and horses are two, then, without the oxen being the non-oxen or the horses being the non-horses there is no difficulty about "oxen-and-horses are non-oxen and non-horses."

There are lots of reasons for the difference in interpretation. Graham takes the passage to be an attack on Kung-sun Lung; I take it to be a centerpiece in the Mohist's own semantic program, from which Kung-sun Lung fashions his argument for "white-horse not horse." So I take the passage to be arguing for the equal *assertability* of "ox-horse is not ox" and "ox-horse is ox," and Graham takes it to be arguing for the (presumably equal) *inassertability* of the two.

The formulas after the first sentence of the explanation constitute one of the most complex actual cases in which the Chinese produces ambiguities of the scope of sentential operators. And Graham and I analyze the structure differently. Graham reads "if A then (B & C)." I read "(if A then B) & C." Graham thinks the grammatical considerations weigh in favor of his reading. I think a language without parentheses can have grammar that settles such issues only if there is a convention about which connectives dominate. I suggest that the otherwise superfluous but parallel *yüeh* 'say' in the formula might be taken as attempts to clarify the scope (in favor of my reading).

But my main argument for grouping the connectives as I have is internal. The formulas concern two sentences: (1) "ox-horse is not ox" and (2) "ox-horse is ox." A consists of "(1) is inadmissible" and "(2) is inadmissible." B says "One (some or part) is admissible, one (some or part) not." C says "'(2) is inadmissible' is not admissible." Graham's parsing results in a seeming contradiction, that is, "(2) is inadmissible" entails "'(2) is inadmissible' is inadmissible." (I will propose removing the negative from the second half of A, but that does not affect the argument for parsing, for in that case having A entail C would be trivial. On my parsing and the deletion of the negative, C has an important logical role to play.)

This is the only canon in which I have made my own textual change. I have removed a *wei* 未 'not-yet' from the second embedded sentence in the very complex second sentence of the explanation. My reasons for doing this are as follows: (1) The physical evidence: there are three nearly identical consecutive sentences all ending in *wei-k'o*. A copyist's eye could have skipped between sentences and made the mistake. (2) The internal coherence evidence: (a) B, the consequent of the conditional, says that to say A entails "some acceptable, some not acceptable" but A as it stands says both are not acceptable. Deleting one *wei* 未 'not-yet' makes the conditional "if A then B" reasonably coherent. (b) The final formula in this complex sequence says: *erh* 'and:yet' *yüeh* 'say' "(2) *wei-k'o* 'is inadmissible'" *i* 'is-also' *pu-k'o* 'inadmissible'. If the *wei* is left in the second formula of A then this final formula is redundant and the stress elements (*i* 'is-also') in it make no sense at all. With the *wei* removed the final formula has a meaningful logical role to play in the structure. (c) The point of the canon is that the case for the assertability of either formula is *t'ung* 同 'the same'. Sentence 1 of the explanation gives the basic rationale for this—since part of the mass sum is non-ox and part is ox, "ox" is assertable of the mass sum if "non-ox" is. The second sentence gives a tight reductio to the conclusion from sentence 1. If we say (1) is inadmissible and (2) is admissible, then we make one admissible and one not (which the previous sentence ruled out). Yet we cannot say (2) is inadmissible, implying therefore that we must conclude that (1) *is* admissible—which is the point of the canon.

29. *Ox* and *horse*, of course, should not be regarded as general nouns. "Oxen 'n' horses" or "ox-stuff-horse-stuff" as translations would be more likely to make Western intuitions regarding the reading of the compound correspond with the intuitions of the Neo-Mohists. If we were to read the compound as consisting of grammatically singular compound terms, that is, as "an ox-horse" rather than as "oxen 'n' horses," the Mohists' explanation would be simply bizarre. "An ox-horse," like "a man-woman," "a lion-tiger," or "a man-horse," suggests a crossbreed, a freak, or some mythological mixed beast that is quite irrelevant to the Mohists' point. The Mohists interpret the compound as a sum—more or less equivalent to "draft animal."
30. Luan Tiao-fu, *Mo Tzu Yen-Chiu Lun-Wen-Ch'i* (Peking: People's Press, 1957), pp. 160–72; A. C. Graham, "The 'Hard and White' Disputations of the Chinese Sophists," *Bulletin of the School of Oriental and African Studies* 30, pt. 2 (1967):358–68.
31. *Chuang-tzu*, SPPY 6:13A:10.
32. Canon II:67 comes close to distinguishing epistemic from ontological separation.
33. *Mo-tzu*, "Hsiao Ch'ü Pien," SPPY 11:6A:6–9.
34. Kung-sun Lung (pp. 163–64) observes that "white-horse fixes something as white," but he does not assert any metaphysical dependence or priority either.
35. A. C. Graham, "Two Dialogues in the *Kung-sun Lung-tzu*," pp. 128–52.
36. If we used the sentential calculus this would be affirming the consequent, or if we used the traditional logic Chmielewski thought was inadequate to deal with Chinese logic, it is a fallacy of distribution—"horse" is distributed in the conclusion but not in the premises. It is a total puzzle to me why, with all the attention the dialogue has had, no one seems to have criticized this argument.
37. Graham, "Two Dialogues," p. 140.
38. Chmielewski, "Logic I," pp. 10–15.
39. This observation of Chmielewski's is explained in the present interpretation as a deliberate attempt to avoid mass-product compounding as a violation of rectification of names.
40. Chmielewski's reconstruction of the first argument goes as follows: first, he translates the premises adding the limiting phrases in parentheses:
    (1) Horse is what commands shape (and only shape);
    (2) white is what commands color (and only color);
    (3) what commands color (and only color) is not what commands shape (and only shape);
    (4) white-horse is not horse.

These are translated into set theory formulas which according to his definitions read:
    (1') The class "horse" has the property "commands shape (and only shape)";
    (2') the class "white" has the property "commands color (and only color)";
    (3') the intersection of the class of classes with the property "commands shape (and only shape)" with the class of classes with the

property "commands color (and only color)" is the unit set consisting of the null class;

(4') the intersection of the classes "white" and "horse" is not identical with the class "horse."

Chmielewski began by criticizing Graham's view that the argument proves only that the color white is not a horse. Yet he says that the reasoning he symbolized proves only:

(3a) The class "white" is not identical with the class "horse."

This seems rather close to justifying Graham's original criticism. Chmielewski, however, engages in some "rational reconstruction." He argues that an obvious suppressed premise will yield the correct conclusion.

(3b) The class "horse" is not a subclass of the class "white."

(3b) is neither obvious (certainly not in a context where it is a crucial premise in a proof whose conclusion is even more obviously false) nor is it the premise required by the argument. (3b) makes all the other premises superfluous. It alone will guarantee Chmielewski's (4). If the class "horse" has members that are not members of the class "white," then it has members that are not members of any subclass of "white."

The minimal premise needed by Chmielewski is:

(3c) The class "horse" is not the null class.

By (3) the intersection of any class of colored things with any class of things with shape is the null class. "White" and "horse," by (1) and (2), are respectively such classes. Therefore, the class formed by their intersection is identical with the class "horse" only if "horse" is the null class.

It does seem implausible that the formalization is Kung-sun Lung's argument. The conditions that do all the logical work are the ones Chmielewski slips in parentheses: "and only color" and "and only shape." Premise (3) is even more remote from the text, which does not seem too problematic in the original. It is a premise that signals the concern for the strict use of names, "the name of a color is not the name of a shape." Chung-ying Cheng and John Swain, "Logic and Ontology in the Chih Wu Lun of Kung-sun Lung-tzu," *Philosophy East and West* 20, no. 2 (April, 1970):137–154, included another attempt to give a formal analysis of the argument, using the first order predicate calculus. They argue that their analysis supports Chmielewski's conclusions. See my criticisms in an earlier version of this chapter, "Mass Nouns and the White Horse Paradox," *Philosophy East and West* 26, no. 2 (April, 1976):202–3, and a similar criticism of their formulation of the Chih Wu Lun argument by James Herne, "A Critical Note on the Cheng-Swain Interpretation of the Chih Wu Lun," in *Philosophy East and West* 26, no. 2 (April, 1976):225–28.

41. Tan Chieh-fu, *Mo-Pien Fa-wei*, p. 16.
42. Graham, "Two Dialogues," p. 145.
43. It is presumably the mention of shape and color that prompts the analyses that attribute an Aristotelian ontology to Kung-sun Lung. But that move ignores the grammatical features discussed in chapter 2 (p. 37) that lie behind the view

of, for instance, horse as *a* thing that is shaped in the sense of being distributed in space in regularly shaped pieces, as opposed to viewing classes of objects as a group of bare individuals or substrata with the attribute of shape. White, by contrast, is apparently viewed as scattered in space in clumps with no regular shape other than that of the *t'i* or stuff it "penetrates."

44. Hsün-tzu, it should be noted, followed the Mohists in loosening the account of the naming relation, especially for compounds. Thus he criticized Kung-sun Lung's paradox as "using names to confuse reality," that is, taking naming so seriously that one makes the reasonable representation of things impossible. He suggests that compounding and general "names" need have no fixed or constant relation to single names.

Selected Bibliography

Books

Chan Wing-tsit, ed. *A Source Book in Chinese Philosophy*. New Jersey: Princeton University Press, 1963.

Chang Shun-yi 張純一. *Moh Ching Chien-ku Chien* 墨經閒詁箋. Taipei: Cheng Chung Bookshop, 1959.

Ch'en Chu 陳柱. *Kung-sun Lung-tzu Chi-chien* 公孫龍子集解. Shanghai: Commercial Press, 1937.

Ch'en Ta-chi 陳大齊. *Ming-li Lun-tsung* 名理論叢. Taipei: Cheng Chung Bookshop, 1956.

Ch'ien Mu 錢穆. *Chung-kuo Ssu-hsiang Shih* 中國思想史. Hong Kong: New Asia Press, 1962.

Creel, H. G. *Chinese Thought from Confucius to Mao Tse-tung*. Chicago: University of Chicago Press, 1953.

Dubs, H. H. *The Works of Hsüntze*. London: Arthur Probsthain, 1928.

Fan Keng-yen 范耕研. *Mo Pien Shu-cheng* 墨辯疏正. Taipei: Commercial Press, 1967.

Forrest, R. A. D. *The Chinese Language*. London: Faber and Faber, 1948.

Fung Yu-lan. *A History of Chinese Philosophy*. Translated by Derk Bodde. Vol. 1. Princeton: Princeton University Press, 1952.

―――. *A Short History of Chinese Philosophy*. Translated by Derk Bodde. New York: Macmillan Co., 1948.

Graham, A. C. *Later-Mohist Logic, Ethics and Science*. Hong Kong: Chinese University of Hong Kong Press, and London: School of Oriental and African Studies, University of London, 1978.

Ho Ch'i-min 何啟民. *Kung-sun Lung Yü Kung-sun Lung-tzu* 公孫龍與公孫龍子. Taipei: Commercial Press, 1967.

Hsü Fu-kuan 徐復觀. *Kung-sun Lung-tzu Chiang-shu* 公孫龍子講疏. Taichung: Central Bookstore, n.d.

Hu Shih. *Chung-kuo Ku-tai Che-hsüeh Shih* 中國古代哲學史. Taipei: Commercial Press, 1968.

———. *Ming-hsüeh Chi-ku* 名學稽古. Shanghai: Commercial Press, 1923.

———. *The Development of Logical Method in Ancient China*. New York: Paragon Press, 1969.

Kao Heng 高亨. *Lao-tzu Cheng-ku* 老子正詁. Reprint. Taipei: World Book Co., 1967.

———. *Mo Ching Chiao-ch'üan* 墨經校詮. Taipei: World Book Co., 1967.

Li Yü-shu 李漁叔. *Moh-pien Hsin-chu* 墨辯新註. Taipei: Commercial Press, 1968.

Liang Ch'i-ch'ao 梁啟超. *Moh-Ching Chiao-shih* 墨經校釋. Taipei: Chung Hua Bookstore, 1936.

Liu Chi 劉奇. *Lun-li Ku-li* 論理故例. Chungking: Commercial Press, n.d.

Liu Tsun-yan, "A New Interpretation of the Canon of the Mohist," *New Asia Journal*, vol. 6 and 7 (1964–1965).

Luan Tiao-fu 欒調甫. *Mo Tzu Yen-chiu Lun-wen-chi* 墨子研究論文集. Peking: People's Press, 1957.

Nakamura, Haijime. *The Ways of Thinking of Eastern Peoples*. Tokyo: Japanese National Commission for UNESCO. Tokyo Japanese Government Publications, 1960.

Perleberg, Max. *The Works of Kung-sun Lung-tzu*. Hong Kong: Local Printing Press, 1952.

Sun Yi-jang 孫詒讓. *Moh Tzu Chien-ku* 墨子閒詁. Taipei: World Book Co., 1967.

T'an Chieh-fu 譚戒甫. *Mo-Pien Fa-wei* 墨辯發微. Taipei: World Book Co., 1961.

———. *Kung-sun Lung-tzu Hsing-ming Fa-wei* 公孫子形名發微. Taipei: World Book Co., 1961.

Waley, Arthur. *Three Ways of Thought in Ancient China*. New York: Macmillan Co., 1939.

Wang Hsien-ch'ien 王先謙. *Chuang-tzu Chi-chieh* 莊子集解. Taipei: San Min Bookshop, 1963.

Wang Tien-chi 汪奠基. *Chung-kuo Lo-chi Ssu-hsiang Shih-liau Fen-hsi* 中國邏輯思想史料分析. Vol. I. Peking: Commercial Press, 1955.

Wu K'ang 吳康. *Lao Chuang Che-hsüeh* 老莊哲學. Taipei: Commercial Press, 1955.

Wu Yü-chiang 吳毓江. *Moh Tzu Chiao-chu* 墨子校注. Peking: Independent Printers, 1944.

Yang K'uan 楊寬. *Moh Ching Che-hsüeh* 墨經哲學. Taipei: Cheng Chung Bookshop, 1942.

Yen Ling-feng 嚴靈峯. *Lao Chuang Yen-chiu* 老莊研究. Taipei: Chung Hua Bookshop, 1966.

———. *Tau-chia Ssu-tzu Hsin-pien* 道家四子新編. Taipei: Commercial Press, 1968.

Yü Yü 虞愚. *Chung-kuo Ming-hsüeh* 中國名學. Taipei: World Book Co., 1967.

Articles

Bodde, Derk. "Types of Chinese Category Thinking." *Journal of the American Oriental Society* 59 (1939):200–219.

Chao, Y. R. "How Chinese Logic Operates." *Anthropological Linguistics* 1, no. 1 (1959):1–8.

———. "Notes on Chinese Grammar and Logic." *Philosophy East and West* 5, no. 1 (1955):31–41.

Cheng Chung-ying. "Inquiries Into Classical Chinese Logic." *Philosophy East and West* 15, nos. 3–4 (1965):195–216.

Ching, C. R. "Concept of Tao." *Review of Religions* 17:126–30.

Chmielewski, Janusz. "Notes on Early Chinese Logic I." *Rocznik Orientalistyczny* 26, no. 1 (1962):7–21.

———. "Notes on Early Chinese Logic II." *Rocznik Orientalistyczny* 26, no. 2 (1963):91–105.

———. "Notes on Early Chinese Logic III." *Rocznik Orientalistyczny* 27 (1963):103–21.

———. "Notes on Early Chinese Logic IV." *Rocznik Orientalistyczny* 28, no. 2 (1964):87–111.

———. "Notes on Early Chinese Logic V." *Rocznik Orientalistyczny* 29, no. 2 (1965):117–38.

———. "Notes on Early Chinese Logic VI." *Rocznik Orientalistyczny* 30 (1966):31–52.

Chu Yu-kuang. "Interplay Between Language and Thought in Chinese." *Etc.*, 22 (September, 1965):307–29.

Dobson, W. A. C. H. "Negation in Archaic Chinese." *Language* 42 (April–June, 1966):278–84.

Duyvendak, J. J. L. "Hsün-tzu on the Rectification of Names." *T'oung Pao* 23 (1924):221–54.

Forke, Alfred. "The Chinese Sophists." *Asiatic Journal of the North Branch of the Royal Chinese Society* 34 (1901–2):1–37.

Graham, A. C. "Being in Western Philosophy Compared with *shih/fei* and *yu/wu* in Chinese Philosophy." *Asia Major*, n.s., 7, nos. 1–2 (1959):79–112.

———. "The Composition of the Gongsuen Long Tzyy." *Asia Major*, n.s., 5, no. 2 (1957):147–83.

———. "The 'Hard and White' Disputations of the Chinese Sophists." *Bulletin of the School of Oriental and African Studies* 30 (1967):358–68.

———. "The Logic of the Mohist *Hsiao ch'ü*." *T'oung Pao* 51, no. 1 (1964):1–54.

———. "Two Dialogues in the Kung-sun Lung-tzu." *Asia Major*, n.s., 11 (1965):128–52.

Lau, D. C. "On Mencius' Use of the Method of Analogy in Argument." *Asia Major*, n.s., 10 (1963):133–94.

———. "Some Logical Problems in Ancient China." *Proceedings of the Aristotelian Society*, n.s., 53 (1952–53):189–204.

Leslie, Donald. "Argument by Contradiction in Pre-Buddhist Chinese Reasoning." *Center for Oriental Studies: Occasional Papers No. 4*, Canberra: Australian National University, 1964.

Lin, T. C. "The Chinese Mind." *Journal of the History of Ideas* 8:259–73.

Liou Kia-hway. "The Configuration of Chinese Reasoning." *Diogenes* (Montreal), no. 49 (Spring, 1965):66–96.

Mei, Y. P. "The Kung-sun Lung-tzu." *Harvard Journal of Asiatic Studies* 16 (1953):404–37.

———. "Some Observations on the Problems of Knowledge Among the Ancient Chinese Logicians." *Tsing Hua Journal* 1, no. 1 (1956):114–21.

———. "Oriental-Western Thought." In *Asia and the Humanities*, edited by H. Frenz, pp. 124–27. Bloomington: Comparative Literature Committee, Indiana University, 1959.

Shiraishi, Bon. "The Chinese Way of Thinking." *Japan Quarterly* 12 (January–March, 1965):87–92.

T'ang Chun-i. "A New Interpretation of 'Pien' in the Mohist Hsiao-chü." *New Asia Journal* 4, no. 2 (1962):65–99.

———. "Hsün-tzu's Theories of Rectification of Names and Three Theories of Names in Pre-Ch'in China." *New Asia Journal* 5, no. 2 (1963):1–22.

Uno, Seiichi. "Some Observations on Ancient Chinese Logic." *Philosophical Studies of Japan* 6 (1965):31–42.

Wright, Arthur F. "The Chinese Language and Foreign Ideas." In *Studies in Chinese Thought*, edited by A. F. Wright. Chicago: University of Chicago Press, 1953.

Index

A priori, 184
Abstraction, 30–49 passim, 52–56, 81, 97–98, 105, 112–16, 119, 125, 138, 141, 144–49, 157, 161, 170–71, 175, 177, 179, 189; denoted by proper nouns, 188; role of, in West, 142.
Action, 77; deliberate, 59. *See also Wei* 'deliberate-action'
Algebraic inference, 163, 166. *See also* Sentence matching
Analects of Confucius, the, 5, 72–73, 80
Analogy, 124
Argument, 127
Argument from anarchy, 80
Aristotle (Artistotelianism), 16–17, 42, 48, 158, 193, 194
Assertability, 41, 151; contrasted with truth, 124. *See also K'o* 'acceptable'; Pragmatics
Attributes, *See* Properties (attributes, qualities)

Bamboo strips, 184
Behavioral implications, 87
Behavioral nominalism, 31, 49, 53–56, 103, 110, 138
Being, 70
Belief, 44, 63, 64, 87, 97, 115; and belief-knowledge distinction, 65; contrasted with behavioral implications, 60

Benefit, 85
Bodde, Derk, 14, 147, 173, 175
Boodberg, Peter, 174
Book of History, 82
Book of Rites, 82
Book of Songs, 82
Buddhism, 139, 140, 171, 183

Cartesianism, *See* Descartes, René
Category mistakes, 41, 117. *See also Lei* 'class'
Causation, 186
Change, problem of, 110
Chang Tung-sun, 16, 17, 20, 60, 173
Chan Wing-tsit, 61
Chao, Y. R., 173
Cheng Chung-ying, 20, 21, 22, 193, 194
Cheng 'govern', 73
Cheng 'rectify', 73, 77
Chien 'compound', 106, 150, 151, 153, 155; corporeal versus noncorporeal, 152; mass-sum analysis of, 152; role in ontology, 158; separation explained, 157. *See also* Compound terms; *Fu* 'compound'; Neo-Mohism
Chien-pai 'hard-white', 150
Chih 'intent', 114. *See also I* 'idea'
Chih 'know', 64, 66, 101, 108, 115. *See also* Epistemology (theory of knowledge); Knowledge.

Index

Chinese grammar, 44, 73; absence of general terms in, 189; abstraction in, 143; adjectives in, 45, 46, 47; alleged inadequacies of, 171; ambiguity of scope of sentential operators in, 191; ambiguity of *shih* 'this' in, 91; articles in, 32; demonstratives in, 91, 175; equational sentences in, 187; inflection in, 40, 45; lack of subject in, 45; malleability of, 101; modification in, 46, 62, 149; nouns in, 42, 44, 45, 176; operators in, 44; pluralization in, 143, 152, 153, 188; propositional contexts in, 63, 64; syntactic mobility in, 44, 45, 54; tense in, 173; "to be" verbs in, 45; verbs in, 44; white-horse paradox and, 144. *See also* Language

Chinese mind, 2, 9–14, 23–28, 56. *See also* Special logic retort

Chmielewski, Janusz, 20–22, 115–16, 143, 162, 174; analysis of white-horse paradox in, 192

Chou 'universal', 135

Chuang-tzu, 25, 88, 93, 94, 96, 98, 139, 140, 183; anthropocentrism in, 93; argument from authority in, 94; butterfly dream in, 183; epistemological interpretation in, 123; and impact of critique of language, 120; indexicality in, 91, 96–97; logic in, 89, 90, 94, 96; monism and mysticism in, 95; nominalism in, 97; on law of excluded middle, 174; On Making Discussions of Things Equal, 92; perspectives in, 90–97 passim, 107, 121; pipes of Heaven in, 92; refutation of idealist Confucianism in, 93; skepticism in, 90–92, 96–97, 122; subjectivism in, 91, 94–98, 121; theory of heart-mind in, 96; theory of language in, 88–96, 121; theory of *pien* 'dispute' in 121; use of *pi* 'that' in, 122; value theory in, 96; and view of argument, 88–92, 95. *See also* Taoism

Ch'ü 'choose', 89

Chü 'pick-out', 30, 89, 106, 109, 114

Ch'ü 'whole', 150

Classes (sets), 34, 111, 143–44, 146, 192

Classical Chinese as natural language, 177

Coherence, 6–7, 10–19 passim, 24–28, 31, 101–2, 142, 170, 174, 177, 181

Communication, argument from, 51; Chinese conception of, 51

Compound terms, 104, 126, 145; in hard-white model, 109; in ox-horse model, 109; scope of, 159; semantics of, 145, 148–49, 150–55, 159, 161, 163, 170, 190, 194; separation of, 159. *See also* Chien 'compound'; Fu 'compound'; Neo-Mohism

Concepts (ideas), 31, 34, 36, 42–43, 47–48, 50–58 passim, 63–66, 72, 81–82, 88, 97–98, 105, 111–12, 115, 119, 132, 137, 144, 150, 153, 170, 184, 189. *See also* Conceptualism; *I* 'idea'; Mentalism; Philosophy of mind

Conceptualism, 115, 119, 179, 186

Confucianism, 59, 83, 88–90, 98, 107, 109, 133, 148, 170; ethics in 76, 88; heart-mind theory in 80, 93; idealist version of 77–78, 80, 93; model emulation in, 78, 80; theory of language in, 72–73, 77–81; traditionalism in, 75, 77, 80, 83. *See also* Confucius; Hsün-tzu; Mencius; Rectification of names

Confucius, 45, 58–59, 67, 72–73, 82–83, 92, 180; ethical theory of, 75

Conservatism, 80

Consistency, 118. *See also* Coherence; Interpretation

Contrast theory of language, 98. *See also* Language; Taoism

Conventions, 43, 49, 52, 61–81 passim,

91–98 passim, 104–6, 109, 120, 137–40, 150, 155, 179, 181, 190
Count nouns (general terms), 32–33, 43, 48, 112, 142, 145, 153, 192; modification of, 149. *See also* Mass nouns
Creel, Hurlee G., 24

Day, Clarence, 82
Definitions, 58, 81, 82, 88, 105, 184–85
Descartes, René, 15, 38, 121, 173
Desires, 59, 67–69, 93
Dialectic, 10. *See also* Hsiao Ch'ü; *Pien* 'dispute'
Dialecticians, 62, 79, 99, 107, 108, 133–34; Taoist ridicule of, 120
Dictionaries, 58; radical translation use of, 141; Shuo Wen, 114; use of, in interpretation, 8
Distinctions discrimination division, 8, 9, 30, 32, 37, 39, 43, 52, 54, 61–79 passim, 84–98 passim, 104–9, 112, 120–26, 137, 179, 183. *See also* Language; Taoism
Dobson, W. A. C. H., 34
Duyvendak, J. J. L., 175

Empiricism, 42, 48, 86, 110
Epistemology (theory of knowledge), 36, 38, 42, 54, 63, 65, 143, 171. *See also* Knowledge
Essences, 31, 36, 43, 58, 81, 82, 98
Ethics (moral theory), 75, 77, 83; conflict of rules in, 76; intuitionism in, 76; reasoning in, 118; role of, in logic, 131; role of language in, 105
Etymologies, 179

Fa 'standard', 113
Fate (destiny), 134, 135
Fei 'not-this', 89, 91, 136; interpretive theory of, 135; use of, in sentence matching, 129. *See also Shih-fei*
Fen 'divisions' 105–6. *See also* Distinctions (discrimination, division)
Fingarette, Herbert, 59, 60.
Fu 'compound' 150. *See also* Compound terms
Fung Yu-lan, 10, 81, 143, 175; on white-horse paradox, 144

Graham, A. C., 21, 102, 103, 116, 125, 127, 134, 146, 156, 159, 161–63, 173, 184–85, 189; mentalistic interpretation of, 184, 191; nominalistic interpretation of, 188
Grandy, Richard, 5, 173

Han Dynasty, 139, 140
Hard-white (stock example of interpenetrating compounds), 104, 148, 149–58, 164; dialogue on, 146; relation of, to white-horse paradox, 159; separation of, 156, 165, 167–68. *See also* Kung-sun Lung; Ox-horse paradigm
Heart-mind, 93, 94, 98
Heaven, 84, 121
Herne, James, 193
Hobbes, Thomas, 84
Holism, 171
Hsiang 'image', 114
Hsiao Ch'ü, 101, 104–7, 114, 118, 124–29, 132–33, 138–40
Hsin 'heart-mind', 115
Hsing 'nature', 177
Hsün-tzu, 59, 72, 77, 79–81, 98, 105, 169, 182, 190; analysis of compound terms in, 194; analysis of white-horse paradox in, 145, 194; prohibition on new names in, 109; scope of names in, 111
Hu Shih, 74, 76, 81, 85, 86, 87, 101, 126, 184, 186
Hui Shih, 88, 124, 134
Hume, David, 145, 148

I Chih, 188
I Ching (Book of Changes), 83
I 'idea', 104, 110, 118, 126, 128, 132,

137, 179, 186; interpreted as intent, 113, 131; interpretive theory of, 115, 138; and role different from "idea," 114; translation problems with, 112. *See also* Concepts (ideas)
Indexical terms, 91, 107. *See also* Chuang-tzu
Indian philosophy, 180
Individualism, 30–31
Inference, 120
Innatism, 78
Intentions, 131, 134, 138; contrasted with denotation, 135
Interpenetration, 46, 151, 152, 158; of concrete noncorporeal stuffs, 155; of hard-white, 156, 157. *See also* Hard-white (stock example of interpenetrating compounds
Interpretation, 56; abstract, 147; Buddhist inspired 57; of Chuang-Tzu, 97; coherence in, 188; comparison of abstract and mass, 146; constraints on, 103; contrasted with translation, 8; effect of philosophical presuppositions on, 103; mass noun hypothesis in, 33, 40, 103; mentalistic, 42; of Mohist Canon, 101; nonabstract, 37, 39, 41; Platonic, 82; of rectification of names, 82; role of logic in, 8; role of tradition in, 8; theory of, 1–28, 43, 102–3, 142, 177; traditional, 57; use of dictionary in, 8; of white-horse paradox, 28, 143, 144, 148, 170. *See also* Textual theory
I-wei 'believe', 64, 97

James, William, 86
Jan 'so' (use in sentence matching), 129
Japanese, 50
Jen 'benevolence', 80
Jen 'people', 34, 136

Kao Heng, 102
Kitcher, Philip, 173

Knowledge, 42, 63, 64, 66, 67; a priori, 184; negative, 67; propositional, 66, 180; skill analysis of, 64, 65, 66; types of, 66
K'o 'acceptable', 59, 89, 129; interpreted as admissability of assertability, 151, 154–55, 160
Ku 'cause', 126
K'ung Ch'uan, 145, 169
Kung-sun Lung, 17, 21, 28, 39, 41, 42, 54, 56, 76, 88, 104, 108, 124, 133, 141–59, 163– 68, 188, 190, 193–94; logic of, 162; not vindicated by analysis, 170; ontology in, 168; as prisoner of language, 148; semantics of compound terms in, 151, 155–56, 160–65; separation of hard-white in, 156, 169; theory of language in, 148. *See also* White-horse paradox
Kung-sun Lung-tzu, the, 41, 141, 143, 147, 188

Language, 9–11, 17–18, 85; Chinese, 13, 14, 15, 17; contrast theory of, 59, 61, 78, 90, 98, 106, 122, 126; conventionalism of, 49; descriptive function of, 61, 98, 137; determinism denied in, 171; evaluative focus of, 106; function of, 26, 59; Han dynasty changes in, 34; inadequacy and paradoxical nature of, 123; indexicality in, 108; learning of, 108; modern and classical Chinese, compared, 32, 33; moral distinction in, 79–80; natural, 177; nominalist assumptions about, 63, 65, 81; pictographic (ideographic) versus phonemic, 47, 49, 50, 53, 147, 179; pragmatic conception of, 103; pre-Han Chinese assumptions about, 57–65, 79, 83, 89, 90, 96, 97, 98, 103, 105, 120, 137, 170, 180; prisoners of, 148; regulative function of, 58– 61, 76, 77, 79, 94, 96, 98, 105; in relation to philosophy, 16, 28,

32, 35, 39, 52, 53, 55, 56; role in moral discrimination, 77; study regarded as trivial, 120; Taoist theories of, 61; traditionalism in, 80; unreliability of, 107, 130, 135, 137, 138, 139, 140, 158, 169; viewed as tool, 109; Western, 16, 17. *See also* Conventions; Distinctions (discrimination, division); Nominalism

Lao-tzu, 25, 58, 59, 61, 66, 69, 70, 71, 96, 180; Ma Wang Tui version of, 4; skepticism in, 97. *See also* Taoism; *Tao-te Ching*

Lau, D. C., 61, 187

Legalism, 4

Lei 'class', 104, 110, 111, 115, 137; and class logic, 118; interpreted as similar stuff, 106; interpretive theory of, 116, 117, 138; no subclass-member distinction in, 113; and possibility of comparison, 117; translation problems of, 112; use in moral reasoning, 118

Lesniewski, 112

Liang 'both', 90

Liang Ch'i-chao, 184

Liang-chih 'intuitive-wisdom', 80

Li-che 'those who separate', 167

Linguistic determinism, 189

Li' 'rites', 75, 77–78, 80

Liu Tsun-yan, 103

Li Yü-shu, 103, 184

Locke, John, 36, 42, 48, 49, 51, 114, 119

Logic, 8–10, 13, 17, 18, 84, 99, 121, 144; Aristotelian, 17; assertability versus truth in, 120, 129; Buddhist, 139, 140; Chinese, 12, 13, 14, 15, 18, 19, 20, 23, 27; of Chinese nouns, 32, 170; disjunction in 174; focus on complements in, 122; focus on compound terms in, 125, 126; logical versus grammatical structure in, 137; of mathematical classes, 162; negation in, 174; nonclassical, 174; principle of excluded middle in, 121; study of inference in, 124, 126, 127, 129, 130, 132, 133, 137, 138, 139, 140; syllogism in, 13, 17; truth and formal inference in, 124. *See also* Chinese mind; Special logic retort

Luan Tiao-fu, 156, 173

Magic, 59, 60

Ma 'horse', 136, 170; radical translation of, 141. *See also* Mass nouns; Ox-horse paradigm; White-horse paradox

Mao Tse-tung, 26, 76, 171; sinification of Marxism, 76

Mass nouns, 14–15, 28, 31–40, 43–46, 53, 62, 104, 113, 117, 124–25, 131, 135–38, 143–44, 149, 151–53, 159, 169, 171, 188, 192; Mao Tse-tung, 26, 76, 171; no principle of individuation in, 176; principle of identity in, 176; sinification of Marxism in, 76

Mathematics, 187

Meaning, 2–3, 5, 30–31, 34, 42, 47, 49, 58, 63, 72, 82, 85–88, 94, 97, 105, 111–12, 119, 150, 153, 170, 185; of general terms, 113; as image or idea, 113; of words versus sentences, 115. *See also* Semantics

Measures, 32, 33. *See also* Sortals

Mei Yi-pao, 85

Mencius, 5, 57–58, 74–80, 88, 90, 98, 118, 124, 133, 180, 182, 188; analogies in, 187. *See also* Confucianism

Mentalism, 105, 141–42, 170–71, 179, 185

Mereology, 14, 16, 31–39 passim, 41, 43, 45, 52–54, 62, 104, 110–12, 138, 142, 158. *See also* Mass nouns; Ontology

Methodology, 2–3, 10–13, 18, 22–27, 56, 101, 142; comparative, 7, 11. *See also* Interpretation

Mind, as discrimination faculty, 30, 31. *See also* Mentalism; Philosophy of mind
Mind-body dualism, 178
Ming 'names', 30, 31, 35, 46, 72, 77, 105, 111, 114–15, 132, 176; and basis of language, 125. *See also* Names; Sentences; Words
Mohism, 75, 82–83, 88–90; authoritarianism in, 84; empiricism in, 85–86; epistemology in, 87; on Heaven, 183; methodology of, 86; nominalism in, 88; on philosophy of language, 83; on philosophy of mind, 88; political theory in, 84; pragmatism in, 85–86; theory of language in, 84–88; three standards of, 84–85, 87–88; traditionalism in, 85; and universal love, 187; and utilitarianism, 183; will of Heaven in, 84. *See also* Neo-Mohism
Mohist Canon, 100; conventionalist assumption in, 106; corruption of text of, 101; dating of, 100; nominalism in, 110; organization of, 100; regulative function of language in, 105; and response to Taoist relativism, 107; use of stock examples in, 185
Mohist dialectics, 100, 103, 110, 167; subject matter of, 101. *See also* Mohist Canon
Monism, 95, 96
Moral responsibility (excuses), 75. *See also* Rectification of names
Mo-tzu, 26, 82–88, 92, 98; standards of language, 83
Mo-tzu, the, 100
Munro, Donald, 60
Museum, myth of, 189; in interpretation of Kung-sun Lung, 147
Mu 'tree:wood', 33
Mysticism, 63, 67, 95

Nakamura, Haijime, 15, 16, 53, 173

Name and Thing, Dialogue on, 146, 148
Name knowledge versus stuff knowledge, 110, 120
Names, 30–31, 35, 43, 46, 50, 53–54, 58, 61–62, 64–65, 69, 77, 79–80, 87, 92, 96, 104–5, 128, 150; argument from, 48, 49; empty and stuff, 178; error of treating all words as, 169; grading function of, 76, 78–79, 98, 182; identified with reference, 166; knowledge of, 67; modification of, 149; and objects, 107; pragmatics of, 182; rigid rule of, 160, 164; scope of, 111, 145, 152–53, 159, 163–64, 166, 169, 189; stuff-naming theory of, 106; stuff-denoting role of, 137; types of, 110–12. *See also Ming* 'names'; words
Natural kinds, 104, 106, 116, 154–55
Needham, Joseph, 11, 85–86, 187
Nehamas, Alexander, 178
Neo-Confucianism, 57, 183
Neo-Mohism, 188; assumptions about language in, 104; criticism of Taoism in, 104, 122–23; definitions in, 105; definition of *pien* 'dispute' in, 121; descriptive project in, 105, 109; epistemology in, 101, 108; ethical theory in, 105–6; importance of ethics in, 120, 132, 133, 136; indexicality in, 108; lack of skepticism in, 109; logic in, 106, 174; name-knowledge and thing-knowledge in, 106, 108–9, 138; names in, 110; and ontology, 158; realism in, 108; rejection of rectification of names in, 106, 108; and rejection of sentence matching, 120, 125–38; semantic theory in, 104; semantics of compound terms in, 148–70; and separation of hard-white, 157; and study of inference, 124; theory of language in, 101–11, 119–21, 123,

125, 130–33, 137–38, 141, 152; and thief-man issue, 133; unreliability of language in, 137, 138; use of *i* 'idea' in, 112
Neo-Mohists, 33–34, 39, 54–56, 62, 79, 96
Niu-ma 'ox-horse', 109, 150, 153
Nivison, David, 59, 187
Nominalism, 37, 39, 104, 120, 141, 143, 150, 170, 185
Nonbeing, 44, 70

One, the, 96
One-many problem, the, 36, 112, 142, 143
One-name-one-thing rule, 133, 150–51, 153, 155, 159, 160, 164, 169. *See also* Kung-sun Lung; Rectification of names
Ontology, 38, 53, 65, 78, 142; Chinese, 30, 31, 35; classes-subclasses in, 162; class-member, 110; Greek, 42; of individuals, 149; interpenetrating stuffs in, 104, 150; Kung-sun Lung's use of, 168; mind-body, 110; of stuffs, 46; and separation from ethics, 131
Ox-horse paradigm, 62, 149–60, 163–65, 168; relation of, to white-horse paradox, 159

Paradox, Kung-sun Lung's use of, 146; role of, 145
Parmenides, 95
Particulars, 30, 36
Part-whole relation, 35, 150, 152
Pei 'perverse', 124
Perspectives, 92
Philosophy, analytic, 8, 9, 12; Chinese, 14–15; Chinese and Western, compared, 11–12, 15–16, 26, 28, 31, 36, 38, 44, 49, 53–55, 58, 60–61, 63–65, 71, 77, 80, 83, 85–86, 88, 95, 97, 118–19, 138, 141, 143–45, 153, 158, 170–71, 175, 178, 180, 183, 189; Indian, 38; Ionian, 38; and relation to language, 16, 28, 33. *See also individual topics (e.g.,* ontology) *and figures (e.g.,* Plato [Platonism])
Philosophy of language, 10, 30–31, 38, 49, 51, 56, 59, 65, 69–72, 96; Chinese, 46. *See also individual philosophers and schools*
Philosophy of mind, 10, 30–31, 38, 42–56 passim, 63–65, 80–81, 94–98 passim, 105, 110, 112, 115, 143, 171; Pre-Han, 31–32. *See also* Concepts (ideas); Conceptualism; Locke, John; Mentalism
Pien 'dispute', 89–92, 94–95, 97, 104, 106, 126–27, 138, 183; defined in Canon, 121–22; interpreted as distinctions, 105; interpretive theory of, 120, 121; translated as dialectics, 125
Pien 'divide', 183
Pi 'that', 91, 96; used as converse in Canon, 122
Plato (Platonism), 10, 14–16, 30–31, 34, 36, 38, 43, 45, 50, 58, 62, 81, 112, 116, 119, 143, 173, 178, 189
Pluralization, 32–33, 35, 188
Poetry, 14–15, 24–27
Positivism, 76
Pragmatics, 58, 87, 127, 191; importance of, 124–26, 134–36, 154; in white-horse paradox, 151. *See also* Assertability; Semantics
Pragmatism, 86–87
Precedent, argument from, 85
Principle of Humanity, 5, 7
Properties (attributes, qualities), 30–31, 36, 42–45, 52, 105, 112, 144, 146, 149, 157
Propositional contexts, 40, 132. *See also* Belief; Chinese grammar; Knowledge
Punishment, 73, 134

Qualities, *See* Properties (attributes, qualities)

Quantification, 136. *See also* Chinese grammar
Quine, W. V. O., 44, 141, 174, 175, 188

Radical translation, 141, 143–44, 188
Reason, 96; in Chinese philosophy, 124
Rectification of names, 59, 62, 72–82, 98, 106–9, 133, 150, 153, 155, 159, 164, 170, 181–82, 192; relation of, to sentence matching, 131; relation of, to white-horse paradox, 141, 148
Redundancy, 108
Relativism versus realism, 62, 88, 98, 104, 107, 108–9, 123, 139, 140, 155, 181–82, 190
Rights, 16
Rosemont, Henry, Jr., 177, 178
Russell, Bertrand, 112, 145

Sage, 67, 78–81
Sellars, Wilfred, 175
Semantic ascent, 43, 44
Semantic mediation argument, 47–49
Semantic paradox, 138
Semantics, 8–9, 13, 28, 35–36, 38, 40, 43, 45, 49, 51, 53–54, 56, 58, 59, 64, 82, 85, 87, 94, 99, 101, 104, 110, 115, 119, 125–27, 132, 137, 140–42, 146, 148–49, 160, 189; and conceptions unwieldy for logic, 120; contrasted with pragmatics, 124; modern class-based, 149; Neo-Mohist theories of, 46; paradoxes in, 123; Pre-Han theories of, 30, 31, 33, 34; and syntax, 138; of term expressions, 130–31
Senses, 86, 92
Sentence matching, 107, 124, 127–28, 132, 134–35, 138
Sentences, 46, 104, 114; discovery of, 187; use in logic, 126
Separation, 157–59, 163; of compounds, 165; of hard-white, 151, 168

Shao 'few:little', 33
Shen Tao, 180
Shih-fei, 90, 92–97, 125, 183
Shih 'stuffs' (reality), 31, 72, 105, 111, 114, 119, 131–32, 158, 176
Shih 'this', 89, 91, 96, 122, 136; use in sentence matching, 129
Shuo 'explanations', 125–26
Singular versus general, 136
Skepticism, 63–66, 71–72, 91, 95, 110, 176, 183; Chinese theories of, 36
Socrates, 50, 58
Solipsism, 189
Sortals, 32, 33, 34. *See also* Mass nouns; Measures
Special logic retort, 11–16, 24, 27
Speech acts, 60
Spinoza, Baruch, 15
Spring and Autumn Annals, 74, 76, 83
Stuff(s), 30–31, 35, 37. *See also* Mass nouns; Mereology; Ontology; *shih* 'stuffs' (reality)
Substance, 28, 42
Sun Yi-jang, 103
Swain, John, 193
Syllogism, 173

Taboo characters, 102
T'an Chieh-fu, 100, 103, 162
T'ang Chün-i, 127
Tang 'correspond-to', 106, 124
Taoism, 36, 59, 61, 62, 63, 88–89, 94, 134; anarchism in, 134; argument against rectification of names in, 107; criticism of dialecticians in, 119; critique of Confucianism and Mohism in, 105; egoism in, 67; Mohist criticisms of, 123; relativism in, 69; skepticism in, 65–66, 71, 80, 92, 97, 109–10, 120, 125, 138, 141, 180; theory of language in, 66, 104, 120
Tao-te Ching, 4, 61, 65–67, 78, 91, 96–98; chap. 1 of, 71; desires in, 68; interpretation of, 70; interpretive

conflict about Wang Pi version of, 174; Ma Wang Tui text of, 70; mysticism in, 68, 69; reversal in, 68; textual theory of, 65; theory of knowledge in, 66–68, 70; theory of language in, 65, 69–70, 72, 180. *See also* Lao-tzu; Taoism

Tao 'ways', 67–69, 77, 83, 95, 121, 180, 181; interpretation of, 67; interpreted as regulative discourse, 105

Taste, 94–95

Textual emendation, circularity in, 102; coherence requirements, 102; constraints on, 103; interpretive grounds for, 185. *See also* Textual theory

Textual theory, 4–6, 24, 27, 101, 184, 185; Graham's example of, 102; role of original in, 102; semantic stimulus for, 102; techniques of, 102

Thief-man example, 76, 133

Thomason, Richmond, 188

Thought, 42, 49, 63. *See also* Concepts (ideas), Mentalism

T'i-chien formula, 154

T'i 'substance:stuff', 106, 116, 150, 153, 194; interpreted as natural kinds, 154–55, 158; separation of, explained, 157; technical use of, as part, 152. *See also* Chien 'compound', Natural kinds

To 'many:much', 33

Tradition, 8, 83, 85. *See also* Confucianism, Conventions

Translation, 8, 9, 33, 50, 88; argument from, 49. *See also* Interpretation

Truth, 16, 42, 46, 59, 60, 64, 82, 85–88, 94, 104, 115, 119, 124; absence of concern with, 126; contrasted with assertability, 124, 129, 136, 141; as goal of interpretation, 146; semantic, 154

Ts'u 'phrases', 114, 125, 128

Tuan 'point', 109
Tui-lei 'analogy', 117
Tung Chung-shu, 74
T'ung 'same', 108, 116

Uncarved block, 61, 72
Universalization, 106
Universal love, 106, 133, 136
Universals, 30, 34, 36, 42, 47, 49, 53, 58, 63, 72, 98, 105, 115–16, 144, 146. *See also* Properties (attributes, qualities)
Use-mention confusions, 40–41, 43–44, 102, 148, 178, 186
Utilitarianism, 106

Wang Ch'ung, 86
Wang, Pi, 4, 70
Wei 'deliberate-action', 64, 95
White-horse Paradox, 28, 39, 41–45, 99, 104, 124, 130, 140–41, 144, 146, 149, 154, 159, 160, 165, 166, 188; analyzed as dilemma, 160–64, 167; argument for, 170; identity argument in, 167; identity interpretation of, 169; nominalist interpretation of, 142; and relation to scope of names, 145
Wisdom, 67. *See also* Knowledge
Wittgenstein, Ludwig, 179
Words, 147–48, 50, 54, 64, 137, 138, 149; contrasted with sentences, 138; grading function of, 78, 79; triviality of, 139. *See also* Names
Worf, Benjamin, 72
Wu 'lack', 44, 68, 70–71
Wu 'thing', interpreted as natural kind, 105

Yeh 'particle', 178
Yen 'language', 85, 87, 97, 138
Yi 'different', 116–17
Yu 'have', 44, 70–71

Zeno, 145

www.ingramcontent.com/pod-product-compliance
Lightning Source LLC
Chambersburg PA
CBHW080602170426
43196CB00017B/2881